THE BREAK-UP OF THE HABSBURG EMPIRE
1914–1918

THE BREAK-UP OF THE HABSBURG EMPIRE 1914–1918

A STUDY IN NATIONAL AND SOCIAL REVOLUTION

Z. A. B. ZEMAN

LONDON
OXFORD UNIVERSITY PRESS
NEW YORK TORONTO
1961

Oxford University Press, Amen House, London E.C.4
GLASGOW NEW YORK TORONTO MELBOURNE WELLINGTON
BOMBAY CALCUTTA MADRAS KARACHI KUALA LUMPUR
CAPE TOWN IBADAN NAIROBI ACCRA

PRINTED IN GREAT BRITAIN
BY RICHARD CLAY AND COMPANY, LTD.,
BUNGAY, SUFFOLK

TO

R. Z. and N. S.

CONTENTS

ILLUSTRATIONS

MAPS

INTRODUCTION

'Austria–Hungary, or the Austro-Hungarian monarchy, the official name of a country situated in central Europe, bounded E by Russia and Rumania, S by Rumania, Servia, Turkey, and Montenegro, W by the Adriatic Sea, Italy, Switzerland, Liechtenstein, and the German Empire, and N by the German Empire and Russia. It occupies about the sixteenth part of the total area of Europe, with an area (1905) of 239,977 sq. m. . . .'

In this manner began the entry on the Habsburg monarchy in the eleventh edition of the *Encyclopaedia Britannica*. The author of the article, writing at the end of 1908—the ominous year of the Bosnian crisis—attempted no speculation as to the multinational Empire's future. The dynasty was still holding sway over its diverse dominions in 'central Europe' that included the ragged Adriatic littoral, the rich soil of Slovenia and of the Hungarian plain, the mighty ranges of the Tirolean Alps and of the Carpathians, the gentle landscape of central Bohemia, the eastern marches of Galicia and the wild woodlands of Bosnia and Transylvania. People and goods of every kind were still moving freely between Vienna and Budapest, and on to Cracow, Lwov or Chernovtsy; between Triest and Zagreb or Prague and Sarajevo. The Empire was a reality which, though its future was often a subject of speculation, was firmly embedded in the minds of men. As Bismarck put it in 1888: 'It is difficult to think without Austria; a state like Austria does not disappear.'

Thirty years later, in November 1918, Austria–Hungary no longer existed; its last ruler was about to go into exile. From its ruins three independent states were coming into existence: Austria, Hungary, and Czechoslovakia. Three other countries—Italy, Serbia, and Rumania—were claiming large tracts of territory and several million new subjects from the defunct Empire. Finally, Poland was in the process of becoming united once again.

The national leaders, busy shaping their states and consolidating their own power inside them, paid little attention to the last pronouncement to 'his peoples' on 11 November 1918 by Emperor Karl. Resigned to the fate of his dynasty, he expressed a hope that 'internal peace may heal the wounds inflicted by the war'. This peace never materialized. The men who had devoted their political skills and energies to the task of destroying the Habsburg monarchy had given but little thought to the hazards of the future in the area vacated by Habsburg power. They were assisted in their effort to break up the Empire first by Tsarist Russia and later, and more effectually, by the western Entente Powers. For the governments of Great Britain, France, and the United States this 'central Europe' of Austria–Hungary was traditionally a territory of no special interest. They turned their attention, for a brief period, to the problem of Austria–Hungary in the spring of 1918 under the impression of military necessity, when the stability of the western front was endangered by the German divisions released from the Russian front. It was then that the Allied governments recognized the expediency of encouraging the national ambitions of the Habsburg peoples: by the middle of the summer, they had given official recognition to the radical (the term 'radical' is used, throughout the book, to denote the plans, of every kind, for the break-up of the Habsburg monarchy) aims of the political exiles.

The Allies had already begun to favour certain Habsburg peoples during the war; later, the distinction between victorious and defeated governments was readily accepted by the 'victorious' successor states of Austria–Hungary. Czechoslovakia, Jugoslavia, Poland, and Rumania found themselves among the first category, while Austria and Hungary were condemned to suffer the privations of defeat. The division of the successor states into these two groups, only partially justified by their histories during the war, did not serve the cause of peaceful development; nor did, for that matter, the experiment tried by the favoured governments to build up national, or rather one-nation states in multiracial territories. In the long run, these new governments were unable to control the destinies of their nations. Although they received a certain amount of patronage from the western Powers, and although they strove to set up a system of alliances linked with Paris and London, they were established at the time of the complete eclipse of the power of both Germany and Russia, the two states most directly interested in this territory. This fact alone boded ill for the future.

After twenty years of precarious existence the new order in central Europe gave way, often with surprising ease, to the ever-growing greed of Nazi Germany: Austria and then Czechoslovakia disappeared before the formal declaration of war; after it, the valiant resistance of the Poles soon collapsed under the concentrated onslaught of Hitler's mechanized forces. Hungary and Rumania were drawn into Germany's orbit; only the Jugoslavs, at the price of great suffering and internal strife, caused severe troubles for the new masters of continental Europe. But Hitler's spell in power brought out the national resentments that had accumulated in peace-time. The powerful Nazi movements in Austria and Hungary bore witness to this resentment; the nationalism of the Slovaks, which had developed between the wars when they were in close contact with the Czechs, and the older nationalism of the Croats that had been thwarted by the centralizing tendencies of Belgrade, found their bizarre fulfilment under Nazi patronage in the states of Slovakia and Croatia.

Dictatorships of the proletariat succeeded Hitler's régime: with or without popular support Stalin extended Russia's influence far into central Europe. Now all the successor states—with the exception of Austria—are run by one-party communist governments. In the thirty years of their existence--from 1919 to 1948—the states that succeeded the Habsburg monarchy went through several adjustments of their frontiers; some of their disputed provinces changed hands three times. These were minor disturbances. The successor states also suffered occupation by the armies of Hitler and Stalin, and the rule by governments sponsored by the dictators. Indeed, it was this aspect of their independence that Sir Winston Churchill must have had in mind when he wrote: 'There is not one of the peoples of provinces that constituted the Empire of the Habsburg to whom gaining their independence has not brought the tortures which ancient poets and theologians had reserved for the damned.'[1]

The historiography of the break-up of the Habsburg Empire reflects the complexity of the subsequent developments. First, there were the personal accounts by the victors and the vanquished: Dmowski, Masaryk, Jovanović on the one hand, and on the other, Czernin, Conrad von Hötzendor and Lammasch are among those who recorded their impressions of the downfall of the Habsburg dynasty. They either exulted or mourned over the event. The biases of the prominent autobiographers were readily accepted by the national schools of historians which flourished between the two wars. Among the peoples that had temporarily profited by the post-war rearrangement of central Europe, the Habsburg monarchy at the time of the outbreak of the war was presented as a decaying structure, hopelessly undermined by the national ambitions of its peoples and committed to the expansionist aims of Imperial Germany; it had lost every justification for its existence. The peoples were habitually divided into the 'dominating', the Germans and the Magyars, and the 'oppressed' nationalities. Such rough division completely obliterated the intricate hieratical order of the races under Habsburg rule. A variation on the same theme was provided by the liberal and socialist historians in Austria and in Hungary. Men like Victor Bibl, Oskar Jaszi, and Otto Bauer viewed the break-up of the Habsburg monarchy as a long process which had started in 1866 or at other critical points in the history of the Empire. This approach deals in general, long-term trends: phrases like 'the dying body of the Austro-Hungarian monarchy' and references to its 'organic decay' do more than hint at the inevitability of its dissolution. These studies are in fact general histories of Austria–Hungary written under the impact of its downfall.

Apart from its strong anti-Habsburg bias, the Czech historiography between the two wars developed a special feature: it concentrated on the study of the exiles' activities during the war, while neglecting the political developments inside Austria–

[1] *The Second World War*, vol. 1, page 8, London 1948.

Hungary itself. There was a good reason for such emphasis. The exiles were all convinced radicals who, soon after the outbreak of the war, went into action against the monarchy; the large majority of the politicians who remained at home, on the other hand, were either loyal to the dynasty or wary of taking a premature action against it. A number of historians (Z. Tobolka, J. Opočenský, M. Paulová) attempted to correct this trend, but their work was interrupted by the war.

Since the end of World War II the Marxist historians in the communist-run successor states have been trying to expound a completely new approach to the break-up of the Habsburg monarchy. They have complicated their task by confusing legitimate historical research and political propaganda; they are pursuing two distinct, but complementary, aims. They have drawn a sharp distinction between national and social revolutions; while playing down the role of the national revolutions and their leaders, they insist that it was the Bolshevik revolution and its aftermath in the Habsburg monarchy that was solely responsible for its downfall. Their thesis, 'Without the November revolution in Russia there would have been no October revolution in Austria–Hungary', is used to destroy the political reputations of the national leaders. There is one exception in this category: it is the work done in Jugoslavia on the Saloniki trials of 1917–18.[1] The post-war production of the Marxist historians is virtually unknown in English; a certain amount of the work that had been done between the two wars was translated. Of the historians who wrote on the Habsburg monarchy in English, the late Professor R. W. Seton-Watson did much of the pioneering work; his remarks on the end of the Habsburg monarchy which are scattered in a number of books he wrote after 1919 favour the views of the 'national', and the Czechoslovak in particular, school of historians. Apart from a number of general studies, covering the second half of the nineteenth and early twentieth centuries,[2] the four years of

[1] B. Nesković, *Istina o Solunskom procesu*, Belgrade 1953 which brought new evidence on the assassination of Archduke Franz Ferdinand.

[2] A. J. P. Taylor, *The Habsburg Monarchy*, London, 1948; R. A. Kann, *The Multinational Empire*, New York 1950; A. May, *The Habsburg Monarchy, 1867–1914*, Cambridge, Mass 1951.

war—the crucial time for the survival or demise of the Habsburg Empire—have received scant attention.

On the following pages, the author attempts to fill this historiographical gap, to correct the misconceptions of both the 'national' and the Marxist schools, and to indicate some of the most rewarding approaches to the study of the subject. He has had access to the archives in Vienna to the period ending 31 October 1918, which were opened in 1956, and also to the documents of the German Foreign Ministry which remained in this country until 1958. Finally, the author has perused most of the relevant material published both before and after World War II in the successor states.

The Vienna archives—the *Haus, Hof und Staatsarchiv*, the *Verwaltungsarchiv*, and the *Kriegsarchiv*—have unfortunately gone through a number of depletions since 1919. Shortly after the end of World War I the governments of the successor states were allowed to take away the documents relating to their countries; some of these were restored to Vienna under Hitler's patronage; after World War II some of the returned documents once more went to Prague, Belgrade and elsewhere. The *Verwaltungsarchiv* did not suffer as much as the Staats- and the Kriegsarchiv from these upheavals; it contains valuable material from the Ministry of Interior, particularly that pertaining to Galicia. (The Poles seem to have been less thorough than the Czechs or the Jugoslavs in their search of the Vienna archives.) On the other hand, the papers of the German Foreign Ministry relating to Austria–Hungary have been well looked after by the Allies in Berlin from the end of World War II until 1948 and, for some ten years, by the British Foreign Office. They contain Ambassadors' situation reports from Vienna, documents on German–Austro-Hungarian relations and finally, the key to the understanding of the relations between Berlin and Vienna during World War I, the papers on the solution of the Polish problem.

The author has not set out to give complete accounts of the histories of the Habsburg nationalities during the war. He has, however, attempted to survey the factors that caused the downfall of the Empire. Of these, radical nationalism proved the most disruptive. But the nature of the radical challenge to the established order went through a number of far-reaching changes during the war. After the outbreak of hostilities no more was heard of the terrorism of the young Serbs in Bosnia that had pushed the Habsburg monarchy into the war; the Russophilism of the Ruthenes in eastern Galicia, regarded by the government shortly before the war as the most dangerous movement in the monarchy, was overshadowed by the Ukrainian movement, protected by the armies of the central Powers; the threat to the Empire by the Neo-Slavism of the Czechs did not survive the demise of the Tsarist régime. After the March revolution, the radicals inside the monarchy came more and more to rely on the support of the western Entente Powers; the political exiles had already been engaged in making their plans acceptable to the Entente governments.

Early in 1918 economic hardships brought about a revolutionary situation in Austria–Hungary; the impact of the Bolshevik revolution and propaganda gave it a new sense of direction. But contrary to the view of the official communist historians, national and social revolutions did not come into conflict in Austria–Hungary; the clash occurred, in special circumstances on Russian soil, where Masaryk's Czech army became involved in fighting the Bolsheviks.

Apart from the controversy between the protagonists of the national and the communist approaches to the break-up of Austria–Hungary, there is another and older argument that is still very much alive. (It was implied in the correspondence columns of *The Times Literary Supplement* in the summer of 1954. In lectures given at the university of Vienna the opinion is still being expressed that the monarchy was broken up by a decision of the victorious Powers at the peace conference.) The author has tried to give a definitive answer to the question: was the Habsburg monarchy broken up from within by a revolutionary explosion, or was its downfall brought about by a decision of the Entente governments? Neither of the two parties engaged in the controversy took into account the co-operation between the radicals inside the monarchy and the political exiles, which became especially intensive in the last months of the war.

Finally, the author has attempted to recreate the background against which the growth of the revolutionary movement took place: the struggle between the military and the civil authorities for power in the Habsburg state in the early stages of the war, the desire of the German politicians to recapture hegemony in the Austrian part of the monarchy, the incompetence of the government and its frequent misreading of the situation, and the inability of both Austria–Hungary and Germany to deal with problems of nationality, which was illustrated by their treatment of the Polish problem and which did not fail to make a profound impression on the peoples of the Habsburg monarchy.

London, May 1960

ACKNOWLEDGEMENTS

The author would like to acknowledge the help he received from Professor R. R. Betts, Mr. D. J. Footman, Mr. J. Joll and Dr. T. Komarnicki, and their kindness in reading the manuscript. He would like to thank the Warden and Fellows of St. Antony's College, where a Research Fellowship made it possible for him to do a large part of the work on this book. He would also like to thank the staff of the British Museum library, Dr. Neck of the *Haus, Hof und Staatsarchiv* and Dr. Goldinger of the *Verwaltungsarchiv* in Vienna for their kind assistance.

ABBREVIATIONS

AA — *Auswärtiges Amt.* Unpublished documents in the Archives of the German Foreign Ministry.

Dokumenty — The documents contained in the third volume of E. Beneš's memoirs, *Světová válka a naše revoluce.* Prague 1935.

HHuSA — *Haus, Hof, und Staatsarchiv.* Unpublished documents in the Vienna State Archives.

MO — *Mezhdunarodnye otnoshenie v epokhu imperialisma.* Documents from the Russian Archives, published in Leningrad in 1931 and the following years.

USFR — *United States Foreign Relations.* The documents pertaining to the period under consideration were published in Washington between 1928 and 1933.

VA — *Verwaltungsarchiv.* Unpublished documents of the Ministry of the Interior in the Vienna Administrative Archives.

The Kingdom of Hungary, within the Empire, is indicated by the broken line - - - - - -

I The Habsburg Empire in 1914

cerned with the Ruthene problem and advised that they should work in closer co-operation.

The recommendations for the solution of the Ruthene problem made by the Minister of Foreign Affairs were moderate and sensible; they showed that Berchtold was aware of the complexity of the problem. Such was not the attitude of Krobatin, the Minister of War, who wrote to the Minister of the Interior in the middle of March.[12] General Krobatin was very impatient with Russia:

> Under the patronage of, or at any rate under the benign sufferance of the Russian government, Slav societies were founded in Moscow, St. Petersburg and elsewhere, whose members are not only official Russian personalities, such as high ecclesiastical dignitaries, retired generals, professors, and others, but also Austrian parliamentary deputies and politicians. Under the guise of material support for a suffering population, they pursue openly a nationalist Russian propaganda.

After a brief description of Russian ambitions on the Danube and on the Balkans, Krobatin's contribution to the solution of the problem was simple: 'We should fight this propaganda by every means at our disposal.' In the differences between the views of Berchtold and those of Krobatin, the conflict between the politicians' and the soldiers' attitude towards the solution of national problems, which flared up with such violence in the first months of the war and which had a powerful effect on the attitude of the Slav nationalities to the monarchy, was already foreshadowed.[13]

In the Czech lands, in Bohemia and Moravia—Silesia was the third land which was united with these two in the concept of the 'lands of the Czech crown' because of historical precedent, but not by administrative practice—there were also some signs of profound dissent. It is, of course, untrue to say either that most Czechs were anti-Habsburg before the war—this is a fallacy shared by many Czech nationalist historians who wrote between the two wars—or, as R. W. Seton-Watson informs us,[14] that they were all loyally Austrian until the outbreak of the war. The Agrarians,

[12] *VA*, 2854 MI ex 1914. [13] See below, page 48.

[14] *A History of the Czechs and Slovaks*, page 285, London 1943.

the party which sent the largest Czech contingent of deputies to the parliament in Vienna, the Social Democrats, the second largest party, and the clerical parties thought and acted, before the war, purely in terms of the Habsburg monarchy. They each had different reasons for doing so: the Agrarians, led ably, though rather unimaginatively, by Švehla, were too conscious of their power and therefore of their responsibility to the nation and to the monarchy to be inclined to entertain any eccentric radical ideas. The Social Democrats, though their unity was put to a severe test under the pressure of national differences between the Czechs and the Germans (the trouble started at the end of the nineteenth century, when the Czechs decided to run their own trade unions, to the exclusion of the Bohemian Germans) shared the Marxist predilection for large economic units such as the Habsburg monarchy; they believed in the brotherhood of the working classes in theory, and they were in close contact with the Social Democrat leaders of other Habsburg nationalities in political practice. The two conservative clerical parties vied with each other in their loyalty to the dynasty, which for them was the paragon of political institutions. These parties representing the majority of the Czechs, although they often stood in opposition to the government in power, were by no means opposed to the existence of the monarchy before the war.

Expressions of a dissent that went beyond opposition to the government among the Czechs were of a purely political nature: the religious issue did not, as it did among the Serbs or the Ruthenes, enter the picture. The Czechs, like the Poles, were mainly Roman Catholics; there was an active Protestant minority among them. In the exploration of subversive political activities we must turn to parties led and supported by urban, middle, and lower-middle class intelligentsia: the Young Czechs, the Progressives,[15] and the National Socialists, a working- and lower middle-class party founded, with a strong support from the Young Czechs, to counteract the spread of Marxism. Its main task was to further national, not class struggle.

Karel Kramář, the leader of the Young Czechs, was one of the

[15] *Strana státoprávně pokroková.*

Radio Times Hulton Picture Library.

The wedding, in 1911, of Archduke Karl (later Karl I, Emperor of Austria), to Princess Zita of Bourbon-Parma. Left to right: Duchess Marie of Bourbon-Parma, the mother of the bride; Duchess Sophie Chotek and her husband, the Archduke Franz Ferdinand, the heir to the Austrian throne (standing in the second row), who were assassinated at Sarajevo on 28 June 1914; Archduchess Maria Josefa, mother of Karl; Franz Josef I, Emperor of Austria; the bridegroom and bride

most influential politicians in the monarchy before the war. He was a forceful personality, often difficult and opinionated; his own party's paper, the *Národní Listy*, hardly ever missed an opportunity to criticise him. His political views were almost identical with those of Roman Dmowski, the leader of the National Democrats in Russian Poland, and one of the party's representatives in the Duma. In 1908, the year of the Bosnian crisis and the Pan-Slav congress in Prague, Dmowski wrote: 'It is in the interests of the western Powers not to weaken, but to strengthen Russia and to make her capable of resistance to Germany.'[16] Like Dmowski, Kramář was pro-Russian and anti-German; the Habsburg monarchy was for him an institution to be moulded to his own image, and if this proved impossible, to be destroyed. Kramář's ideas on foreign policy were a curious mixture of Slav emotionalism, clearly a substitute for the absence, among the Czechs, of Orthodoxy, and power politics; his home policy was completely conservative, intended to protect the comparatively recent acquisition, by the middle-classes, of prosperity and political prominence. But problems of foreign affairs were his main interest: Kramář on several occasions before the war made determined bids to become the monarchy's Foreign Minister. In the years between 1908 and 1914, he attempted to attract the attention of foreign politicians, especially Russian, to the 'Czech question' and to find its solution within the wider framework of Slav politics. This attempt took the form of Neo-Slavism, closely related to the Pan-Slavism of the previous century; it laid, however, more stress on the equality of all Slav peoples: Russia was merely a *primus inter pares*. There were two flaws in Kramář's romantic picture of the Slavs: the Austrian Poles and the Ukrainians. The anti-Russian Ukrainians he regarded as beneath contempt; the Poles were too important to be ignored. Kramář calculated that if the dislike of the Austrian Poles for Russia could be removed, he would win them over for a common Slav front in the Viennese *Reichsrat*. With this aim in mind, he invited representatives of the Austrian Poles to the Slav congress in Prague in 1908; he was disappointed when the chairman of the

[16] *Niemcy, Rosya i kwestia polska*, page 251, Lwow 1908.

club of the Polish deputies grudgingly agreed to detail two of its members to attend the festivities.

Kramář thought that a united front would increase the influence of the Slavs not only on the internal affairs of the monarchy but also on its foreign policy. This would have meant drawing away from Germany and the building up of closer ties with Russia. Indeed, the aim of Kramář's Neo-Slavism was a Habsburg monarchy ruled by its Slav majority. It was a policy in the tradition of the early Czech national leaders, Palacký the historian and Rieger the politician, who had taken the continued existence of the Habsburg monarchy for granted.

There is evidence, however, that Kramář had already strayed from the narrow path of loyalty to the monarchy before the war. He was a friend of Svatkovski, a representative of the official St. Petersburg Telegraph Agency, who was in close contact with the Russian Foreign Ministry. Svatkovski was the only man to whom Kramář fully revealed his alternative, secret plan for the future of the Slavs and of his own nation. It was built on the assumption that a war would occur between Austria–Hungary and Russia, as a result of which the Habsburg Empire would break up. Kramář discussed with his Russian friend a plan for a Slav confederation ruled from St. Petersburg. In May 1914 he wrote down his suggestions; on 16 June Svatkovski transmitted the memorandum to Sazonov, the Russian Foreign Minister, and also to Shebeko, the Ambassador in Vienna. Shebeko commented on Kramář's proposals: 'The project is of a fantastic nature, and because of the serious consequences it might have for its authors, should it become known, I regard it as my duty to request most humbly that it be kept in strict confidence.'[17]

Shebeko's verdict was right. The new states on the Balkans could hardly have been expected to give up even a small part of their hard-won independence; the Poles would have been forced into an undesired union with Russia; finally, in the confederation proposed by Kramář, the smaller Slav nations would have had no

[17] This document was discovered in the Soviet archives by Jaroslav Papoušek shortly after the war; he reported on his find in the Prague *Národní Osvobození*, on 24 June and 5 July 1934.

I

BEFORE THE WAR

The sixty-fifth anniversary of Franz Josef's succession to the throne was celebrated with High Masses in Vienna on 2 December 1913. His reign, while establishing a European record for longevity, had seen the rise of mass movements—of nationalism, and later of socialism—among the peoples of the monarchy. The Emperor did not look on these developments as potential threats to the very existence of the Empire. He was by nature averse to taking drastic political measures and had determined early in his reign that the order of the Empire was best served by hard administrative work. By 1913, merely to administer rapid social and national changes had become a very demanding task indeed.

On the surface, the political ambitions of the Habsburg subjects appeared to be maintaining a working relationship with the established order in these last months of peace: the internal balance of power was still based on the compromise between the dynasty and the Hungarian nobles—the *Ausgleich* of 1867. Although the compromise was originally regarded, at any rate in Vienna, as a way out of temporary difficulties, it ossified into a rigid system; it not only divided the monarchy into two separately governed parts, but it also made a common treatment of the nationality problems impossible. The architects of the *Ausgleich* believed that while the Germans would be able to strengthen their position as the ruling nation in the Austrian part of the monarchy, the Magyars would remain in control of Hungary and its national minorities. But while the rulers in Budapest, aided by their sense of a civilizing mission among the backward peoples, encountered little resistance among the Rumanians, the Slovaks, and the Ruthenes—in Croatia they struck a bargain similar to their own with Vienna—the hegemony of the Germans in the Austrian part of the monarchy was to be seriously undermined after 1867. In fact, whereas the Magyars were able to pursue a tough policy towards the peoples living under their rule, the government in Vienna had not only to temporize with its nationalities but even to co-opt Slav politicians as its members in order to strengthen its own position. The Poles in Galicia enjoyed a high degree of autonomy, they never failed to be represented in the Austrian cabinet, and their representatives in the Viennese parliament, together with the German deputies, supported the government in power. The German national extremists in the *Reichsrat* were largely recruited from the ethnical borderlands, from the territories where the German element was in constant touch with the Slav population, and with the Czechs in particular. The Czechs in Bohemia, though less successful in settling their differences with the Germans than were their fellow-countrymen in Moravia, were by no means opposed to the existence of the monarchy. Their major political parties were loyally Austrian, even when they stood in opposition to the government. The Social Democrat movement in both parts of the monarchy suffered from the rising temper of nationalism; the national feeling of many of the Social Democrat politicians cut across their loyalty to the working class.

On the international scene the monarchy was favourably regarded by the western Powers as the protector of law and order in territories where political chaos was endemic and lawlessness always near the surface. Outwardly, the monolithic area of the Habsburg dominions compared favourably with the kaleidoscopic arrangement of the territories beyond the south-east frontier. Balkan wars, assassinations, and poverty set off the comparative peace reigning inside the Habsburg monarchy. Her dynasty and aristocracy were international in their connexions: the English aristocracy appreciated the great houses in the mountains of Austria and the hunts and horses in the Hungarian plains. Those conservatives in France who regretted the passing of the *ancien régime* in their own country could rejoice over its preservation elsewhere. The progressives in western Europe could find a reflection of their opinions in the liberal, Jewish-run press of Vienna and Budapest, while Roman Catholics everywhere could see in the Habsburgs the most powerful secular pillar of their faith. And seekers after a European balance of power could regard Austria–Hungary as a check on the ambitions of Russia in the Balkans and in central Europe and, to some extent, even on those of Germany.

But no one in the West—apart from a handful of learned men—took an interest in the individual races of the Habsburg Empire. This was not the case in Tsarist Russia: its attitude to the Habsburg dominions was more complex. While giving official support, through Serbia, to the irredentist movement in the south, the unofficial Pan-Slav groups in Russia took an interest in the Slav subjects in the north-eastern corner of the monarchy. Three days before the Habsburg Imperial anniversary, on 30 November 1913, a meeting of the Galician–Russian society took place in St. Petersburg. It was attended by politicians, army officers, church dignitaries, and two guests of honour: Demetrius Markov—a deputy in the Viennese parliament from eastern Galicia, and a Ruthene peasant. The Duma deputy, Count Bobrinski, was in the chair. The main purpose of the meeting was to describe the desperate economic situation in Galicia and Bukovina, the result of a disastrous harvest. Bobrinski invited the society to help the needy Ruthene population; in his opinion, he said, the 110,000,000 Russians should be able to support the 4,000,000 of their brothers on the other side of the frontier. Markov and the authentic peasant he had brought with him described, in their own ways, the emergency situation in their province, pointed out the cultural and ethnical unity between the Russians and the Ruthenes and appealed to the Russian nation for help in their hour of need. After his speech, Markov received a wreath with the inscription 'To the brave fighter for the Russian language'. Count Bobrinski was the most active leader of the Pan-Slav group, recruited mainly from the higher reaches of Russian society. Several newspapers—the *Novoe Vremia* among them—and the higher echelons of the army were the Russian Pan-Slav strongholds; the Foreign Ministry, on the other hand, proved to be an institution completely resilient to their ideas. Although Pan-Slavism in Russia, like Pan-Germanism in Germany, had little influence on official foreign policy, the activities of this group, and of societies such as the Galician–Russian, found some response among the Slav nationalities of the monarchy. It would be a mistake to present this movement as one with precisely defined policy and aims. The forms it took varied among the different Slav peoples of the Habsburg monarchy. But in spite of local variations its backbone was political. It was, among the Habsburg Slavs, an expression of dissent from the official foreign policy of the monarchy, and an expression of protest against their treatment by the central authorities.

In eastern Galicia, the 1911 elections to the *Reichsrat*, the first general elections following the introduction of general suffrage in the Austrian part of the monarchy and the last elections before the war, brought about a sharpening of the differences between the Poles and the Ruthenes. The Ruthene representation in Vienna was increased; their perennial demand for a university of their own in Lwow and for a reform of the system of elections to the Galician Diet became louder. But at the same time the elections of 1911 reduced considerably the number of deputies the Old Ruthene party sent to Vienna: it was represented by two deputies only, while the Ukrainian party's number of deputies increased to twenty-one. This change was of great importance: while the Old Ruthenes maintained that their nation was unquestionably a part, historically and linguistically, of the Great Russian nation, the Ukrainian party claimed significant differences between the two peoples, and on this they based their political programme. They were as much anti-Russian as they were anti-Polish; from the uncomfortable position between their powerful enemies they tended to look towards Vienna for the support of their national ambitions. In the Austrian capital there were signs of delight that yet another nationality was in the making which, if need be, might be used as a balance in the traditional Habsburg manner: in this case, to counteract excessive claims from the Polish side and at the same time to fight Russophil tendencies among their own people.

The Old Ruthene party, on the other hand, had become smaller and more radical. The introduction of general suffrage had worked against it; the Balkan wars and the tension between Austria–Hungary and Russia at the end of 1912 and the beginning of 1913 had contributed towards its radicalization. The younger generation started taking over the leadership of the party; its transformation into an irredentist movement was merely a question of time. As late as June 1914, however, there were some members of the Old Ruthenes who resented or ignored this development, and continued to regard the party as a political organization entirely loyal to the Habsburg dynasty. On 12 June this group sent a memorandum to the Ministry of the Interior in Vienna[1] in which they complained about the persecution of their party and societies, which they argued drove some of their 'younger and more hot-blooded' members into treason. They wrote:

> The traditional and unshakeable loyalty of the Ruthene nation, these 'Tiroleans of the East', to His Majesty, the ruling house, and to the Austro-Hungarian monarchy has been confirmed by the sacrifice of earthly goods, of life and of blood; for several decades now this [conduct], under the leadership of the Old Ruthene societies, has been repeatedly acknowledged by the Emperor and by the government. These years were the most fruitful time for the Ruthene nation, and it was during these years that many societies and clubs were founded, some of which are now of historical importance, especially the Ruthene National House in Lwow, which was founded at the instigation of His Majesty the Emperor himself.

The Old Ruthenes who drafted and signed this memorandum entirely overlooked the effect on their party of tension between Austria–Hungary and Russia. Markov, one of the party's leaders, appeared more often at meetings of the Galician–Russian society in the last year of peace than he had done before; in his speeches he was outspokenly pro-Russian and anti-Habsburg. Although eastern Galicia alone sent Russophil deputies to the parliament in Vienna, the pro-Russian movement branched out into all territories with Ruthene population; into Bukovina and the north-eastern corner of Hungary, Carpathian Russia. The Orthodox church proved a strong ally of the political agitators: its efforts to

[1] *VA*, 7258 MI ex 1914.

convert Ruthene peasants from Greek Catholic—the Uniate—to the Orthodox faith proved even more insidious than Markov's flirtations with Russia. The Uniate church recognised the Roman Catholic hierarchy but the rites of the two creeds were deceptively similar. In the prayer books introduced by the Orthodox priests into Ruthene territories there were scattered, among devotional literature of routine nature, prayers for the Tsar and his family, the Russian army, and other institutions of the Russian state.

On 19 January 1914 Korytowski, the Governor of Galicia, reported to the Ministry of the Interior that:

> . . . recently, the agitation of the Russophil party of Dr. Dudykiewicz[2] has become more lively; it is partly concerned with strengthening its political organization and partly with the education of the younger generation in its own spirit. . . . The schismatic propaganda is also gaining in strength; new Orthodox emissaries have appeared in the district. . . . The continuing Russification of Galicia, aided by Orthodoxy, requires greater attention on the part of administrative officers if they are to be able to combat it.[3]

At the same time, the Governor of Galicia requested district officers (*Bezirkshauptmann*) in the eastern part of his province to supervise the movement with vigilance, and to give particular attention to the Michael Kaczkowski societies, originally founded for the political enlightenment of the Ruthene peasants. Korytowski also pointed out that although the expulsion of Orthodox priests from his province was difficult, as they were Austrian subjects, there were various administrative measures at the disposal of the district officers which could be used to restrict their activities. Here, the Governor touched on the key problem in countering the pro-Russian political and religious propaganda in the Ruthene provinces. The Ukrainian, anti-Russian societies such as the *Prosvita*, though very useful in this respect, were incapable of countering such propaganda entirely on their own. The Old Ruthene political traditions died hard; they had had a

[2] Wladimir Dudykiewicz, stood as an Old Ruthene candidate in the Medenice district in 1911. In a straight fight between him and the candidate of the Ukrainian party, Dudykiewicz received only 581 out of a total of 25,788 votes.

[3] *VA*, 604 MI ex 1914.

longer run than the Ukrainian. Parishes which were under the influence of a Russophil priest, especially those near the Russian frontier, became impenetrable bastions of Orthodoxy. And finally, to some of the Polish landed nobility in eastern Galicia, the conservatism of the Old Ruthenes was more congenial than the democratic politics of the Ukrainian party. These were the weightiest reasons why the Austrian administrative authorities felt themselves obliged to help the Ukrainians in their fight against the pro-Russian and Orthodox propaganda. But though all Austrian administration, from the Minister of the Interior to the district officers, were agreed to fight such propaganda, they had no legal tools at their disposal. They were aware that only a slight shift of emphasis was needed to turn such propaganda into treason; and since they had no suitable legal provisions at their disposal they were forced into adopting methods that resembled, and often in fact were, a low form of administrative chicanery.

These difficulties were demonstrated in February and March 1914, when some of the leading Ruthene pro-Russian propagandists were put on trial both in Austria and in Hungary. The most radical pro-Russian paper in Lwow, the *Prykarpatskaja Rus*, commented at the time of the opening of the trial at Marmaros-Sziget:

> Russia listen! Today, there begins at Marmaros a trial of the Hungarian–Russian peasants and of their priest, Father Alexander Kabalyuk. They have been accused of treason; they have apparently intended to detach Carpathian Russia from the Kingdom of Hungary and to incorporate it into Russia. What does this treason of the Hungarian–Jewish clique consist of?

On 3 March thirty-two Ruthenes were sentenced to short terms of imprisonment, in spite of the intervention of Count Bobrinski, who had appeared at Marmaros as a voluntary witness. Father Kabalyuk received the severest penalty—four years and six months' imprisonment and a fine of 100 crowns.

In the evidence for the prosecution, pamphlets distributed by pro-Russian agitators were produced, and quotations from them were read at the trial. The pamphlets attacked the Uniate church, and accused the Hungarian state of cruel oppression of the Ruthenes. The Tsar, on the other hand, was hailed as the protector of the true faith and as a potential liberator of the Ruthenes from the Magyar yoke. 'Every Russian, even if he is not a subject of the Tsar, everyone in whom there flows a drop of Slav blood has the duty to pray for him and for his family, because he is the only protector the Slavs have on this earth. The fame of great Russia is infinite; she is a sister of the Russians in Hungary.' And the pamphlet concluded with the words: 'Fear not, the Russian nation is great and powerful and it is on our side. We shall be victorious.'[4] The conclusions which the prosecution drew from such evidence were that the defendants had worked for the conversion of their fellow-countrymen from the Greek Catholic to the Orthodox faith, in order to facilitate the annexation of the north-eastern counties of Hungary by Russia.

A week after the sentences had been passed at Marmaros the Ruthene trial at Lwow began. There were only four defendants; the charges were high treason and espionage. The chief defendant was Simeon Bendasiuk—an associate of Count Bobrinski, who had worked on the two most radical pro-Russian newspapers, the *Prykarpatskaja Rus* and the *Halicanin*; at the time of the trial he was a district secretary of the Old Ruthene party. Two of the defendants at Lwow were Orthodox priests. After long and tortuous proceedings the jury declared all the defendants innocent.

The charges of the prosecution in Lwow were similar to those in Marmaros: the accused were presented as the leaders of a pro-Russian irredentist movement. Indeed, when the evidence for the prosecution was being gathered, new connexions between the Ruthenes and the Russians were discovered; the administration acquired more knowledge and understanding of the techniques of pro-Russian propaganda. The danger to the state, especially at times of tension between the Habsburg monarchy and Russia, not to speak of war, was evident. Yet at Lwow the jury, consisting entirely of Poles, let the defendants go free. The Ukrainian press accused the jury of bias in favour of Old Ruthenes and of traitors;

[4] *Politische Chronik*, 1914, page 97.

some of the Polish newspapers greeted the decision with self-congratulations on their national tolerance, which extended as far as the contemptible Ruthenes.

However, the legal grounds on which the jury had to make their decision were not completely clear. Pro-Russian ideas were not illegal in themselves. The defendants had to be tried for treason and the jury, quite rightly, refused to make the equation between treason and Russophil convictions. Whereas the Hungarians, because of their more united political front and their tougher attitude to subject peoples, had been successful in passing sentences, however mild, at Marmaros, for the Austrians the meaning of treason had become obscured by 1914. At the same time, political trials became discredited after the fiasco of the 'Friedjung trial' of the Serbs: although the Austrian judicial authorities were on the right track when prosecuting both the Serbs and the Ruthenes they were incapable of producing conclusive evidence. After the trial in Lwow, the Viennese *Neue Freie Presse* expressed the opinion that political trials were unsuitable means for the fighting of religious or political agitation; it commented, in a rather high-minded manner: 'In a civilized state, the jury cannot convict anyone unless it is absolutely convinced of the defendant's guilt. There is only one answer to activity for idealistic reasons: idealistic activity in the opposite direction.'

During the preliminary investigations for the Ruthene trials, new information on the Russophil movement emerged, the threads of which led to Bukovina. The Hungarian frontier police confiscated a box containing Cyrillic Russian printing types, which had been sent by Julius Jaworski, a secondary school teacher and the secretary of the Galician–Russian society in Kiev, to the offices of the *Ruskaia Pravda*, a Russophil paper published by Alex Gerovski in Czernowitz in Bukovina.[5] Gerovski was one of three brothers who contributed much to the spread of the pro-Russian movement among the Ruthenes, and who proved to be, from the point of view of the Austrian authorities, extremely elusive. Alex and Georgi were both university students; Roman, the eldest of them, was a doctor who

[5] *VA*, 574 MI ex 1914.

practised in St. Petersburg in the winter and among the Russian guests at the Karlsbad spa in the summer.

The investigation of the activities of these brothers, carried out jointly by the Austrian and the Hungarian administration and police, revealed some new features of the movement. It was established that the Gerovskis were in close contact with Kabalyuk and Koldra, the latter having been one of the defendants at the Lwow trial, and also with Count Bobrinski and with Vosnesenski, another prominent member of the Pan-Slav group in St. Petersburg. They had also received financial support from unofficial sources in Russia, which they distributed among the Russophils in eastern Galicia and in Carpathian Russia. On 10 January the Czernowitz police sent a report to the Ministry of the Interior on the results of a search in Gerovski's house. They had found a letter from Denasi, a monk at the Mount Athos monastery, and a number of copies of a pamphlet by him; an enthusiastic account of the conversion of Father Kabalyuk from Greek Catholic to the Orthodox faith; a bundle of declarations by Count Bobrinski; a memorandum on the persecution of the 'Russian nation' in Galicia; a number of letters from Ruthene peasants in Hungary on their persecution by the local authorities. Neither did Gerovski's mother remain inactive: at the end of 1913 she opened a shop in Czernowitz, where she sold objects of Orthodox devotion imported from Russia. While Roman Gerovski was still in St. Petersburg, his two younger brothers were arrested. They did not remain in prison long: on 7 June they escaped and joined their brother in Russia.

Apart from the investigations of Russophil activities and the Lwow trial, the Austrians had to deal with the Russian relief action for Galicia which, as we have seen, had been initiated in St. Petersburg in November 1913. On 13 January 1914 the Minister of the Interior wrote to Stürgkh, the Prime Minister:[6]

> I informed the Governor of Galicia in my communication of 5 January that there was no basis for a legal or police action against the Russian relief activities in Galicia and Bukovina. In order to paralyze

[6] *VA*, 184 MI ex 1914.

their political effect as much as possible, I recommend that our own relief action be speeded up, in order to make the concern of the state clear to the population in a suitable manner. . . . At the same time I would like to point out that the sum of 500,000 crowns was put at the disposal of the Governor of Bukovina for the relief action, while the Governor in Lwow received 3,200,000 crowns; of this 2,200,000 for food and 1,000,000 for seeds. Apart from these sums, there is a remainder of 800,000 crowns for employment in Galicia.

While the Governor of Galicia recommended absolute fairness to his district officers in distribution of aid in the distressed areas, and especially the avoidance of any national or political discrimination, the aid organized by the Galician–Russian society was distributed at the discretion of the Old Ruthene 'Kaczkowski' societies. In February the Austrian Consul General in Odessa reported that more funds were being collected in Russia for use in Austria–Hungary; in Odessa alone, 30,000 roubles had been contributed to the relief action in Galicia. The consul added that on St. Nicholas' day about 3,000,000 roubles had been collected in Russia for Pan-Slav propaganda.[7] Most of the funds for the Galician Russophil party and the aid for distressed areas were transmitted through the *Živnostenská* bank[8] in Prague, whose chairman Preiss was a prominent Czech Russophil and a friend of Klofáč, the pro-Russian political leader.[9]

Problems like the treatment of pro-Russian agitation made the co-ordination of foreign policy with the attitude of the central authorities to the nationalities imperative. Sometimes the Ministry of the Interior resented, sometimes it gladly followed the lead of the Ministry of Foreign Affairs. On 24 April 1914 Heinold, the Minister of the Interior, acknowledged the initiative of the State Secretary for Foreign Affairs,[10] who had suggested that three separate lists should be introduced, dealing with Russophil agitators, newspapers, and societies; Heinold commented that this would be a most valuable method of producing a complete survey of the movement.

The doctrine of 'inter-dependence of foreign and internal

[7] *VA*, 2628 MI ex 1914.
[8] *VA*, 3935 MI ex 1914.
[9] See below, page 17.
[10] *VA*, 4452 MI ex 1914.

policy' was clearly formulated for the first time in a note by Berchtold, the Minister of Foreign Affairs, to Stürgkh.[11] Berchtold wrote:

Because of the events of the last years, an intensive relationship has been formed between foreign policy and those national questions which are connected with an irredentist movement supported from abroad, so that a firm conduct of foreign affairs, without the knowledge of internal treatment of these national questions has become impossible.

Further, Berchtold wrote that of all these questions he regarded the Ruthene problem as the most important, because of its repercussions on his country's relations with Russia:

This means that the problem consists of the political treatment of our Ruthenes on the one hand, and on the other, of the fight of the pro-Russian and Orthodox agitation. It is no exaggeration when I say that our relations with Russia, which are of such great importance, will depend in the future on our success in preventing the Russification of the Ruthenes, which is being vigorously pursued on our territory, and in preserving the separate character of this nation, and by raising its civilization.

But the Foreign Minister was aware of the difficulties of this policy.

We must absolutely avoid, when supporting the Ukrainians, putting the Poles in such a position that they might one day become receptive to Russian influences. We should also not go so far in our fight against schismatic propaganda as to awake suspicions of latinizing tendencies among the members of the Greek Catholic confession and participants in the Orthodox rites, which would give our enemies the strongest weapon against us.

At the end of his note Berchtold remarked that he was perfectly aware of the difficulties of making a precise distinction between the Greek Catholic clergy who were merely strict adherents of Orthodox rites, and those priests who, under the guise of the fight for the preservation of these rites, entertained schismatic designs. Berchtold also suggested a conference of the Ministers con-

[11] *VA*, a Note of 5 June 1914, 2976 MP and 7262 MI ex 1914.

more autonomy than within Austria–Hungary. Nevertheless, this plan was a political second string for the leader of the Young Czechs: until the last moment before the outbreak of the war, Kramář remained hopeful that his attempt to transform the foreign and internal policy of the monarchy would meet with success. On 4 July, three weeks after his proposal for the Slav confederation had been handed over to the Russian Foreign Minister, Kramář poured the vials of his wrath on the Serb assassins of the Archduke Franz Ferdinand; he concluded the speech by declaring; '. . . we very much deplore the insinuation that our sincere Slavism implies acts inimical to the Habsburg Empire. We do not intend to disassociate ourselves from this Empire; it has no reason to fear our attitude.'[18]

Though Kramář's pro-Russian inclinations had a strong influence not only on the policy of his party, but on the whole of Czech political life, he acted solely on his own initiative in drafting the memorandum on the future of the Slavs. On the executive committee of his party there were a number of men who would have strongly disapproved of such a plan had they known about it.

The National Socialists, represented in the parliament by thirteen deputies, were more radical in internal politics of the Empire than their sister party, the Young Czechs. In 1912, when Kramář's party voted for the military reform laws in Vienna, the National Socialists took a firm stand against them. The National Socialists were conducting at the time a ferocious anti-military campaign: this feature of their policy, directed against one of the most important mainstays of the monarchy, made this party one of the most suspect of the political associations in the Czech lands. Klofáč, its chairman, shared Kramář's enthusiasm for Russia: an unusual attitude for a socialist politician, even though non-Marxist, when to European socialists Russia was the 'bulwark of reaction'. While Kramář took an interest in the Poles, Klofáč turned his attention to South Slav and Ruthene problems. He visited Belgrade on many occasions after the Bosnian crisis; the Pan-Slav society in St. Petersburg, at one of their meetings in

[18] *Národní Listy*, 5 July 1914.

January 1914, sent Klofáč a telegram of thanks for having organized a protest meeting against the Marmaros trial of the Ruthenes. Like Kramář, Klofáč liked to keep himself a few jumps ahead of his party.

On 22 January 1914 Zhukovski, the Russian consul in Prague, telegraphed the Foreign Ministry in St. Petersburg: 'On Saturday, deputy Klofáč will arrive in St. Petersburg. He and the director of *Živnostenská Banka*[19] ask that newspapers should not report on their arrival and stay in the capital.'[20] Klofáč visited St. Petersburg because he wanted to consult Russian authorities on the organization of underground resistance to the Habsburg monarchy in the Czech lands. Following the example of the Serbs, he intended to create a network of agents in Bohemia who, in the event of war, would conduct anti-Austrian propaganda and carry out acts of sabotage. This organization was to be particularly strong and active in Silesia and Moravia, that is in the eastern provinces which were most likely to be occupied by the advancing Russian forces. Zhukovski defined Klofáč's suggestion as an attempt to 'facilitate Russian intelligence activities'. At the time of his visit to Russia, Klofáč was convinced that war between Austria-Hungary and Russia was not only inevitable but imminent.

The Russian Foreign Minister received Klofáč on 24 January. Sazonov opened the conversation by reference to 'war-mongering adventurers' like Enver Pasha, Archduke Franz Ferdinand and Ferdinand, the King of Bulgaria. But he added that reports from Berlin and Vienna gave him confidence in peace, and that France and Britain certainly did not want war either. After their talk on the possibility of an armed conflict, Sazanov asked Klofáč how the Czechs would behave if it really occurred. Would they revolt? Klofáč replied evasively that the Czechs would not have the 'means' for a successful revolt.[21]

A few days later Klofáč saw the Chief of the General Staff who told him that although Russia did not want a war, she was pre-

[19] This was Preiss, who had organized the transfer of funds for the relief action in Galicia and Bukovina. See above, page 11.

[20] *Mezhdunarodnye otnoshenia v epokhu imperialisma*, series III, vol. 1, page 88.

[21] Klofáč in *České Slovo*, in an article entitled 'Ze vspomínek na naši velezradu', 7 December 1933.

pared for any eventuality. It was to him that Klofáč described his plan for creating a network of agents, and explained the necessity of sabotaging Austrian mobilization in the event of hostilities. At the end of their talk Klofáč agreed to discuss the details of his plan with the Russian military attaché in Vienna. However Klofáč was probably afraid to make any more contacts with Russian official representatives in the monarchy; he visited Zhukovski after his return, and gave the Russian consul an account of his interviews in St. Petersburg. His talk with Sazonov had very likely convinced the National Socialist leader that war was not imminent: it was only in the middle of April that he drafted a memorandum on his plans. Zhukovski forwarded it to St. Petersburg on 25 April.[22]

In the memorandum Klofáč identified the interests of his party with those of the Tsarist Empire in central Europe. He advised the Russians to help the National Socialists to carry their propaganda into those regions where the 'Slav spirit' was weak, especially in eastern Moravia and Silesia, 'territories of exceptional importance in the event of war'; he reminded the Russians that 'in Bohemia, simple people are politically educated in the Slav and Russophil spirit by the National Socialist party'. He gave exact figures, in roubles, as to how much it would cost to open new party secretariats and subsidize newspapers. Klofáč concluded the memorandum:

> In eastern Moravia and in Silesia the secret aim of the secretariats should be the building up of a network based on every town and village so that in the case of a Russian advance across Silesia into eastern Moravia people should be available on whom the Russian army could completely rely. The aim now is to conduct a well-planned propaganda in the Slav and Russophil spirit and to widen the organization.

A copy of this project also reached Shebeko in Vienna, who, as usual, advised caution in his dispatch to Sazonov:[23]

> Owing to the atmosphere of distrust of everything Russian which is prevalent here, a feeling which is partly due to the careless behaviour

[22] *MO*, series III, vol. 2, pages 381–384.
[23] Idem, page 473.

of our agents, I think it necessary to ask my colleague Zhukovski to be extremely careful in his contacts with local politicians and members of opposition parties, and to refrain from any action which might compromise our consular representation in Austria–Hungary.

Kramář and Klofáč had to act independently of the executive committees of their parties when they plotted against the Habsburg state. The only Czech political party which openly took a stand against the monarchy before the war were the Progressives, a small group represented in the parliament by two deputies. Lev Borský, the Vienna correspondent of the Progressive *Samostatnost* exercised a strong influence on the party's policy. He was unhampered by the provincialism which was the most characteristic feature of Czech political life; he took a broad, though often one-sided view of European political affairs.

Borský had been consistently forecasting a general war ever since the Bosnian crisis; in the *Samostatnost* he ran a military column, a rather unusual feature for an opposition paper. In April 1914 he started conducting a press campaign to draw the attention of the Czech public to international affairs and to the necessity of a new direction of Czech policy because, Borský argued, the international situation was propitious for the furthering of Czech interests. In his military column he made an imaginary English statesman say that an independent Czech state could mobilize 500,000 men, while it was unlikely that Great Britain could send more than 150,000 troops to the Continent.[24] However, Borský's campaign found little public response. Only a small independent magazine answered him[25]

We could not possibly be tempted . . . by the creation of an independent Czech statelet, which would find itself at the mercy of its more powerful neighbours. And if world events gave us such a state against our will, it would certainly be the first concern of all reasonable Czech politicians to incorporate it by prudent treaties into a powerful Austria–Hungary, justly reorganized.

[24] Lev Borský, *Před válkou or válce. In Minulost a Přítomnost.* Volumes 12, 69, 73 and 74.

[25] Krejčí in *Přehled*, 1 May 1914.

Inside the Progressive party Borský's campaign was more successful. A party congress in Prague on 16 and 17 May discussed the Czech question in the context not of Austro-Hungarian, but of European politics. Its outcome was the 'Manifesto to Europe', which was translated into French and Russian; of the two drafts of the Manifesto presented to the congress, one was prepared by Borský. His draft was turned down on the grounds that it was too radical and liable not only to be confiscated, but also to cause persecution of the Czechs.[26] Defending his draft before the congress, Borský said that he meant to incite persecution against the Czechs for two reasons: firstly, to wake his fellow-countrymen from their political indifference, and secondly, to interest the Entente Powers in the Czech problem. Thus at the congress of the Progressive party a political and moral question was raised for the first time, a question the exiles were to face frequently during the war: should politicians consciously invite persecution of their own nation? The majority of the Progressive party leaders answered it in the negative in May 1914.

The draft of the Manifesto which was finally approved was radical enough. It developed the idea that the Czech question could no longer be solved by the government in Vienna, and it argued that an army of at least 500,000 troops could be drawn from the Czech lands, who would fight either on the side of the Triple Entente or of the Central Powers; that is, as the Progressive politicians saw it, either on the German or on the Slav side. From this point the Manifesto went on:

> . . . we cannot betray either our past or the Slav idea and we advise against the reliance on the Austro-German, anti-Russian partnership. We are against the policy of the Triple Alliance, and Europe and Germany know that the restoration of the Czech state implies the utter failure of this policy. If it is not in our power to forestall the consequences of the present Austro-Hungarian policy, we do not intend to bear even partial responsibility for the catastrophe which this policy will bring. . . . We are convinced that the Czech question would be solved more justly by war than it has been hitherto solved by peace.

[26] V. Dyk, *Vzpomínky a komentáře*, Vol. 1, page 309.

In the spring of 1914 the leaders of the Progressive party were very busy. Apart from Borský's press campaign and the surprisingly radical Manifesto, they also set up a special commission, the task of which was to enter into contact with Zhukovski, the Russian consul in Prague. His attitude to the overtures by the Progressives was, however, rather forbidding.[27] Zhukovski may have become more cautious after Shebeko's admonition to take no part in local politics; he also may have regarded the Progressive party as too insignificant to be of any practical use to him. In spite of all their activities, the influence of the Progressives and their press remained negligible. They did, however, touch on problems which were to become of considerable importance later, and some of their members and sympathizers became the first Czech political exiles shortly after the outbreak of the war.

Thomas Masaryk, who was to become the leader of the Czech political emigrés, was the only deputy the Realist party sent to Vienna. Like Klofáč, he took a keen interest in the South Slavs. To the Serb, Croat, and Slovene students at Prague University, where Masaryk taught philosophy, he often talked about the idea of South Slav national unity; the seeds sown by Masaryk often fell on fertile soil. But Masaryk at no point before the general mobilization turned to Russia for help or advice. Like the Social Democrats he was highly critical of the Tsarist regime: his sympathies, from the time of his student days at Vienna, lay in the West. He admired Hume, and many of his ideas were derived from the radical liberal philosopher; his personal contacts abroad were in France and in England, his wife was American. His three pre-war visits to the United States gave him some knowledge of the conditions among the Czech and Slovak immigrants there, which was to be useful to him during the war. In the differences between the political attitudes of Masaryk and Kramář before the war the origins of their later conflict could be discerned; but Kramář's political ideas had an incomparably larger following than those of Masaryk: in his secret plan for a Slav confederation, Kramář was planning for the event of war. Masaryk, on the other hand, did not make an allowance, in his

[27] V. Dyk, op. cit., page 314.

political calculations, for war: when it finally came he was unprepared for it. Such unpreparedness was, of course, typical of the majority of Czech politicians. They were too absorbed, in the last months of peace, in their own parochial issues: there were negotiations for a compromise between the Czechs and the Germans in Bohemia and the political scandal of Šviha who, while chairman of the National Socialists, had been co-operating closely with the police in Prague.

While Czech political life was, on the surface, little affected by the explosive situation in the Balkans, the Slavs in the south of the monarchy were much more sensitive to the momentous events taking place on the other side of the frontier. The attraction exercised by Serbia on the Serb and Croat subjects of the Habsburg dynasty increased after the success of the young state in the Balkan wars; but the degree of this attraction varied considerably from one South Slav province to another. In Croatia, which occupied a similar position in the Hungarian part of the monarchy to that of Galicia in the Austrian half, the Croats were little susceptible to the pull of Belgrade. Indeed, many Croats, convinced of their cultural superiority, regarded the Serbs as Balkan barbarians, unfit to live in a civilized state. Even the Croat–Serb Coalition, the strongest party in the Croatian Diet, with its programme based on the co-operation between the Serbs and the Croats, regarded the solution of the South Slav problem as an internal affair of the monarchy: although there were, from the Habsburg point of view, disloyal elements in the Coalition, it took the declaration of war on Serbia to separate them from the loyal majority of the party. The politicians from the Adriatic provinces of Istria and Dalmatia were the most internationally minded of the deputies in the *Reichsrat:* they had observed the unification of Italy at close quarters and learned their lesson. By 1913 some of the younger politicians in the Adriatic provinces began to ask themselves whether Serbia might become the Piedmont of the South Slavs. Shortly after the partial mobilization of Austria–Hungary against Serbia in 1913 Meštrović, the Dalmatian sculptor and amateur politician went to see Pašić, the Serbian Prime Minister, in Belgrade. The Premier, just back from St. Petersburg, told

Meštrović that war between Austria–Hungary and Serbia was, sooner or later, inevitable.[28] Meštrović told Frano Supilo, the Rjeka journalist and Ante Trumbić, the Croat politician from Split, who later became the chairman of the South Slav committee in exile, about his talk with Pašić. At the end of 1913, these men discussed the possibility of a war on a larger scale than the local Balkan hostilities; in such an event, they decided, they would have to look to Serbia for help. Although these provinces later supplied the anti-Habsburg movement abroad with most of its leaders, they were not much affected by the revolutionary terrorism, a feature of the South Slav national movement that distinguished it from others in the monarchy, and which, several months later, was to drive Vienna into the war.

The terrorist movement, aiming at the unification of South Slav territories under the leadership of Serbia, found the most suitable ground for its activities in Bosnia and Hercegovina. These two provinces were the latest territorial acquisitions of the Habsburgs (they were occupied by Austria–Hungary, following a decision of the Congress of Berlin and they were formally annexed thirty years later, in 1908); before they passed under the control of Vienna they had suffered centuries of Turkish maladministration; even under Austro-Hungarian administration they were treated as a backward, outlying colonial possession. They were far removed from the important centres of Austrian industry and communications; because of the rapidly changing political situation on the Balkans, and because of the frequent switches in the foreign policy of Vienna, Austria–Hungary had made little progress towards their assimilation. This uncertainty was reflected in their constitutional position: since neither Vienna nor Budapest wished for further increase of their Slav population, Bosnia and Hercegovina belonged, technically, in neither part of the monarchy; they were administered by the Ministry of Finance, one of the three ministries common to both Austria and Hungary.

Since the terrorist movement was to a high degree inspired and directed by Belgrade, it is necessary at this point to consider the internal changes in Serbia which made possible the pursuit of a

[28] Milada Paulová, *Dějiny Maffie*, page 16, Prague 1937.

policy directed against the Habsburg Empire. Until 1903 Serbia was, from the point of view of the Ministry of Foreign Affairs in Vienna, an unimportant and friendly state, with a marked streak of corruption running through its government and administration, on the south-eastern frontier of the monarchy. In this year, after a bloody palace revolution in Belgrade, the picture started to change. The assassination of the last Obrenović ruler put an end to a system of government and foreign policy. Alexander Obrenović, like his father King Milan, had valued good relations with Austria–Hungary; under the new King, Peter Karadjordjević, Serbia switched its sympathies from Vienna to St. Petersburg. Such change in foreign policy was completely acceptable to the men who had brought King Peter to power and who now came to dominate Serbian politics. The conspiracy of 1903 brought two groups into prominence: the military, which included Dragutin Dimitrijević and Voja Tankosić, and the political, among whom Pašić and the Old Radicals were most powerful. They succeeded in shaking Serbia out of her political lethargy; they maintained that she would remain economically dependent on Austria without her own access to the sea. They realized, and learned to exploit, the opportunities presented by the existence of their Orthodox fellow-countrymen in the Habsburg monarchy on the one hand, and of the Russian alliance on the other. The military clique and Pašić instilled new life into Serbia. Both groups were striving for power: for themselves at home, for their country abroad. But whereas their identical interests abroad led to co-operation between them, their struggle for power inside Serbia ended in a violent clash and victory for the politicians.[29]

The annexation of Bosnia and Hercegovina was the last major move on Austrian initiative in the Balkans before the war. Although the position of the two provinces was changed only formally, the Serbs in Belgrade, who coveted these territories, were indignant. They thought of the annexation as of yet another barrier erected on their way to the Adriatic sea in the West. Serbia had to capitulate to a superior force, especially when it became clear that the government of Russia, still uncertain of its

[29] See below, page 33.

strength after the setbacks in the Far East, was in no position to assist Serbia. On 2 November 1908 Pašić telegraphed from St. Petersburg: 'Russia cannot and will not go to war on account of Bosnia at the present time.'[30]

The events of 1908 had a stimulating effect on Belgrade. Shortly after the annexation several high-ranking civil servants and senior officers founded the *Narodna Odbrana*—National Defence—which was to serve as a voluntary fighting organization against Austria–Hungary; the society was intended to train its members in partisan warfare. But instead of war, Serbia was forced into recognizing the annexation on 31 March 1909. After six months' existence, *Narodna Odbrana* was transformed from a military into a cultural organization. It remained violently anti-Austrian: in a pamphlet published in 1911 by the society's central committee, the victory of Serbia over the waning power of the Turks was taken for granted; the main effort now had to be directed against the 'new Turks, who come from the North and who are more powerful and terrible than the old enemy'.[31]

The Austro-Hungarian frontier districts, and Bosnia and Hercegovina in particular, were, from the point of view of the *Narodna Odbrana*'s leaders, the most interesting territories. A network of agents had to be built up who would infiltrate into South Slav societies on the territory of the Habsburg monarchy; if no such societies were in existence they had to be founded. Moreover, all the societies preaching Great Serbian propaganda had to appear harmless to the Austro-Hungarian authorities: the existing *Sokol* gymnastic societies, for instance, were unsuitable for this purpose; the Pan-Slav tendencies of these organizations in other Slav provinces of the Empire were well known to the Austrian administration. Nevertheless, the men who conducted pro-Serb propaganda in these territories were resourceful. The Great Serbian idea was preached behind the smoke-screen of various gymnastic, anti-alcoholic, and literary societies. Here the Serbs and the Croats could learn the simple message 'Against Vienna, for Belgrade'. The Orthodox priest and the village teacher

[30] *Die auswärtige Politik Serbiens*, edited by M. Boghitschewitsch, vol. 1, Document 27
[31] *Kriegsschuldfrage*, vol. 5, page 210.

were often very helpful in this respect; the priest, of course, could not appeal to the Roman Catholic Croats; for them the idea of Greater Serbia had to be translated into terms of unity and co-operation between the Serbs and the Croats.

In the period between 1908 and 1911 there was no need for clandestine contacts with Belgrade. Serbian schools and universities were open to young men from the South Slav provinces of the Habsburg monarchy. Government offices in Belgrade did not hesitate to employ Serbs from Austria–Hungary, although technically they were foreign subjects. A large number of student delegations crossed the Austrian frontier on their way to the Serbian capital. At school or university in the monarchy, students could read books and periodicals supplied by the Serbian government. There was a colony of young Serbs from Bosnia in Belgrade: they were a highly inflammable material.

In 1910 Vienna made an attempt to introduce a certain degree of self-government into Bosnia and Hercegovina. In June the first Bosnian Diet was opened. Four months later, Bogdan Žerajić, a Serbian student from Bosnia, fired five shots at the Governor of the province. But Zerajić missed his target and committed suicide on the spot. It was one of Dragutin Dimitrijević's friends, Bogdan Simić, who had taught Žerajić to shoot in Belgrade, and had provided him with the revolver and ammunition.[32] The Serbian press hailed Žerajić as a martyr. Gacinović, who later became the leader of the Bosnian revolutionary youth, celebrated Žerajić's death in a romantic and violently nationalist poem, *The Death of a Hero*. The manuscript of the poem was sent from Vienna to Belgrade where it was printed and then sent back to the monarchy in thousands of copies.[33] Žerajić became the first Bosnian nationalist saint: the foundation had been laid for the legend of the Habsburg Serbs' struggle against the monarchy. The young Serbs on the Austro-Hungarian side of the frontier were profoundly impressed by Gacinović's poem; it was more wood on the fire fanned by their nationalist societies. The poem and the writings of the Russian revolutionaries, and Prince Kropotkin in

[32] H. Bauer, *Sarajevo*, page 31, Stuttgart 1930.
[33] H. Uebersberger, *Der Saloniki Prozess*, page xxiii, Berlin 1933.

particular, helped to maintain these young men—most of them under twenty years of age—at a high pitch of revolutionary and nationalist enthusiasm. Most of them had passed, on their spiritual pilgrimage, the familiar landmarks of anarchism, Marxist, and non-Marxist socialism, before they ended up as completely dedicated, romantic nationalists.[34]

Between 1908 and 1910 Serb irredentist activities on the territory of the Habsburg monarchy were limited to cultural propaganda for South Slav unity and, more frequently, of the Greater Serbian ideal. After Žerajić's unsuccessful attempt on the life of the Governor of Bosnia the tone of Serbian nationalist activities changed. In 1911 the period began in which the Serbs concentrated on terrorist rather than on cultural activities; a period that ended in the assassination of Archduke Franz Ferdinand, the successor to the Habsburg throne.

In May 1911 a group of Belgrade Serbs, among whom the military conspirators in the palace revolution of 1903, Dimitrijević and Tankosić, were prominent, founded the society *Ujedinenije ili Smert*—Unity or Death, also known as the Black Hand. From the time of its foundation it was in close contact with the *Narodna Odbrana*: a member of the central committee of the Black Hand, for instance, Major Milan Vasić, was the acting secretary of the *Narodna Odbrana* until June 1913 when he died fighting the Bulgarians. The new organization preferred terror to propaganda. Its statutes clearly indicate the determination and ruthlessness of the men who founded it.[35] At the Saloniki trial in 1917 Major Vulović said that he had regarded the assassinations and other illegal activities committed in the territories 'not yet liberated' as necessary evils, essential in the interests of the nation.[36]

Members of the Black Hand could be found in many branches of

[34] Cf. Princips *Bekenntnisse*, Vienna 1926. This is a record of conversations between Gavrilo Princip, the assassin of Archduke Franz Ferdinand and Dr. Papenheimer, the doctor at the Theresienstadt fortress prison in Bohemia where Princip spent the last three years of his life. In this unique document, Princip unwillingly and in halting, abrupt German, described and defended his own and his friends' ideological development.

[35] H. Uebersberger, op. cit., page 397 et seq.

[36] Idem, page 162.

Serbian administration, but the core of the society was recruited among regular army officers. It received support and protection from the highest places. Crown Prince Alexander, who was in frequent contact with the members of the secret society before the war, contributed a large sum towards the foundations funds of its newspaper, the *Pijemont*. Milovanović,[37] when Dimitrijević acquainted him with the aims of the organization, was enthusiastic about it. He apparently told Dimitrijević: 'Young friend, put your society at my disposal, and you will see what Milovanović will do for Serbia in no time.'[38]

Shortly after the foundation of the Black Hand, the Serbian General Staff, with the approval of the Ministry of War, worked out a plan for the appointment of special duty officers to certain sectors of the Austro-Hungarian and Turkish frontier. Three such posts were created on the border between Serbia and Austria–Hungary: at Šabac for north-eastern Bosnia and Syrmia, and through Syrmia for Croatia; at Loznica for central Bosnia, and finally at Užice for southern Bosnia and northern Sandjak. The original plan was worked out by Lieutenant-Colonel Milovanović together with Major Dimitrijević. Officially, the appointment of the special duty officers was made by the General Staff; in fact, all three of them were members of the Black Hand organization, and as such they were expected to further the Great Serbian revolutionary idea on both sides of the frontier. Because of this confusion of functions and responsibilities, which we encounter so often in pre-war Serbia, it is often difficult to define precisely the limits of official duty and unofficial activities; the question of 'official responsibility' is frequently ambiguous.

The work of the special duty officers against the Habsburg monarchy was supervised by Captain Popović, one of the founder members of the Black Hand who was based on Šabac. In Popović's opinion, the prestige the *Narodna Odbrana* had won for itself among the South Slavs of the monarchy was worth exploiting.[39] In spite of its exclusively 'cultural' activity, the Serbs in

[37] Foreign Minister since 1907, Prime Minister from 1911 until his death in 1912.
[38] Bauer, op. cit., page 22.
[39] Popović, *Nova Evropa*, *XVI*, page 139 et seq.

Bosnia and Hercegovina regarded the older society as a revolutionary organization. Popović therefore opposed the introduction of the Habsburg South Slavs into the Black Hand, and maintained that its work could be carried on just as effectively by the *Narodna Odbrana*. Popović's policy was also aimed at preventing a split of the revolutionary movement into two groups; it helps to explain why the Austro-Hungarian authorities, though well-informed about the activities of the *Narodna Odbrana*, knew very little about the Black Hand.[40]

The influence of Belgrade by no means remained limited to the young generation in Bosnia and Hercegovina, although these two provinces were best suited for its exercise. In April 1912, 176 Serb and Croat students from Croatia visited the Serbian capital.[41] They were received by cabinet ministers; a military parade was organized for their benefit; the Belgrade officers' corps gave a ball in their honour. King Peter greeted these subjects of the Emperor of Austria as his 'Croat Brothers' who, in their turn, addressed him as the 'King of the Jugoslavs'. Colonel Dimitrijević gave a private dinner for a few selected members of the delegation. It was at this dinner that Oscar Tartaglia, the future Mayor of Split, heard about the aims of the secret organization; he was the first Croat and the first Catholic who was won over for them.[42]

On the occasion of the Zagreb students' visit to Belgrade, another political assassination was decided on. This time the victim was to be von Cuvaj, the Governor of Croatia. Apparently, it had been in Sarajevo in February 1912 that the plan was first discussed between Tartaglia and his friend Jukić, a student from Bosnia. In Belgrade, Tartaglia introduced Jukić to Dimitrijević and told him about their plan. Dimitrijević handed Jukić over to Major Tankosić, who taught him to shoot and to throw bombs, and who provided Jukić with the weapons necessary for the assassination. In June 1912 Jukić fired several shots at the Governor, but missed, and injured one of the officials accompanying Cuvaj. During the two following years, three more attempts on the life of the Governor of Croatia were made.

[40] See below, page 39. [41] Lončarević, *Jugoslawiens Entstehung*, page 409 et seq.
[42] Bauer, op. cit., page 29.

The attempts to assassinate high officials in the Austro-Hungarian administration in the South Slav territories were all made by Serbs who were Habsburg subjects, mostly of Bosnian origin. In every case their connexion with Belgrade has been, to a higher or lesser degree, established. The ages of the terrorists hardly ever exceeded twenty; they were used, as exceedingly willing tools, for the ends of the 'unofficial' policy of Belgrade. Yet looked at from Vienna, these terrorist activities could not be regarded merely as a form of political protest against the intractability of the Austro-Hungarian authorities. Their motivation was more complex. Acts of terror invited acts of suppression by the Habsburg administration, which on occasions exceeded the limits of legality and good sense. By employing a small number of resolute terrorists it was possible to keep the population of the South Slav provinces in a state of constant uncertainty, fear, and even hatred not only of the local authorities, but of the whole Habsburg system. Žerajić's attempt on the life of the head of administration of Bosnia[43] can best illustrate this point. It was made a few months after the opening of the first Bosnian Diet, at a time when there was a risk that the political aspiration of the majority of the inhabitants of the province might well be satisfied. Such a state of political contentment would have been highly undesirable from the point of view of the young radicals. In the interests of Greater Serbia, the Austro-Hungarian authorities had to be incited to acts of suppression which would drive the Serbs into the revolutionary movement, or at least into opposition to the Habsburg state. Borský, when he drafted the manifesto for the congress of the Progressive party in Prague,[44] entertained precisely the same idea: he wanted to 'wake up' the Czechs by inviting their persecution. Whereas Borský's own party declined the offer, some Serbs, on both sides of the frontier, accepted it.

There can be no doubt, in spite of contradictory evidence, that the men in Belgrade were encouraged in pursuing the 'unofficial' policy of supporting terrorism in Austria–Hungary by

[43] See above, page 27.
[44] See above, page 21 et seq.

St. Petersburg. Whereas the Pan-Slav societies in Russia took a mild interest in the Ruthenes and a still milder one in the Czechs, there are indications that in official quarters and military circles in particular, the Serbs aroused a more direct and active interest. They could be, of course, regarded as the 'Orthodox brethren' by the Russians; they also occupied an important strategic position in the south as Russia's natural allies against the Ottoman Empire and later against Austria–Hungary. Hartwig, the Russian Ambassador in Belgrade, himself regarded his position in the Serb capital, in a dispatch to Sazonov in March 1913, as 'quite exceptional'; Lieutenant-Colonel Simić, a member of the Black Hand, described the situation in Belgrade before the war in no uncertain terms: 'During the Balkan war Hartwig completely dictated our foreign policy, and partly also our internal policy. In all important matters Pašić was merely a mouthpiece of Hartwig's plans and decisions.'[45] Artamanov, the military attaché in the Russian Embassy, was in frequent touch with Colonel Dimitrijević; it is likely that he knew, and approved of, the last and most momentous action of the Black Hand. Nevertheless, it is certain that the men in Belgrade, whether they were exponents of the 'official' or the 'unofficial' policy, could not indulge, without the support of Russia or without the knowledge that it was forthcoming, in hostile and aggressive acts against the Habsburg monarchy.

The assassination of the Archduke Franz Ferdinand, the successor to the Habsburg throne, was the last act of political terrorism in the Balkans before World War I. Many answers have been given to the question of why this man should have attracted such vengeance. Colonel Dimitrijević himself has provided one of them: '. . . feeling that Austria–Hungary was making preparations for war against us, I thought that with the disappearance of Franz Ferdinand the party and the climate of opinion he repre-

[45] Hans Uebersberger, *Oesterreich zwischen Russland und Serbien*, pages 297 and 298, Köln-Gratz, 1958. Dr. Uebersberger presents the evidence of Serbia's dependence on Russia in some detail. The study of this problem, however, is made difficult by the fact that Hartwig's dispatches from Belgrade for the crucial period between May and July 1914 were destroyed, by a person unknown, in the archives of the Russian Foreign Ministry in the first days of the revolution in November 1917.

sented would lose its impetus, and that the danger of war would thus be removed, or at any rate postponed, from Serbia.'[46]

If this is a genuine statement of what Dimitrijević thought before the assassination, his sources of information were singularly unreliable. Franz Ferdinand was opposed to the plans of the party led by Conrad von Hötzendor, the Chief of the Austro-Hungarian General Staff, which maintained that the Serbian problem could be solved only by war.[47] Neither did the Archduke plan an attack on Serbia at either of his meetings with the German Emperor at Konopiště in October 1913 and at the beginning of June 1914.[48] At any rate, the preparations for his assassination had been completed some time before his second meeting with the Kaiser. Franz Ferdinand did, however, take an active interest in the solution of the South Slav problem. He favoured the 'trialist' plan for the reform of the monarchy, which would have transformed the South Slav provinces into its third constituent part. Colonel Dimitrijević and his friends might have regarded such a solution as disastrous for Great Serbian aspirations: previous terrorist acts in Austria–Hungary point to the fact that it was not so much the suppression as the protection of Serb and Croat interests within the monarchy that invited their, and the young terrorists', resentment.

Throughout the years between the foundation of the Black Hand and the summer of 1914 Dimitrijević's influence in the secret organization was on the increase. Ambitious, charming, and secretive, the young conspirator of 1903 had made his way to the top in the Serbian army; in 1914 he was, as a Brigadier, the head of the intelligence section of the General Staff. But as his power increased Dimitrijević's conflict with the politicians became sharper. In March and April 1914 Serbia was going through an acute internal crisis caused by the differences, between the Radical party and the military, on the treatment of the Macedonian

[46] From a statement signed by Dimitrijević at the time of the Saloniki trial in 1917. Stoyan Gavrilović, *New Evidence on the Sarajevo Assassination*, Journal of Modern History, December 1955.

[47] L. Albertini, *The Origins of the War of 1914*, vol. 2, page 8, Oxford University Press 1953.

[48] *Die Grosse Politik*, vol. 39, documents Nos. 15709 to 15711 and notes; 1573.

territories, which Serbia had won in the Balkan war. This conflict brought Pašić sharply up against the threat of the military clique to the power of his own party. Pašić never forgave the soldiers, and Dimitrijević in particular, for the trouble they had caused him in the spring of 1914: his opportunity to settle accounts with the worst offenders came only in 1917 when Dimitrijević was sentenced to death at the Saloniki trial. The political situation in Belgrade in the spring of 1914 partly explains why Pašić, though he knew of the preparations for the assassination of the Habsburg Crown Prince, did not take more active steps to intervene.[49] The political power of the soldiers may have been too much for him to try to break in peace-time; he must have known that the organizers of assassinations on the other side of the frontier would have had no scruples in turning their skill against him.

Thus in Belgrade, Dimitrijević and his friends were able to proceed with the preparations for the assassination of Franz Ferdinand undisturbed. In March 1914 it became known in Belgrade that the Archduke would visit Bosnia sometime in June; it was at the end of the month that Princip discussed the impending event with his friend Čabrinović.[50] By the middle of May there was a group of Bosnians in Belgrade determined to use this opportunity to murder the Archduke; Dimitrijević and Tankosić approved of the young terrorists' intentions, and they did everything to assist them.[51] On 28 May Ciganović—Dimitrijević's and Tankosić's contact man with the Bosnians, a Serb from Croatia and an employee of the Serbian state railways, and also possibly Pašić's confidant in the Black Hand organization—sent three Bosnian students, Princip, Grabež, and Čabrinović from Belgrade to Sarajevo. He provided them with a number of introductions, among them one to Major Popović, the special duty officer at Šabac. Popović and one of his colleagues on the frontier farther south found no difficulty in securing illegal entry into Austro-Hungarian territory for these young men.

[49] Albertini, op. cit., vol. 2, page 97 et seq.

[50] Princips *Bekenntnisse*, page 15.

[51] Mr. Joachim Remak's *Sarajevo*, published in London in 1959, is the best study of the assassinations available in English; it follows the argument first convincingly expounded by Professor Hans Uebersberger.

They had been sent to Sarajevo with the approval of Dimitrijević; they had been provided with arms from the Serbian army arsenal at Kragujevac, and they had been trained in using them at a terrorist school near Belgrade; they were seen safely across the frontier by Serbian special duty officers. The fuse had been laid: now Gavrilo Princip and his friends had to spend a month in Bosnia, awaiting the arrival of their victim.

II

THE EASTERN FRONT

The mid-summer of 1914 was exceptionally hot. The Archduke Franz Ferdinand was attending army manœuvres in Bosnia; on 28 June he visited Sarajevo, accompanied by his wife and General Potiorek, the Governor of Bosnia and Hercegovina. Soon after the beginning of the majestic procession through the provincial town, Čabrinović made the first attempt to assassinate the Archduke: the bomb he threw exploded only a few seconds after the Imperial car had passed. As soon as the excitement had died down the journey was continued according to plan. After speech-making at the Town Hall the convoy of cars was slowly proceeding down the embankment: a confusion as to which route should be taken at a crossroads gave Princip his opportunity. He fired two shots in quick succession; the Archduke remained sitting upright; his wife leaning slightly towards him. The glittering heat of the day must have affected the senses of the spectators in the tightly packed crowd: some eye-witnesses heard no shots being fired; nobody, including General Potiorek, who was sharing the Archduke's vehicle, realized that the Archduke and his wife had been mortally wounded. It was only after the General had ordered the driver to go to his residence on the other side of the bridge that he noticed a trickle of blood on the Archduke's tunic. At the Governor's Residence the doctors could do nothing for the Archduke and his wife.

In Vienna, the Sarajevo murders failed at first to make an impression; only the thick black headlines in the newspapers bore witness to the gravity of the events. On Monday night, Josef Redlich recorded in his diary: 'There is no mood of mourning in the town; in Prater and here in Grinzig music was played all over the place on both days.'[1] And a day later, the Russian Ambassador reported to St. Petersburg:

> The tragic end of Archduke Franz Ferdinand found little response in financial circles here and on the stock-exchange—this index of the mood in business circles. The value of government stocks did not change, which is explained here by confidence in the continuation of peace.[2]

Nevertheless, the Austro-Hungarian press soon began to speculate on the connexion between the assassination and the government in Belgrade: collusion was suspected but no concrete evidence could be produced. The journalists in Belgrade were not slow to retaliate: on 1 July *Politika* complained that less than half an hour after the assassination the 'Jewish press in Vienna flooded the world with news about money and bombs from Serbia'. The anti-Serb riots after the assassination, which spread from Sarajevo as far as Croatia, and the failure of the Austro-Hungarian authorities to check them, gave a new weapon into the hands of the Belgrade propagandists: on 30 June the Serbian daily *Straža* produced a pamphlet which described the riots in terms of 'extermination of the Serbs in Bosnia' by 'mobs bought with Austrian money'.

While the journalists were engaged in verbal warfare, discussions between Vienna and Berlin were opened on an official level. At a luncheon on 5 July Szögyeny, the Austrian Ambassador to Berlin, handed over a letter from his Emperor to the Kaiser, together with a memorandum on the Balkan situation. Emperor Wilhelm read both documents carefully in the Ambassador's presence: he said that he expected Austria–Hungary to act against Serbia, but since the conflict might have serious European repercussions, he had to consult his Chancellor before replying.[3] On the following day, the Austrian Ambassador reported that the German government, in the person of the Chancellor, Bethmann-Hollweg, 'recognizes the danger presented to Austria–Hungary

[1] J. Redlich, *Tagebücher*, edited by Fritz Fellner. Vienna, 1953. Vol. 2, entry for 29 June 1914.

[2] *M.O.*, III, vol. 4, Document No. 32.

[3] *Österreich-Ungarns Aussenpolitik*, vol. 7, Document No. 10058.

and to the Triple Alliance by the Russian policy of alliances on the Balkans. It also recognizes the fact that in the present situation Bulgaria ought formally to join the Triple Alliance, but that this must happen in such a way as to avoid cutting across our commitments to Rumania. As far as our [i.e. Austria–Hungary's,] relations with Serbia are concerned, the German government's standpoint is that we should judge ourselves what is to be done to clear up the relationship; in this respect, we can rely on Germany as an ally and as a friend, whatever course we take'. Later in the conversation, the Ambassador reported, he was able to ascertain that 'the Chancellor, like his Imperial master, regards our immediate intervention against Serbia as the most radical and best solution of our difficulties on the Balkans'.[4]

Certain of Germany's support, but uncertain as to the manner in which other European Powers would react, the Austro-Hungarian government took the fatal decision to embark on a military action against Serbia. At six o'clock in the afternoon on 23 July the Austro-Hungarian Minister in Belgrade handed over an ultimatum to the Serbian government. It was a stiff ultimatum: the time it gave the Serbs to fulfil its ten conditions was ominously brief. Yet in its conclusions the note and its enclosure were not widely off the mark:

> The history of the last few years and the sad events of June 28th have proved the existence of a subversive movement in Serbia, the aim of which is the detachment of certain territories from Austria–Hungary. This movement, which originated in the full view of the Serbian government, found its expression on this side of the frontier in a number of terrorist acts. The Serbian government not only did not respect the formal obligations of the declaration of 31 March 1909, it did nothing to suppress this movement.

Though the ultimatum proved that the Austro-Hungarian authorities knew of the existence of the *Narodna Odbrana*, it made no reference to the activities of the Black Hand

[4] *Österreich-Ungarns Aussenpolitik*, vol. 7, Document No. 10076.

organization.[5] A few minutes before the forty-eight hours' grace granted to the Serbs expired, Pašić appeared at the Austro-Hungarian mission in Belgrade. His reply to the note was officially described as 'unsatisfactory'. Half an hour later von Giesl and other members of the Austrian mission in Belgrade left the town: the declaration of war by Austria–Hungary on Serbia followed on 28 July.

The Habsburg monarchy was driven into an armed conflict by the ambitions of Belgrade and by the response these ambitions found on the Austro-Hungarian territory; having abandoned hope of solving the South Slav question peacefully, the rulers of the Dual Monarchy delivered the future of their state into the hands of the soldiers.

The army which was to fight this war reflected faithfully the national composition of the Empire. It was a reliable instrument at the disposal of the established order; more than any other institution of the state it had retained, even in its higher echelons, a multi-national character. Although German was the language of command, it consisted of no more than sixty words; national considerations played little or no role in the recruitment for the officers' corps; it contained many dedicated, and some very able men. For a young Croat, Pole, or Czech the army offered a tempting career. Although it was exposed to the same strains and stresses as the other institutions of the Empire, the army remained on the whole an effective instrument until the summer of 1918. Contrary to the opinion of many historians, the balance sheets of the Austro-Hungarian army in the four years of the war speak in its favour.

From the beginning of hostilities until February 1917 Conrad von Hötzendor was Chief of the General Staff. In his overall strategy he attempted to avoid war on two fronts; relying on the slow and cumbrous procedure of Russian mobilization, he expected to deal Serbia a decisive blow before Russia's effective intervention. After a brief Serbian campaign, the Austro-Hungarian

[5] The ignorance of the Austro-Hungarian authorities may be explained partly by insufficient reporting by their Belgrade mission, and partly by the policy of Major Popović and of other Serbian special duty officers on the frontier. See above, page 30.

army was expected to divert most of its potential to the Russian front, to participate there in a joint action with the German army.

The bulge of Russian Poland was to be the first objective of the campaign. But, like the German plan for an early victory in the West, the Austrian scheme was frustrated. Serbia offered an unexpectedly stubborn resistance; because of Falkenhayn's commitments in the West, the Germans neglected the eastern front. The lack of coordination of military effort became apparent soon after the outbreak of the war; it was the cause of the first serious disagreements between the Central European allies.

Finally, when Italy entered the war on the side of the Allies, the Austro-Hungarian army found itself engaged on several fronts simultaneously. Although Hötzendor's strategy misfired, he had achieved, when war on Serbia was declared, one of his most important pre-war objectives: the possibility that the South Slav problem might be solved by the force of arms. Like many Austro-Hungarian high-ranking officers, Conrad was a pre-eminently political soldier: the political interests of the military and especially their views on national problems were to have a disastrous effect on the developments in the Habsburg monarchy.

At this point we should stress the fact that it was the Russian and Serbian, and later the Italian, fronts that attracted the attention of war-lords and public alike in Austria–Hungary. Indeed, they can be said to have taken a rather parochial interest in the European struggle. The degree of self-confidence of the rulers of the Danubian monarchy was directly related to the fortunes of the war in the East; the hopes of the radical minority among the Slavs were raised every time the front moved westward, and dashed to the ground whenever the armies of the Central Powers scored a success in the Russian or Serbian theatres of war.

The declaration of war deeply affected the constitutional and legal situation in Austria–Hungary: it brought about a considerable increase in the political power of the army.[6] Imperial edicts

[6] See J. Redlich, *Austrian War Government*, page 55 et seq., Yale University Press, 1929.

replaced some of the civil law code, and the paragraphs relating to civil liberties in particular. Courts of law including a jury were abolished, and 'extraordinary criminal senates' were introduced. By an Imperial edict of 24 July high treason, offences against the Emperor and the members of his House, disturbances of public order, revolt and acts of sabotage were withdrawn from the jurisdiction of civil courts and placed in the hands of military authorities. The war also gave virtually unlimited administrative powers to the military in the territories of the battle-front, but in some cases the 'military zone' extended far into the hinterland. The Teschen and Ostrava districts in Silesia and north-eastern Moravia, for instance, passed under military administration when they were over a hundred miles distant from the actual front line.

The constitutional checks on the powers of the military also disappeared in the Austrian part of the monarchy. While the parliament in Budapest met in regular sessions throughout the war, the *Reichsrat* in Vienna had been prorogued since March 1914; it was not to meet again until May 1917. The dissolution of the parliament had been originally facilitated by the support the German middle-class parties gave to the plan; after the outbreak of the war they continued their opposition to the summoning of the parliament. The Prime Minister shared the feelings of the Austrian Germans: he himself hesitated to re-open a representative body with a Slav majority. Stürgkh's attitude towards the parliament shows that he was uncertain about the effect the declaration of war on Serbia and Russia might have had on the Slavs in Austria. Like many other German politicians, the Premier suspected them of a marked proclivity for treason and rebellion; at times of crisis he found it difficult to believe that men like Klofáč, Markov, Kramář, and Supilo were isolated rebels among the Slavs, the majority of whom were either pro-Habsburg or, at worst, undecided or indifferent. Stürgkh's government failed to give encouragement to these loyal politicians; it did not appreciate the fact that attacks on official policy in the *Reichsrat* were less dangerous to the monarchy than the agitation of the radicals in Bohemia, Dalmatia, or Croatia. Indeed, the work of the anti-Habsburg politicians was facilitated by the panic-stricken atmosphere of the provincial towns, by the absence of the moderating influence that Vienna had exercised on the politicians of different races and creeds, and by the scarcity of reliable news under a stiff censorship.

In spite of the fears of the government and the high hopes in some quarters abroad, no revolution occurred in the Slav lands at the beginning of the war.[7]

The general mobilization, apart from some minor incidents, ran smoothly: the reports of the Supreme Command (*Armee-oberkommando*), which never tried to flatter the Slavs on their behaviour during the war, confirmed this. However, some Czech and South Slav historians, who wrote between the two wars, although they were unable to introduce any concrete evidence of revolt, maintained that the majority of their compatriots in the armed forces were unwilling to engage in a 'fratricidal struggle'—meaning the war on the Russians and the Serbs—and that 'not only their actions, but also their feelings were forced on the Slavs'.[8] Such arguments, while aiming to prove that the 'national masses' were anti-Habsburg from the beginning of the war, discounted the loyalty of the majority of the politicians to the monarchy. These, on their part, could take one of the following choices: they could remain loyal, or pursue an opportunist policy—while keeping a close watch on the fortunes of the war—or, finally, they could take action against the Habsburg state.

In Bohemia Klofáč, the leader of the National Socialists, was arrested on a suspicion of treason in September; there was no one in the top echelons of his party forceful enough to carry on his pre-war radical policy. Kramář, however, managed to keep out of prison longer than his friend. On 4 August, the day the Germans invaded Belgium, he wrote an article in the *Národní Listy*, in

[7] In a letter to a Czech named Rohla, Professor Denis, the historian of central and eastern Europe at the Sorbonne, expressed his disappointment with the loyal behaviour of the Czechs after the outbreak of the war. See M. Paulová, *Dějiny Maffie*, page 470.

[8] J. Werstadt, *Politické plány české Maffie v prvním roce války*. *Naše Revoluce*, volume 6, page 369. Prague, 1929–30.

which he presented the war as a struggle between the Slavs and the Germans:

The historical moment which so many have feared and so many have expected, has arrived. The words of the German Chancellor about the fight between the Slavs and the Teutons have become a reality. The policy of the European Powers will be brought to judgement—now all the mistakes of internal policy will have to be accounted for . . . we are prepared to state that at the end of this war we shall hardly recognize the map of Europe. Bismarck pointed out that the future war would have to be fought until the complete destruction of the enemy, so that the enemy would no longer present a threat. *Saigner a blanc*. . . . At this moment all of us have the future of our nation in mind. Many may think how wise it would have been had we not wasted our strength on squabbles and had used it for a firm organization of our national forces, so that we could await the blows of fate without trepidation.

Kramář, without being too explicit (his article, with its obscure references and veiled criticism, is a good example of the radical, anti-Habsburg journalism in the first three years of the war) made his point. Playing on the pro-Russian sympathies of the Czechs, he pointed the way his fellow-countrymen should take. Once the problem of the war was formulated as a struggle between the Slavs and the Germans, it should have been obvious to every Czech on whose side he was. But Kramář was the only leading politician who indicated what the attitude of the nation to the war should be. The Progressives, the National Socialists, and Masaryk's Realists, some of them surprised by the outbreak of the war and most of them uncertain as to their own attitude towards it, gave free rein to their party organs which, unwilling to take any risks, confined themselves to factual reporting and to quotations from other newspapers. Nevertheless, the attitude of the majority of the Czech and Moravian press made it abundantly clear that there were political parties that were loyally Austrian, without any opportunist considerations or fear of the censor. On the day Kramář's article appeared, all the clerical press published a declaration of the Catholic party in Moravia, signed by its leaders, Hruban and Šrámek. The declaration read:

Our whole nation is aware of the fact that it has the most secure guarantee for its development in an Austria which is strong and just to all her nationalities. At this grave moment in which our Empire, and with it our nation and our country find themselves, we and all our people are unswervingly faithful and devoted to the state and to its exalted monarch.

At the other end of the political spectrum, *Právo Lidu*, the Prague Social Democrat daily organ, expressed a day later similar sentiments in different terms:

The Czech nation, because of its international position, has to rely on Austria in the future, and it must work for a reform of the state according to its needs. It is in the situation of a man who temporarily occupies small rooms in the house best suited to his requirements. His endeavour should therefore not be directed towards either demolishing the house or moving somewhere else, but to negotiating better living conditions for himself.

And further on the *Právo Lidu* wrote, indirectly addressing Kramář, his party, and other Czech Russophils:

We are inclined to believe that we express the views of the majority of the working class if we say: the sympathies of the Czech people are not with those who represent official Russia nowadays, but who are in fact the biggest enemies and the cruellest oppressors of the Russian nation. Our sympathies are with those whom the Tsarist government shoot and kill in the streets of the Russian cities, whom they torture in their prisons, whom they deport to the icy plains of Siberia. We are proud that we have been able to render some good services to these real representatives of Russia and that they can always rely on us. Had we had our own way, there would have been no war. Yet if there is war, which we could not prevent, the Russian government must share the responsibility for its origins, and it cannot expect the Czechs to stake their future for the selfish ends of Russian Tsarism.

The policy of the Social Democrat party was to move on these lines until the spring of 1917 with regard to Russia, and, as far as the Habsburg monarchy was concerned, until a few months after the Russian revolution. It was a policy different in kind from that of the Young Czechs and the National Socialists. These parties pursued, especially after the arrest of Kramář,

Rašín and other radicals at the end of 1915, an official policy loyal to the monarchy: apart from the fear of persecution, such a course was made possible by the fact that these parties contained, among their leaders, men who did not share the views of Kramář or Klofáč, and who took over the direction of policy. Whereas the attitude to the monarchy of the Young Czechs and the National Socialists changed with the changes in their leadership, the opportunism of the Agrarians remained vested in the person of Švehla who, throughout the duration of hostilities, was an exponent of a 'policy of two irons': he was waiting for the outcome of the war before he made a decision for or against the monarchy. In fact, the loyal policy, whether of the Agrarians, the Young Czechs, and the National Socialists, was based on the conviction that either the Central Powers would emerge victorious from the war, or, if the struggle were concluded by a compromise, the future of the Czechs would continue to be bound up with Vienna. They took a pessimistic view and pursued an opportunist policy. While Šmeral, the leader of the Social Democrats, who did much to steer his party's policy on loyal lines, was simply not interested in a small and independent Czech state, the Young Czech politicians who took over the direction of the policy of their party after Kramář's arrest maintained that the Czechs would be forced to find a *modus vivendi* within the Empire, and therefore regarded a policy of cutting off all their ties with the government and the court as unjustified.

In a talk at the end of November between Šmeral and Beneš, two attitudes to the monarchy—the radical and the genuinely loyal—were sharply contrasted. Eduard Beneš was at the time a young socialist teaching at a secondary school, keenly interested in politics but without any practical experience. He had gone abroad in 1905 at the age of twenty-one; he returned to Prague after three years in Paris, London, and Berlin. He wrote about his experiences: 'I came back home strengthened in my original deep dislike of our political and social conditions. In comparison with England, France, and western Europe in general, Austria–Hungary seemed to me a paragon of the reactionary state.'[9] In 1908 he became a pupil, and later a friend, of Masaryk. When the war broke out Beneš, under the influence of his former teacher,[10] and also under the impression of Britain's entry into the war, decided that the end of Austria–Hungary was within sight and that the Czechs should take an active part in speeding up the process of dissolution. This was the point of view Beneš expressed, in November 1914, during his talk with Šmeral, and to which he tried to win over the leader of the Social Democrats. Beneš recorded Šmeral's answer in the following words:

> Šmeral simply told me that we were mad, that Masaryk was leading the nation into another disaster, that a politician who was responsible for a large party, and, in fact, for the whole nation could not and must not take part in such a gamble as that of Professor Masaryk. Besides, the plans we had made were fantastic.[10a] The Triple Entente cared nothing about us and it was not concerned with us. Šmeral asked me to give him a single guarantee from the side of the Allies that would justify such a policy on our part.[11]

Šmeral met Beneš's argument on its own ground: he refrained from discussing the more fundamental principles which made it impossible for him to commit himself and his party to co-operation with the anti-Habsburg radicals. Being a socialist Šmeral, like Beneš, could not even consider soliciting in Tsarist Russia for the break-up of the Habsburg monarchy; but he was also acutely aware of the fact that the radical plan would run into difficulties in the western Allied countries as Beneš and other political emigrés discovered for themselves during the first hard years of exile.

Although the reactions of the Czechs to the war were varied, they followed the lines of pre-war political divisions, which did not entail any startling changes—apart from Masaryk's radical plans—in the politicians' attitude towards the state. At no point of the war, however, did the front line divide the nation: whereas the sound of heavy guns never even reached the Czech lands, for

[9] E. Beneš, *Světová válka anaše revoluce*, vol. 1, page 5, Prague 1935.

[10] See below, page 82.

[10a] A detailed discussion of the radical plans and the development of the anti-Habsburg movement after the outbreak of the war will be found in Chapter III.

[11] Beneš, op. cit., vol. 1, page 25.

Drzavni Arhiv, Sarajevo

Archduke Franz Ferdinand's car on the Appel Quay at Sarajevo, a few seconds before Gavrilo Princip fired two shots on 28 June 1914

Drzavni Arhiv, Sarajevo.

Execution of Serbs by Austro-Hungarian military authorities at Rebinja in 1914

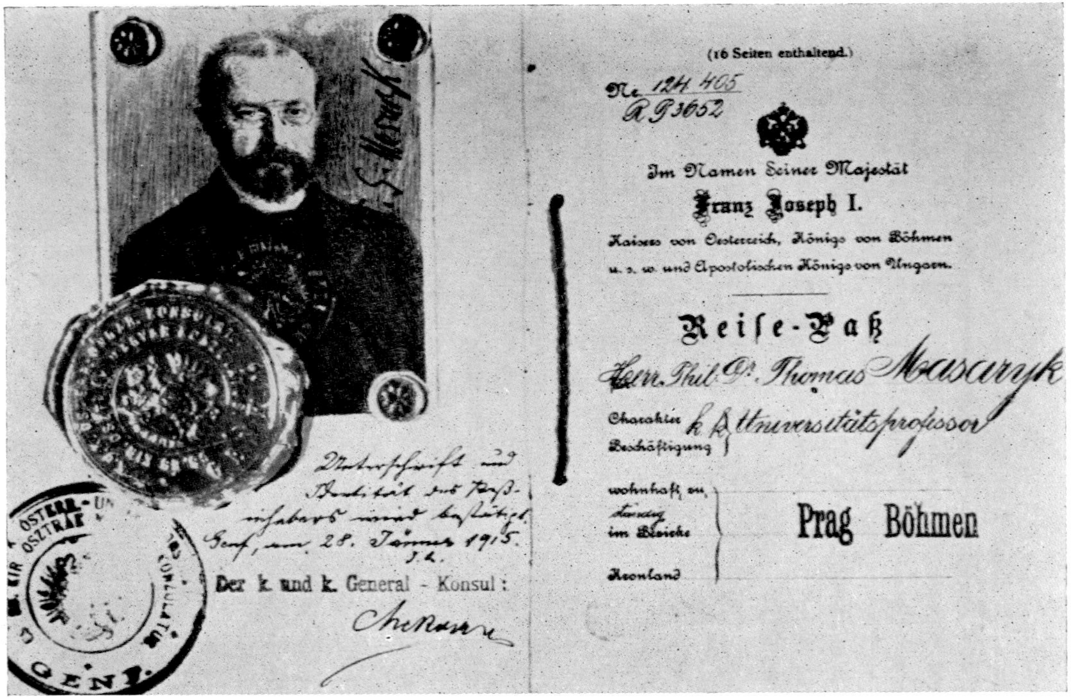

The first pages of the passport Thomas Masaryk, who became the first President of the Czechoslovak Republic, carried when he went into exile on 18 December 1914. The signature on his photograph was witnessed on 28 January 1915 by the Austro-Hungarian Consul-General in Geneva

the Poles and the Ruthenes in eastern Galicia, and for the Serbs and the Croats living on both sides of the south-eastern front, the war and the government by the heavy hand of the military were a concrete reality. The future of the Poles in particular appeared, during the initial stages of the war, completely dependent upon the movement of the eastern fronts: the main effort here of the armed forces of Germany and Austria–Hungary was directed against Russian Poland, a westward bulge some 250 miles long and of approximately the same depth. Of all the Austro-Hungarian peoples, the outbreak of the war confronted the Poles with the gravest dilemma. They were not only fighting each other on the opposite sides of the battle-line; their official representatives were committed to support their respective partitioning powers: in the circumstances, a united Poland appeared a practicable possibility only under the patronage of Russia or of Austria–Hungary and Germany, which meant unification without any prospect for independence. The divisions among the Poles deepened after the events of July 1914.

Dmowski's National Democrats monopolized Polish representation in the Russian *Duma*: their international outlook was strikingly similar to that of Kramář's Young Czechs. Although its original programme had favoured the idea of Polish independence, a steady retreat from this policy had been taking place since 1905, the year of the revolution in Russia. The National Democrats were a middle-class party, a political by-product of the fast rate of the industrialization of Russian Poland that had begun in the last two decades of the nineteenth century; its leaders were fully aware of the importance of the Russian hinterland for their country's economy. The threat of socialism and social unrest drove them into a higher degree of reliance on the established régime in Russia: in 1905, the idea of independence was superseded by that of unification, i.e. of an autonomous Poland within the Russian Empire. The autonomy the Poles in Russia aimed at had been achieved by their compatriots in Austria–Hungary. The December constitution of 1867 made it possible for Count Goluchowski, the Governor of Galicia, to introduce far-reaching self-government in his province. But the Poles did not only run

Galicia; they played an active role in the Austrian government and in the central offices in Vienna. In spite of the introduction of general suffrage and the subsequent emergence of middle- and lower middle-class parties and politicians, the nobility remained the most powerful political force in Galicia: it owed its position of power to its exceptionally good relations with the court and the government in the Austrian capital. The privilege of self-government, the opportunity for an unrestricted cultural life, and also the freedom of the Polish landlords and administrators in eastern Galicia to manage the Ruthenes, secured the loyalty of the Galician Poles to the Habsburg dynasty.

Like other European socialists, the Polish movement both in Austria–Hungary and in the Congress Kingdom violently resented the existence of the Tsarist Empire: a Polish socialist did, however, have the added stimulus of regarding the Tsarist government as the most implacable enemy and oppressor of his nation. Thus the socialism of Josef Pilsudski, who emerged during the war in the front ranks of the national movement, was mixed with a strong dose of national sentiment. But his activities, already before the war, indicated that Pilsudski, unlike the majority of the Poles, entertained hopes of achieving a complete independence for his nation. And as far as unification of the Poles was concerned he turned to Austria for help. In 1908, Pilsudski took over control of the League of Military Action, which Sosnkowski had founded in Lwow; two years later he converted it into a para-military organization known as the League of Riflemen, and soon he succeeded in gaining the Austrian government's support for it. On 6 August 1914 Pilsudski's small unit advanced into Russian Poland. But the success of Pilsudski's unit was short-lived; by the third week of August the armies were ranged against each other alongside the old Austro-Hungarian–Russian frontier. It was only after the spring and summer offensive in 1915, when the armies of Germany and Austria–Hungary succeeded not only in regaining the territories previously lost to the Russians, but also in executing their original plan—that is, the occupation of Russian Poland—that some of the troops of the Polish Legion reached Warsaw. Once again, the gulf between the Russian and the

Austro-Hungarian parts of Poland was made abundantly clear: neither the troops of the Legion nor the armies of the Central Powers were welcomed with enthusiasm in the capital. Only a resolute action in favour of a united Poland could have won the inhabitants of the Congress Kingdom over to the side of the Central Powers: although they remained in occupation of the Russian part of Poland throughout the duration of hostilities, both Vienna and Berlin proved themselves incapable of such action.[12]

While the military successes gave Austria–Hungary and Germany an opportunity to solve certain outstanding national problems—the Polish question was by far the most important—the war itself gave the military authorities ample opportunities to deal, unhampered by too much control by the government and the civil administration, with some political phenomena they had regarded as treasonable even in peace-time. Although inside the army itself men had little cause to complain of national discrimination, the treatment of the nationalities by the army during the war was abominable. In those parts of Galicia and the South Slav territories that came under direct military control, the army commands behaved towards the local population as an occupying power in enemy territory.

But the military were not content with arrests and executions of the Ruthenes or Serbs who were suspected of pro-Russian or pro-Serbian sympathies. At the end of 1914 they began vigorously to contest the power of the civil administrative authorities: a struggle between the army and the civil administration developed that went on behind the scenes in Vienna and in several provinces during the first two years of the war. In Bohemia and Croatia, both lands some distance from the actual battle front, it became a fierce contest for political power. After the outbreak of the war, the governments in Budapest and in Vienna had begun to wield a higher degree of executive power, which they did not hesitate to use in order to enforce obedience on those elements in the state they thought unreliable. Yet the military regarded the governments' policies, especially those towards the

[12] See below, pages 100 et seq.

Czechs and the South Slavs, as unsatisfactory and indulgent. Although on a few occasions they had a genuine cause for complaint, they frequently made gross mistakes in their calculations and arguments. They tended to generalize isolated cases of disloyalty and treason; they believed that not individuals but whole nations could be put on trial. They regarded the Habsburg Slavs either as traitors or as potential candidates for treason; they maintained that the unruly and unreliable peoples could be coerced, by ruthless measures, into loyalty to the monarchy. The civil servants and the government, on the other hand, with their long experience of the intricacies of the national problem, resented the impetuous and impatient attitudes of the military.

The creation of an institution known as the War Supervisory Office (*Kriegsüberwachungsamt*, *KÜA*), under the auspices of the Supreme Army Command at the beginning of the war, contributed much to the friction; the new department soon became one of the most important instruments in the bid for power by the military authorities. Since it was designed to safeguard the armed forces against both external and internal enemies, it could interfere in all branches of civil administration; it acquired a net of agents whose reports were distinguished by their singular unreliability. The War Supervisory Office was intended to cover both parts of the monarchy: in Hungary, however, its activities were severely curtailed by Tisza's disapproval. Inevitably, the new organization devoted most of its attention to the Slav nationalities in Austria and Bosnia–Hercegovina: its reports soon convinced the Supreme Command that local authorities were not severe enough in the treatment of treason. The Supreme Command, with Archduke Friedrich at its head, tried to impress the two Premiers, Stürgkh and Tisza, that civil administration in the Slav provinces in both parts of the monarchy should be abolished.

The most time-consuming efforts of Prince Thun, the Governor of Bohemia, were directed, from the last months of 1914 until his resignation in March 1915, towards preserving civil administration in his province and also towards the protection of the civilian population against the more outrageous and irresponsible behaviour of the military. The conflict between Thun and

General Schwerdtner, the commander of the Prague garrison, began in earnest when the Governor complained to Heinold, the Minister of the Interior, about some of the verdicts of the local military court in the middle of November. Shortly afterwards the Governor found out that Schwerdtner, in spite of their agreement to exchange political reports before sending them off to Vienna, had started submitting reports to the Ministry of War that contained serious charges against the Czechs, without having consulted him beforehand.

But the origins of the conflict went back to the first concrete incident, to which the attitude of the military and that of Thun sharply differed, and that had occurred on 22–23 September when the 8th and 28th Prague Battalions were leaving the town for the Russian front. In his first report on the incident, in a letter to Stürgkh, the Governor wrote:[13]

> Yesterday and the day before, troops were departing for the frontline. The manner of their departure left a lot to be desired. The soldiers, though most of them older people, were accompanied by relatives and by children; they were obviously drunk. The day before yesterday they were wearing badges in national colours on their forage-caps; some, though not very many, wore the Slav colours. Yesterday, their behaviour was still worse . . . they carried three large white, red and blue flags, and a red flag with the inscription: we are marching against the Russians and we do not know why. . . . I spoke to the local commander who had received reports on these events; he hopes to prevent their repetition by severe measures.

While Schwerdtner interpreted this incident as a sign of animosity to the state, common to all Czechs, which Thun and the civil authorities preferred to ignore, the Governor, on the other hand, put the blame on the lack of discipline for which the officers were responsible. Incidentally, there was a third party interested in the interpretation of the incident: the anti-Habsburg radicals in Prague. Their attitude resembled closely that of the military authorities. In a conversation in Rotterdam with R. W. Seton-Watson,[14] Masaryk maintained that the demonstration had

[13] 8508 ex 1914, Min. L.V., printed in Paulová, *Dějiny Maffie*, page 205.
[14] See below, page 79.

clearly been directed against the Habsburg state and that it had taken place on a much larger scale; Lev Sychrava, a sympathizer of the Progressive party, who was soon to become the first Czech political emigré, when reporting to one of the Czech societies in the United States, magnified the incident into an incipient revolt. Both the soldiers and the radicals wanted to prove that all Czechs were traitors: at this time of the war they were mistaken. Although there was a strain of pro-Russian feeling in the demonstration, it was neither the beginning of a revolution nor a unanimous expression of popular will against the Habsburg monarchy. Most of the troops that made up these two battalions were recruited from working-class districts, where the organization of the National Socialist party was strong: most of the recruits had spent the years before the war under the influence of the party's anti-militarist and Pan-Slav propaganda. Thun was also right when he blamed lack of discipline in these units; the unwillingness of the men to be ordered about by the military, or any other organ of the state, was certainly an additional reason for their behaviour.

Another, and more disturbing event, that aroused the suspicions of the military and which made them press their claims for the transfer of administration into their own hands, was the spread of Russian leaflets, some genuine and others forged, in several provinces of the monarchy. As early as 7 September the head of the civil administration of Bukovina reported to the Ministry of the Interior that a number of leaflets had been found in his province, addressed to the Ruthenes by Father Vitali, the Archimandrite of the Pochaev monastery. (A monastery some seven miles east of the Austrian frontier, with a long tradition of printing that dated back to the seventeenth century.) The leaflet was written and printed at the monastery shortly after the beginning of the war in the style of the pre-war Russophil propaganda among the Ruthenes:

> Our dear brothers who suffer under the German yoke! The Holy Mother of God has heard your prayers and she will reunite you with the Orthodox Russian Empire. In the name of Father, Son and the Holy Ghost, renounce your involuntary oath to the Austrian Emperor. The time for your liberation, decided by our Lord, has come. The time

has come to fight for the Holy Empire. Hurray! Join the Russian troops who were sent by our wise Tsar to liberate you. Help us to liberate you and the rest of the Slavs from the Germans.

The Austrian government made a rather mild attempt to counteract such crude but effective propaganda: it produced a leaflet, signed by the Emperor, which expressed deep regret at the fact that the Russian ruler had stooped to using the Orthodox church for his own political ends.[15] At the end of October the appearance of another leaflet, unsigned but very likely produced by the notorious Gerovski brothers, was reported from Galicia.[16]

On 16 September, another declaration was published in Russia, in which the Supreme Commander, the Grand Duke Nikolai Nikolaevich, addressed the nationalities of Austria–Hungary. It was printed in all the Slav languages spoken in the monarchy, and it announced in the name of the Tsar that Russia, 'who has sacrificed on several occasions the blood of her sons for the liberation of nations' entered the war in order to bring liberty and the 'fulfilment of national desires' to the peoples of Austria–Hungary.[17] The first news about the declaration reached the monarchy via the Italian newspaper *Corriere della Serra*, which could be freely bought in Austria–Hungary and which printed the Grand Duke's declaration in full on 18 September. Four days later it was reprinted by the *Reichenberger Zeitung*, and on 23 September it appeared in a Czech provincial newspaper.[18] Soon, copies of the manifesto were spread in northern Bohemia, where they reached some troops of the 11th Battalion stationed at Jíčín, who were denounced and arrested.

From the end of September a number of Russian declarations were in circulation in Bohemia, Moravia, Bukovina, and Galicia. Some of them, like the Gerovski declaration, were brought from Galicia to the Czech lands by railwaymen. Some were forged in Bohemia: the special declaration of the Grand Duke to the Czechs (the Grand Duke, apart from his declaration to the Habsburg nations, issued a special declaration only to the Poles) and

[15] *VA*, 12325 MI ex 1914.
[16] *HHuSA*, P.A.I. 816, Krieg 1b.
[17] *Dokumenty*, pages 553 and 554.
[18] In the *Královodvorské nejnovější zprávy*.

the manifesto signed by General Rennenkampf were two widespread forgeries. In December some 170,000 copies of the genuine Grand Duke's address were distributed in Prague. They were smuggled into Bohemia from the office of the Russian Military Attaché in Berne and they were distributed, rather carelessly and hastily, by members of the Progressive party. On 8 January 1915 Svatkovski—Kramář's friend—reported to St. Petersburg from Switzerland: 'The Czech people received the Russian manifesto with sympathy . . . posters were issued, announcing that spreading the leaflets would be punished by death.'[19]

The affair of the Russian leaflets gave the military authorities an opportunity for taking, for the first time, a firm action against the disloyal elements among the Slavs. Whereas in the territory near the front line in Galicia and Bukovina traitors were dealt with in a summary manner, in the Czech lands the military were obliged to pay more regard to the letter of the law. Nevertheless, by the first day of November thirty-three people had been arrested in Prague and the number of arrests was steadily increasing; in Moravia, sixty-five people had been arrested before the end of January and transferred to Vienna for trial. On a higher level, the Supreme Command also made good use of the affair. Archduke Friedrich, the Commander-in-Chief, clearly irritated by some of the reports from the Slav provinces, and also by what he and his military friends considered as too easy-going an attitude towards treason by the civil authorities, began to bombard Krobatin, the Minister of War, and the Emperor himself with requests for the transfer of administration in certain territories to the 'strong hands' of the military. Archduke Friedrich fired the first shot on the home front at the end of October, shortly after the first appearance of the Russian leaflets: the intensity of the home front campaign was to vary with the amount of evidence on the disloyal behaviour of the Slav subjects that reached the Supreme Command.

While the last prosecutions in connexion with the Russian leaflets were being concluded, another proof of Slav disloyalty to the monarchy fell into the hands of the military. After the battle

[19] A. Popov, *Chekho-Slovacki vopros is carskaia diplomacia.* Krasnyi Arkhiv Vol. 2 1933), pages 10–11; cf. Paulová, *Dějiny Maffie*, page 216 et seq.

at Štebnická Huta, a village north-west of Zborov, on 3 April 1915, only 20 officers and 236 troops were gradually reassembled from the 2,000 men of which the 28th Prague Infantry Battalion—one of the two units that had already behaved in an indisciplined manner at the time of its departure for the battle front—had originally consisted. The capture of a large part of the battalion became a highly controversial subject. There had been some contact between the Czechs in the Austrian lines and their compatriots in the Czech unit in the Russian army. A small number of reconnaissance troops sent from the Austrian side had already been reported missing in this section of the front line before 3 April. It is a matter of conjecture whether the desertion of the battalion had been prearranged: the question whether it was a desertion at all became the subject of one of the fiercest arguments inside the Austro-Hungarian army. The Czech historians largely regarded the capture of the battalion as a straight-forward desertion. While the Austrian military reports expressed the same opinion, Karl Nowak[20] and later, General Kunz[21] maintained that the unit was captured only after it had offered resistance to the Russian attack. The evidence given at an official enquiry by officers of the battalion who had escaped capture supported, on the whole, the latter view. However, the most balanced account of the events of 3 April came from an eye-witness, a Captain Kubala. He wrote:[22]

It is very likely that most of the men of the 28th Battalion were captured voluntarily. This of course did not happen without a shot being fired from either side. Parts of the unit defended themselves of their own accord, others were shooting only under the pressure from their officers. It will, however, remain the key fact that only the remnants of the unit could be salvaged.

The senior Austrian officers directly concerned with the events of 3 April were thoroughly alarmed by them. On 8 April the Headquarters of the Third Army received a report from the divisional commander:[23]

[20] In *Der Sturz der Mittelmächte*, page 110, München 1921.
[21] *Tajnosti z rakouského generálního štábu*, an article in *Pestrý Týden*, Prague 1931.
[22] *Referát o spisu Generála Klecandy. Naše Revoluce*, vol. 2, page 114 et seq.
[23] *Kuk Korpskommando*, Nr. 359–32. Paulová, *Dějiny Maffie*, page 386.

A provisional enquiry into the behaviour of the 28th Infantry Battalion established, mainly on the basis of the evidence supplied by the unit's commanding officer, that the battalion was captured by one Russian company and more or less led away from its positions, without having once fired at the enemy. . . . The original troops may have been quite reliable; but only several days before the battle one company was added to the battalion, which had been infected by Pan-Slav ideas at home. From this reserve unit several reconnaissance groups had deserted to the enemy, on the day before the battle. . . . It is obvious that the deserters informed the Russians about the mood of the battalion. Similar complaints about unsatisfactory morale of the troops arriving at the front line were reported by the 97th Infantry Battalion, though the outcome was not so frightful. These reports concern recruits of Slovene nationality from Ljubljana. A report on these events will be sent before the end of the official enquiry, because it has been demonstrated that it is essential to take great care over the supervision of fresh recruits who are not engaged in fighting.

The Commander-in-Chief was also outraged by the incident. He wrote to the Emperor demanding the dissolution of the regiment: his request reached Vienna on 16 April and it was granted the following day. At the same time, the campaign of the military to take over political control of Bohemia was intensified: once again, the administration was accused of weakness and indecision. In the heat of the struggle with the civil authorities, the military were little concerned with an analysis of such incidents as the desertion of the 28th Battalion: it was merely another argument in favour of a tighter political control supervised by themselves. We have already discussed the reasons why this particular unit should have suffered from lack of discipline.[24] Masaryk, often inclined to impute idealistic motives to people's actions, did not do so when he talked about the deserters from the Austro-Hungarian army on the Russian front. In a conversation with Karel Čapek after the war,[25] Masaryk maintained that the desertions were the result of the dislike of the troops for war, rather than of patriotic—that is, anti-Habsburg—motives. He mentioned, in this connexion, the difficulties the political emigrés encountered when they were recruiting for the Czech unit in the

[24] See above, page 52. [25] *Hovory s Masarykem*, page 166, London 1941.

Russian army among the prisoners of war.[26] But whatever the Czech troops' motives were, the Štebnická Huta incident was the first clear writing on the wall. The Austro-Hungarian authorities, civil and military alike, should have noticed that the war was unpopular with the Czechs, and that it was likely to become more so the longer it lasted.

A contest between the military and the civil administration similar to that in Bohemia developed in Croatia. It hinged on the same problem: the question of loyalty and disloyalty to the monarchy, and the conflicting attitudes of the Austro-Hungarian authorities towards it. Like the Czechs the South Slavs were suspect. The picture was, however, complicated by the relations between the Croats and the Serbs. The relations between the two peoples had reached the breaking point soon after the assassination of Archduke Franz Ferdinand when there was excitement and a feeling of sympathy among the Croats for the victims of Sarajevo; as early as the evening of 28 June anti-Serb riots spread to Hercegovina and Croatia. The three main Serb newspapers in Bosnia and Hercegovina[27] ceased to appear because the demonstrators had smashed their printing presses. In Croatia, Ivo Frank's Party of Law started to exploit the wave of resentment against the Serbs for its own purposes. Two days after the assassination the Croat Diet in Zagreb held a special *in memoriam* meeting for the Archduke. During this meeting scenes unique even in the history of a Balkan parliamentary body developed. Members of Frank's party hurled violent abuse at the deputies of the Croat–Serb Coalition, and in particular at Světozar Pribičević, one of its Serbian leaders, whose brother was a senior officer in the Serb army. The Speaker was not successful in restoring order; subsequently he decided to ban three of the leaders of the Party of Law, including Frank himself, from sixty meetings of the Diet.

Nevertheless, restrictive measures against the Serbs had already been introduced by the civil administration before the war. On 23 July, five days before the declaration of war on Serbia, the

[26] See below, page 132.
[27] *Srpska Rijec*, *Narod*, and *Odtažbiana*.

Minister of the Interior sent a circular to all the heads of provincial administration in Austria on the subject of the supervision of South Slav students.[28] The Minister pointed to the fact that the Great Serbian ideas were popular among the Slav students in the south of the monarchy, and requested the administration to employ every legal means to counter their propaganda. On the same day *Sokol*, the gymnastic society, was banned in Croatia. Three days later the first arrests were being carried out in Dalmatia: Josip Smodlaka, a deputy to the *Reichsrat*, and Oscar Tartaglia, who was at the time editing a newspaper in Split, were among the victims. But the measures taken by the civil administration in the South Slav provinces did not satisfy the military. Whereas, in Bohemia, they had no friends among the Czechs, the military found a valuable ally among the Croat political parties. Ivo Frank's organization was only too keen to help the army. Frank and his fellow party members regarded the soldiers, and Conrad von Hötzendor in particular, as the protectors of the trialist solution of the national problem. For Frank and his followers, the corner-stone of the third constituent state of the monarchy would be neither the Serbs, nor the Serbs and the Croats jointly, but the Croats alone. The Party of Law was a militant Great Croat party; it expected the soldiers to help them in their endeavours to reduce the political influence of the Serbs, in or out of the Croat–Serb Coalition. Although the Frankists numbered some inoffensive Croat patriots among its ranks, their leaders frequently encouraged acts of political hooliganism. The party was in a frustrating position: it was the second largest political organization in Croatia, with strong branches in other South Slav provinces, and as such it expected to take a bigger share in the running of Croatia than it actually did. They bitterly resented the Hungarian Premier's support and protection of the Croat–Serb Coalition; but men who shared the opinions of Frank could hardly expect Budapest politicians to approve of a party that advocated trialism and with it the detachment of Croatia from the Hungarian part of the monarchy. Thus the war on Serbia and the possibility that the military authorities might assume a decisive political role did not,

[28] *VA*, 8516 MI ex 1914.

as far as Frank and his followers were concerned, present altogether gloomy prospects.

The Supreme Command soon became convinced that the attitude of the civil authorities to treason was not severe enough. This impression was created not only by the reports of the War Supervisory Office, but also by the denunciations—mainly of the leaders of the Serbo-Croat Coalition—by members of the Party of Law. General Scheure embarked on a ruthless campaign against Baron Skerlecz, the Governor of Croatia.

The origins of the conflict dated back to the time immediately after the short-lived occupation by the Serbian army of the Srjem and Banat districts: the Austro-Hungarian offensive that began on 7 September forced the Serbs to retreat beyond the right bank of the river Sava. The first complaint about the behaviour of the Serbian population was made three days later, and many more followed. They all dwelt on the assistance rendered by the local Serbs to the enemy: signals to guide the fire of Serbian artillery, the ringing of bells indicating the presence of Austro-Hungarian troops, and other acts of sabotage. The Serbian population paid dearly for the suspicions the military entertained against them. More than 120 were executed, many more were arrested, and on 18 September the first contingent of 516 Serbs from Srjem was deported.[29] The local administration in Croatia was well informed about, and enraged by, the measures the army had taken against the civilian population in the battle-zone; it had to take care of the resettlement of the deported Serbs.

From this point onwards, the controversy developed on familiar lines. Accusations against the Serbs that reached the Supreme Command from the local military authorities were forwarded to Tisza, the Hungarian Prime Minister, accompanied with requests for the transfer of political control. It was mainly due to Tisza's resolute stand and several threats of resignation that the civil administration was able to continue functioning in Croatia. Unlike the situation in Bohemia, however, the campaign of the military was mainly directed against a minority section of the population, namely the Serbs; at the same time, from the point of view of the

[29] Paulová, *Dějiny Maffie*, page 101.

Hungarian Premier, it was a dangerous political move against his alliance with the Croat–Serb Coalition. It was supported by the trialist Frank's Party of Law, and it aimed at undermining the dualist system of government.

Because of ethnical complications, the conflict between the military and the civil authorities assumed some unusual forms in the South Slav provinces. On 26 January 1915 the head of the administration in Dalmatia reported from Zara to the Ministry of the Interior[30] several cases of arbitrary behaviour towards the Serbs by the local military commander, such as illegal arrests of Orthodox priests and even the prohibition of the use of the word 'Serb'. On 20 July Sarkotić, the Governor of Bosnia, agreed with the military on the question of the use of Cyrillic script, and related the problem to a wider framework:

> The Cyrillic script is part and parcel of the eastern attitude to the world and therefore it represents a foreign body in the western character of both parts of the monarchy. Regarded from this highest point of view, the present use of the script in the monarchy is nothing but an advanced position of the eastern way of life in the frontier battle zone of the West, which we are defending.

Such high-minded philosophizing from an uncomfortable position between the East and the West did not, however, appeal to the Minister of the Interior. He pointed out, when pressed hard by the military, who received unexpected support from the Minister of Education, what the exact legal position was, and what the interpretation of the Imperial law of 25 April 1882 should have been; that in Croatia the Cyrillic script was still being preserved and protected and that, anyway, even among the Ruthenes, the military authorities had made no attempt to ban the script.[31] However, in the south of the monarchy the soldiers did not mind riding roughshod over Imperial laws whenever an opportunity presented itself.

Paradoxically, as the army began to be more successful on the battlefields, its chances of taking over administration in the hinterland began to recede. The civil authorities were more liable to

[30] *VA*, Ad 25095 MI ex 1915. [31] *VA*, 25095 MI ex 1915.

fumble at times of military disaster; the Slavs, on the other hand, aware of the failures of the Habsburg armies, ceased being impressed by the power of the state. In Croatia, however, as soon as there were signs that the military were about to abandon their struggle for power, the Party of Law began to fill the breach, ready to carry on the fight alone. At the same time, victories on the battlefield encouraged Frank and his followers to pursue their aims more vigorously.

Although the co-operation between the Party of Law and the military in Croatia did not result in a decisive victory for either of the allies—civil authorities continued to administer the country and trialism remained a plan for reform—the time of the successful spring and summer offensive on the eastern front witnessed an important advancement of the political aims of the Croats. On 14 June 1915 the Diet in Zagreb resumed its meetings; a few weeks before this date the politicians in Croatia had begun to discuss the formulation of the opening declaration by the whole Diet. While the Serbs had little to contribute to the discussion, Lorković, the leader of the Croats in the Coalition, expressed the opinion that, in the situation brought about by the war, the Diet should demand the unification of all the Croats. Lorković regarded such a demand as a stepping-stone towards trialism in the event of the survival of the Habsburg monarchy; he argued, on the other hand, that if a victory of the Entente Powers was to be followed by the monarchy's dissolution, then the unified Croats would be in a better position to enter into an agreement with the government in Belgrade.[32] The final draft of this part of the address, delivered on 14 June by the Deputy Speaker, read:

Bearing in mind the sacrifices the Croats are making in order to bring about a successful conclusion of the war, I regard it as my duty to express the unshakeable conviction of the whole Diet, the mouthpiece of our political and national ambitions, that all these sacrifices will bear fruit if the constant demand of the Croat nation for unification in one state organization on the basis of the principle of nationality and of the positive and historical state rights is recognized. This would

[32] Paulová, *Dějiny Maffie*, pages 482–483.

facilitate free development of the Croat nation in the interests of civilization and progress and in the interests of the Habsburg monarchy.

The declaration of the Diet offended the Serbs as much as the Hungarian Premier. It was conclusive evidence of the decline of Serb influence in the political life of Croatia since the beginning of the war. Tisza, who disapproved of its tone and aims, which attacked the dualist arrangement, made an attempt to have it altered by the deputies themselves or, failing this, to have it suppressed by the official Croat paper, the *Narodne Novine*, and by the official press agency. The line taken by the declaration corresponded to the programme of the Party of Law; it made no reference to co-operation between the Serbs and the Croats: it was in fact a complete negation of the pre-war policy of the Croat–Serb Coalition.

In the stifled political atmosphere of war-time Austria–Hungary, the opening meeting of the Croat Diet sounded an unusually clear note. The deputies declared themselves for the Habsburg monarchy without any pressure from official quarters, but at the same time they made a public pronouncement criticizing the internal arrangements of the state. The opening of the Diet had a relaxing effect on the political life of Croatia: some of the deputies who had been called up returned to take part in its sessions; the question of parliamentary immunity was openly discussed. In such an atmosphere, the machinations of the military against civil administration behind the scenes were threatened with exposure by discussion in the open; at the same time the Croats staked their claims to hegemony in the south, declared their loyalty to the monarchy and, by implication, expressed their readiness to coerce the Serbs into loyalty to the Habsburgs. In the Austrian part of the monarchy, on the other hand, political life remained severely restricted: neither the parliament in Vienna nor the provincial Diets had assembled since the beginning of the war. The Czechs in particular proved themselves sensitive to the political changes brought about by the war: they feared encroachments on their national rights by Imperial edicts;

Josef Pilsudski Inst., London.

Josef Pilsudski, the Polish national leader. In Vienna, 1915

A Rumanian soldier of the Austro-Hungarian army accompanying Václav Klofáč, the Chairman of the Czech National Socialist party, from the fortress prison in Prague to the prosecuting counsel in 1915. Klofáč was sentenced to death but amnestied in the summer of 1917

Bildarchiv d. Ost. Nationalbibliothek.

Barricade fight in Belgrade, October 1915. An oil painting by Oskar Laske, an Austrian impressionist painter and official war artist

they observed the activities of the military with grave misgivings. Although the Supreme Command had not succeeded in its attempts to gain more administrative and political powers for the army, its policy, and the behaviour of the military, succeeded in the long run in convincing the Slavs that their position in the state was an underprivileged one; it may have led, in a number of individual cases, to complete estrangement from the monarchy. In such conditions a new type of radical anti-Habsburg movement made its first furtive appearance during the war.

II Central and eastern Europe after World War I, showing the successor states—Poland, Czechoslovakia, Austria, Hungary,

III

AUSTRIA DELENDA EST

The encouragement of refractory nationalist movements in enemy territories was not a game at which any of the European Powers were very skilled at the time of the outbreak of the war. The value of such a policy was questionable; under dynastic governments, it might have proved a double-edged weapon. Only in Russia were there signs that the High Command under Grand Duke Nikolai Nikolaevich intended to explore the ground that had been prepared by the activities of men like Count Bobrinski—who was in fact appointed the military governor of the Austro-Hungarian territory during its short-lived occupation by the Tsarist army—by Kramář, Klofáč, and others. The Russians made the first move on the field of political warfare with the Grand Duke's declaration to the nationalities of the Habsburg Empire of 16 September 1914. Soon afterwards, the Imperial German government began to experiment, with its customary vigour and thoroughness, on the Tsarist Empire itself. In the West, France and England did not appreciate the value of this weapon until late in the war. Austria–Hungary was not their principal enemy and their attitude to it changed little with the formal declaration of war. It may have been of some concern to English and French scholars and journalists but the politicians and soldiers showed little or no interest in it.

It was the conviction of some of the politicians in Austria–Hungary that they would suffer persecution or that they would be restricted in their political activities, rather than the attitude of the Entente Powers towards the monarchy, that decided them to go into exile. The South Slav provinces, and Dalmatia and Istria in particular, provided the anti-Habsburg emigration with its first and largest contingent; Meštrović, the sculptor, had left Dalmatia for Italy a fortnight before the declaration of war on Serbia. Trumbić followed him on 4 August and Supilo shortly afterwards. The political organization of the South Slavs in exile grew up from the nucleus of these three men. At the end of 1914 they moved from Rome to Paris; in April of the following year the South Slav Committee in exile was formally established. Trumbić, the leader of the Croat National party in the Zagreb Diet, former Mayor of Split in Dalmatia and deputy for Zara in the Viennese parliament, became its chairman. Its members were: Ante Biankini, another Dalmatian, who became a leading worker for the unity of the South Slavs in Chicago at the beginning of the war; Ivo de Giulli, a lawyer and formerly an alderman in Dubrovnik; Julije Gazzari, a lawyer from Šebenico; Niko Grsković, chairman of the Croat League in Cleveland; Hinko Hinković, a lawyer and a member of the Croat Diet and a member of the Diet's delegation to the parliament in Budapest; Josef Jedlovský, a Slovene journalist; Niko Stojanović, a Serb member of the Bosnian Diet, and Frano Supilo, editor of the Rjeka *Novi List* and a former member of the Croat Diet. The Dalmatians were strongly represented on the Committee: they were perhaps more internationally minded than any other politicians in the Habsburg monarchy. There were also several members of the Committee who had settled before the war in the United States; indeed the plan of Trumbić and Supilo was eventually to draw the older, non-political emigration into supporting their activities.

In May the Committee began to put out its first feelers to the statesmen of the Entente countries. On 1 May it presented itself to Delcassé, the French Foreign Minister, and to Izvolsky, the Russian Ambassador in Paris. After establishing contacts in France, the Committee moved to London where, on 12 May, Trumbić and his friends issued a 'manifesto to the English nation and parliament'. At the beginning of June they were received by Lord Crewe in the Foreign Office, who expressed his sympathy and assured the South Slavs of the 'goodwill' of the British government. Although these first steps could not have been expected to bring about concrete political results, they at least brought to the attention of the politicians in the West the fact that a national problem existed in the south of the Habsburg monarchy. Indeed, persistent publicity and propaganda work was the first task of the political emigration. The South Slav Committee was publishing the *Bulletin Jugoslave*; they founded an information bureau in London. The arguments of the exiles were simple and underwent little change throughout the war. They attempted to convince the Entente politicians and public alike that the Habsburg monarchy was an artificial and monstrous structure, despised by the majority of the people who had to live in it; that, in complete dependence on Germany, it ruthlessly pursued its own expansionist aims or, more often, supported those of its ally and that they, the political emigrés, were the true representatives of their nations either by a direct mandate—this was usually the argument of the Czechs—or because the people at home had no other means of expressing their will—the line the South Slavs usually took. The reports of the exiles on the situation inside the monarchy were, especially at the beginning of the war, highly coloured. They in fact resembled, in their underlying assumption that all the Slavs were traitors to the Habsburg dynasty, the reports, on the same subject, by the Austro-Hungarian military authorities.[1]

But the progress of the South Slav cause was seriously interrupted by the conclusion of the secret pact of London in April 1915. Although many exiles regarded Italy as a paragon of national unification, the ambitions of the South Slavs came into a sharp conflict with the plans of the Italian government with regard to the Adriatic littoral. The Entente promised Italy, if she entered the war on the Allied side, large tracts of the Habsburg territory on the Adriatic sea. The Serbian government was at first not informed of the pact; it was not long, however, before the Serbs and the South Slav exiles became aware of its existence. It affected especially Dalmatia; it was one of the Dalmatian members of the South Slav Committee, Frano Supilo, who first found out about the existence of the pact when he visited Sazonov in St. Petersburg at the end of April.[2] The first intimations of the existence of the pact reached Pašić shortly after Supilo's conversation with the Russian Foreign Minister, when Ljuba Mihailović, the Serbian Ambassador

[1] See above, page 51. [2] Paulová, *Dějiny Maffie*, page 409.

to Rome, was informed by Sonnino that the safety of Italy on the Adriatic sea demanded bases on the eastern littoral. When Mihailović asked the Foreign Minister what was the Italian attitude towards the unification of the South Slavs, Sonnino curtly replied that 'if Italy gets what she needs for the maintenance of peace and her own safety, she would have no objections to unification'.[3]

The situation became still more delicate when, on 23 May, Italy declared war on Austria–Hungary and became Serbia's ally. By that time the Serbian government had declared the unification of all South Slavs as its principal aim in the war. Although the Serbs missed no opportunity to criticize the pact, the fact that they were not officially informed of its existence hampered their attempts to get it rescinded. (It was made public by the Bolshevik government shortly after the November revolution and then by Seton-Watson in his *New Europe* in January 1918.) In the meanwhile, however, the unofficial South Slav Committee was not tied down by the same considerations as Pašić; it rendered the Serb Premier valuable services in fighting against the pact's provisions.

While defending the Adriatic littoral against the Italian demands, the Committee began extending its activities beyond mere propaganda work. After the failure of the appeal at Christmas 1914 for volunteers to fight in the Serbian army before the Committee was properly constituted, the South Slav leaders in exile realized that their movement, for political and financial reasons, would have to be put on a broader basis. Work among the numerous South Slav immigrants and their societies in the United States and in South America was the only way open to them. To a certain extent the ground had been prepared for their activities by the itinerant agitators for South Slav unity before the war. In May 1914, for instance, the following leaflet was spread among the Serbs, Croats, and Slovenes in New York; it is a good example of pre-war propaganda of the South Slav idea:

Declaration. You are invited to a public and free lecture on the settlement of New Serbia, [i.e. the territorial acquisitions by Serbia in

[3] Paulová, *Dějiny Maffie*, page 410.

the Balkan wars] and the decline of Austria–Hungary, which will be given by Todor Dimitrijević, Philosopher. The lecture will take place on May 10th, at 9.30 a.m. in the Sokol Hall No. 14 in New York. All brother Serbs, Croats and Slovenes are therefore invited to attend the lecture in maximum numbers. This is the only talk brother Dimitrijević will give in this town. Entrance free, only Socialists will pay 25 cents.

There were also pamphlets produced by the *Narodna Odbrana* in Belgrade that circulated in the settlements of South Slav immigrants before the war; the *Sokol* organizations were also active in spreading the idea of unity. After the outbreak of the war such agitation was carried on more intensively, but until the beginning of 1915, when the South Slav Committee entered the field, without any central co-ordination. The first emissaries sent to the United States as early as January 1915 by the men who were to form the South Slav Committee were Potoćnjak and Smodlaka; on their arrival in New York, they published a 'proclamation to all South Slav patriots, Croats, Serbs and Slovenes'.

A fateful war, the decisive fight between the Slavs and the Germans is taking place in Europe. While our free brothers, the Russians and the Serbs are combating our hereditary enemies, our own brothers, the Slovene, Serb and Croat subjects of the Habsburg monarchy, bleed in their struggle against their liberators; in fact, they are fighting against themselves.[4]

At the beginning of May 1915 Potočnjak completed his exploratory mission to the United States and returned to Europe. Two months later Father Nikolai Velimirović, an Orthodox preacher and writer, whose aim was to tone down the religious differences between the Serbs and the Croats,[5] was sent to America by the South Slav Committee. His mission succeeded in patching up a number of differences of long standing among the various societies of immigrants and their newspapers; twenty-eight

[4] An official pamphlet on the anti-Habsburg movement in the United States in the political archives of *HHuSA*.

[5] Father Velimirović pursued this aim in his study *La religion et la nationalité en Serbie*, dedicated to the memory of the Catholic bishop of Zagreb, Strossmayer, and published in Paris in the summer of 1915.

editors of South Slav papers in North America subscribed to a resolution that committed them to writing for the 'liberation and unification' of the South Slavs. Father Velimirović also organized a meeting between Catholic and Orthodox priests who undertook to work for the same aims as the journalists.

Whereas Velimirović's mission was regarded by the Committee as an unqualified success, the opinions as to the value of Milan Marjanović's work in the United States were divided. Marjanović was the secretary of the *Bulletin Jugoslave*; he left Paris shortly after Velimirović's return in the middle of October 1915. In December the Pittsburg *Narodni List*[6] reported that at a lecture given by Marjanović a fight developed between the partisans of the Committee and their opponents, which had to be settled by the intervention of the police. There were indeed several groups of immigrants in America that opposed the policy of the Committee, and Marjanović, in his proselytizing zeal, chose to visit the unconverted South Slav communities. Whereas the Serb and Dalmatian immigrants gave support to the movement for South Slav unity, some Slovene and Croat societies and their newspapers, especially those controlled by the Catholic clergy, opposed the plans of the Committee in London. The political situation among the immigrants in America reflected faithfully the divisions among the South Slavs in the Habsburg monarchy itself. The Slovene League and its organ, the *Glas Naroda* and the influential Croat *Narodni List*, published in New York and in Pittsburg, defended until late in the war the policy of autonomy for their countries, preferably within the framework of the Habsburg monarchy. They argued that the South Slav Committee was under the influence of the Serbian government and that it pursued exclusively Great Serb aims, while taking little or no notice of the Croat and Slovene aspirations. There was evidence that this was the case: in an article in the third issue of *Libre Serbie*, the Serbs were cast in the role of the leading nationality in the future state; in the 'Statute of Organization of South Slav National Defence in Latin America', concluded in Antofagasta on 23 January 1916, Serbia

[6] 26 December 1915; the *Narodni List* was a Croat newspaper with no particular liking for the activities of the South Slav Committee.

was described as the 'carrier' of the South Slav idea and as the 'founder and the heart of the South Slav state'.[7]

The Austro-Hungarian Embassy in Washington was uneasy about the spread of anti-Habsburg trends among the South Slavs in the Americas; although it has been suggested that it actively supported the movement that disagreed with the London Committtee's policy, this was not the case. Though proposals to combat the pro-Serb policy came from various quarters, the Embassy had at its disposal neither the men nor the means to carry out a successful propaganda counter-offensive.[8]

The South Slav Committee itself had to fight against financial difficulties. As early as February 1915 Trumbić published an appeal to all South Slavs to make financial contributions to their cause. Later, when the connexions between the immigrants in the Americas and the Committee in London were established, the financing of the movement somewhat improved. In fact, the activities of the Committee were supported throughout the war by contributions from private sources in the United States and Latin America. Although the large majority of the immigrants were poor, some of their societies and clubs had succeeded in amassing considerable sums of money before the war; the Serbian government, which commanded considerable funds—mainly loans from the Entente governments—made no direct financial contribution to the work of the South Slav Committee. Indirectly, however, by financing the recruitment of the South Slavs in the Russian and the Serbian prisoner-of-war camps, it relieved the Committee of heavy expenditure.

The recruiting drive among the immigrants in the United States and Latin America, on the other hand, was carried out entirely under the auspices of the Committee. Recruitment for the Adriatic Legion was regarded as one of the most important activities of the South Slav Committee: the contemporary sources were sharply divided in the assessment of its success. The Austro-Hungarian Embassy in Washington was sceptical: it

[7] *HHuSA*, official pamphlet on the anti-Habsburg movement among the South Slav emigrants, section on Latin America. Also in *VA*, 1953 MI ex 1916.

[8] *HHuSA*, PA I 768, Z 401–550.

reported in November 1915 that only a few hundred volunteers had left for Europe. The consulate in Geneva, usually well-informed about South Slav activities, had put the figure much higher in July. One of the consulate's agents intercepted a letter from the United States to a Serb exile in Switzerland indicating that by the middle of May 8,000 volunteers had been recruited in the Americas, of whom 3,500 had left for Europe. Although this figure is probably too high, and since the difficulties of shipping the volunteers to Europe were considerable, there can be no doubt that by the end of 1915 there were several thousand South Slav volunteers in the Serbian army.

The reaction to the war by the radicals in the South of the Habsburg monarchy was unequivocal and immediate. Those who decided to work abroad for their cause did so in complete isolation from their home country: although Trumbić had, early in his exile, made an attempt to obtain approval for his action abroad from the politicians who stayed behind, it failed, and Trumbić never tried again. There was really no reason why he should have done. His South Slav Committee represented the pro-Belgrade trend in the movement for unification; the success of its policy depended on the success of Serbia in the war. The attitude of the South Slav politicians in the monarchy to Trumbić's plan was of no importance to him. The political developments in Croatia and Slovenia during 1915 and the victory of the Great Croat plans at the opening of the Diet in Zagreb[9] further widened the gulf between the policies of the South Slavs in the monarchy and those in exile: the impasse could now be solved by a decisive victory of one side or the other in the war. Nevertheless, the lack of contact between the Jugoslav politicians abroad and those in the monarchy, and the complete disregard for domestic political developments by the exiles, worked out to their advantage in the early stages of their work. Unhampered by considerations of the reactions of the politicians at home, they were able to put their plans into practice swiftly.

The Czech radicals, on the other hand, embarked on their action against the monarchy more cautiously; they had no Serbia

[9] See above, page 61.

to rely on, and they were entering uncharted waters. After the outbreak of the war there were three groups in Prague ready to work against the monarchy: the Young Czechs, and the Progressives; the place of the National Socialists—after the arrest of their leader, Klofáč, in September—was taken by Masaryk's Realists. The war, for which the Progressives had been preparing themselves for a long time, had come at last. Nevertheless, their plans were hampered by the lack of funds; at the time when the question arose of sending a representative abroad at the end of September, the party did not have enough money even to continue the publication of its newspaper. On 8 October the Progressives were relieved of this care by an order of the censor, which forbade them to continue the publication of their organ.

The first political emigré had already left Prague on 21 September. Lev Sychrava, a young lawyer and journalist, was a sympathizer, though not a member, of the Progressive party: he went abroad on his own initiative. Shortly before his departure and Klofáč's arrest, Sychrava met the National Socialist leader. Klofáč was very optimistic; he told the young man that 'everything was well arranged': he was probably referring to the plan he had given the Russians.[10] Sychrava himself was surprised to find that Klofáč 'expected a speedy Russian victory and the arrival of the Russians in Bohemia'.[11] Having seen Klofáč, the young man sought interviews with other potential leaders of the anti-Habsburg movement. He obtained an introduction to Scheiner, a prominent Young Czech and the head of the *Sokol* gymnastic society who gave him a message for the Russian Ambassador in Berne to the effect that the Russian money which had been transferred to the *Sokol* account for the support of the Ruthenes in eastern Galicia was in safe hands. After these preparations, without knowing what the precise nature of activities abroad would be, Sychrava left Prague, officially on a study visit to Geneva.

Kramář and the radicals in the Young Czech party did not confine themselves to the ambiguous anti-Habsburg pronouncement

[10] See above, page 18.

[11] L. Sychrava, in *Národní Osvobození*, Nos. 194, 199, 205, Prague 1926, *Jak jsem se dostal za hranice.*

published in their party's newspaper; they began secretly to plot against the state. Their group by no means embraced the whole leadership of the party: it had originally consisted of Kramář, Rašín, and Sís; in November it was joined by Franta, a Young Czech deputy in the *Reichsrat*. The members of this group differed, however, in their estimation of the nature of the war, and their differences hampered their conspiratorial activities. The Young Czech radicals did not contribute a single politician to the small contingent of Czech exiles: this was due to Kramář's conviction that the war would be one of short duration and that the Russian army would soon occupy the Czech lands. Rašín, on the other hand, though he agreed that the war would end in a defeat of the Central Powers, was confident, like Masaryk, of the strength of the British Empire; he was prepared for a long war. Kramář's view prevailed in the end: the Young Czech radicals remained in Prague, expecting the arrival of the Russian army, until the arrests, on charges of high treason, of both Kramář and Rašín in 1915.

The value of František Sís, the youngest and the least prominent member of the group lay in the fact that his brother, Vladimír Sís, was the Balkan correspondent of the Young Czech daily newspaper: he was to become the most important link between the conspirators in Prague and the outside world. Sís was in Sofia when the war broke out; after an agreement with Kramář, his brother informed him that he had full powers to negotiate in the Bulgarian capital in the name of the party chairman. Vladimír went to work immediately; at the end of September he reported to Prague the results of his first interviews in Sofia. Apart from describing the attitude of the local politicians to the war and to the Habsburg monarchy, Sís informed his friends of the result of his conversations with the Russian and the British Ministers in Bulgaria. Tabarinov, the Russian Military Attaché, introduced him to Savinsky, the Minister; Bourchie, the Balkan correspondent of *The Times* arranged an interview for Sís with Sir Henry Bax-Ironside, the head of the British mission. Sir Henry expressed himself for the preservation of Austria–Hungary and against the spread of the influence of Russia westward. When Sís referred to the possibility of the defeat and break-up of the Habsburg monarchy, and the creation of an independent Czech state, the British Minister's first question concerned the relations of this state with Russia.[12] While Savinsky had nothing more interesting to tell Sís than that Russia was fighting for a just cause, Tabarinov, the Military Attaché, let him know that the creation of an intelligence service in the Czech lands was highly desirable.

When the report reached Prague at the end of September, Kramář, Rašín, and František Sís met to consider it. This was their first war-time excursion into the field of high treason; they made a few notes on the basis of the report and then burnt it. Tabarinov's proposal stimulated the conspirators to take immediate action. Soon after the meeting, Sís began to organize an intelligence service: he tried, in fact, to put into practice Klofáč's pre-war plan. Nevertheless, at the beginning of his intelligence activities, Sís found it difficult to recruit agents and to collect sufficient information. His attempt to use the party's apparatus proved dangerous; Sís then began gathering the intelligence himself from those members of the party who had access to official in-
Union of Railway Officials and at the Wollersdorf, one of the largest ammunition factories in Austria. Most of Sís's friends were, however, unaware of the use the conversations about their work were being put to. The information Sís succeeded in collecting largely concerned the economic situation in Austria–Hungary, the mood of the population, and, less frequently, the movements of troops.

While Sís was busy compiling reports for his brother in Sofia, Kramář made an attempt to contact his pre-war friend Svatkovski, who was now representing the official St. Petersburg Telegraph Agency in Switzerland. The necessity of consulting Svatkovski became even more urgent after the unexpected arrival of Vaněk from Russia at the beginning of November. Václav Vaněk was one of the four members of the *Družina*, a unit of Czech immigrants in the Russian army,[13] who penetrated behind the Austro-Hungarian lines in an attempt to reach Prague. Of the four men, only Vaněk succeeded in reaching the capital.

[12] Paulová, *Dějiny Maffie*, page 153. [13] See below, page 93.

He brought a message for Kramář from the political representative of the Czech unit: it asked the Czechs to organize a revolution as soon as the Russian army reached the frontiers of their country.[14] During their conversation, Kramář pointed out to Vaněk that, although it was unnecessary to stimulate 'passive resistance'—this was already conducted by the whole nation—it was impossible to organize a revolution. Kramář may have been afraid at this time of a temporary occupation of the Czech lands by the Russians; during a short-lived occupation, Kramář feared, the Czechs might compromise themselves too much and, after the withdrawal of the Russians, the vengeance of the Austrian military would be swift and ruthless. Kramář had the example of the Srjem Serbs before his eyes;[15] the Russian steam-roller, after three months of war had demonstrated its ability to change suddenly into reverse gear. Finally, Kramář's unwillingness to commit himself to a decisive action might also have been due to his uncertainty as to whether the nation would join in the revolution; all these factors forced the leader of the Young Czechs to answer Vaněk's enquiry in the negative. Kramář did not, however, want to give the Russians the impression that he had changed his position: this was why he wanted to assure his friend Svatkovski that he still believed in his plan for a Slavonic confederation under the leadership of Russia. It was not until the beginning of December that Kramář and his friends established contact with Svatkovski. Franta, who was known to the Austrian authorities as a moderate politician, found no difficulty in securing a passport for a visit to Switzerland and in transmitting Kramář's assurances to Svatkovski.

Apart from the Progressive party and the radicals among the Young Czechs, the Realists led by Thomas Masaryk made an early contribution to the anti-Habsburg movement. There were, however, sharp differences between Masaryk and the leader of the Young Czechs, which made co-operation between the two men difficult. Masaryk was critical of Kramář's thesis that the war was a struggle between the Teutons and the Slavs and that it would

[14] V. Vaněk, *Moje válečná Odyssea*, page 56 et seq., Prague 1925.
[15] See above, page 59.

bring about profound changes in the political map of Europe. On 20 August, in an article in a weekly magazine, Masaryk argued that the war had neither a national nor a racial character: it was a struggle for mastery in Europe. He added that 'the change of the map of Europe after the war may not be very considerable, but the war is certain to bring about far-reaching changes in social organism'. Indeed, Masaryk's hostility to the Habsburg monarchy is more difficult to understand than that of Kramář. Whereas Kramář's dedicated pro-Russian policy provided the basis for his radicalism, Masaryk's development into an enemy of the Habsburg state was a more empirical process. His own post-war explanation of the change in his attitude is not completely satisfactory. He wrote in his memoirs:[16] 'talks with the politicians at home convinced me that the vast majority of the members of parliament was anti-Habsburg, even though some individual leaders were pro-Habsburg.' In this sentence, Masaryk underestimated the courage and the visionary aspect of his anti-Habsburg action. Since his statement had little relation to political realities in Prague at the beginning of the war,[17] it could hardly have been the reason for Masaryk's change of mind. In fact, other considerations are likely to have played a greater role when he made his decision. The war had interrupted the negotiations on a compromise between the Czechs and the Germans in Bohemia: like the majority of the politicians in Prague, Masaryk was afraid that the dispute might, especially in war-time, be settled by an Imperial edict in favour of the Germans. He also was convinced that the Austro-Hungarian Supreme Commander, the whole army, and even the civil service were violently anti-Czech at the time. For Masaryk, as for many other radicals, revolutionary action against the Habsburgs was also a short-cut to establishing the supremacy of their own nation in Bohemia and Moravia. When Great Britain entered the war, he became convinced that the Entente states were stronger, from the military point of view, than the Central Powers: he clearly did not want the Czechs to give their wholehearted backing to the losing side. Finally, at the end of 1914, Masaryk received a message from his English friend,

[16] *Světová revoluce*, page 12, Prague 1926. [17] See above, page 43.

Wickham Steed, the foreign editor of *The Times*, that the possibility of a long war was being discussed in English political and army circles. This was another factor which convinced Masaryk that there should be a Czech representative in the Entente countries.

The exchange of notes between Wickham Steed and Masaryk began at the end of August. It was made possible by the good services of an American Czech called Voska, who had been staying in Prague since the beginning of May; it was through him that Masaryk sent his first message to England on 28 August. The information Voska transmitted to England was similar to that passing between the Sís brothers. Masaryk drew Steed's attention to the discontent among the Czech troops, and he suggested that the Russian Supreme Command should do something to facilitate their desertion. Before Voska left London for the United States, he was informed by Steed that 'they took note of the matter in St. Petersburg and everything necessary would be arranged'.[18]

Nevertheless, Masaryk was not satisfied with this indirect correspondence; he spent the second half of September in Rotterdam, and he wrote from there to Steed, R. W. Seton-Watson, and to Professor Denis at the Sorbonne. He wanted to see at least one of them personally, but as this proved impossible he let them know that he would be returning to Holland soon. Between the two visits to Rotterdam, Masaryk organized a nucleus of members of his party who were prepared to fight against the Habsburg monarchy; he also discussed the situation with numbers of other parties. He reported on the trip to Holland to his Realist friends; they agreed with Masaryk that as many politicians as possible should go into exile, and that they should go on working against the monarchy even in the event of the victory of the Central Powers.

In the discussions with his political colleagues, Masaryk was not merely interested in what they had to say about the current situation; his main purpose was to secure credentials for his action in the Entente countries. Sometime in Septem-

[18] V. Voska, *Z účasti zaocenánského emigranta v československém odboji. Naše revoluce,* volume I, page 241, Prague 1923.

ber he met four National Socialist deputies and confided in them his intention of leaving the country. It seems doubtful, however, that the question of full powers for Masaryk's action abroad was discussed at these meetings. Masaryk also consulted Stránský, his friend and former party colleague, now the leader of the People's party in Moravia. Stránský agreed with Masaryk that it was necessary to work for an independent Czech state abroad during the war; himself and the leaders of the Progressive party were the only men who gave a ready consent to Masaryk's revolutionary plans.

Masaryk spent the days between 13 and 29 October on his second visit to Rotterdam; for two days he remained closeted in his hotel room with Seton-Watson, discussing the situation in Austria–Hungary. After their meeting, Masaryk's friend drafted a memorandum based on their conversation, which he passed on to the British government.[19] Masaryk told his Scottish friend that, apart from his own party, he was 'speaking for' the Young Czechs, the Progressives (called 'Constitutionals' in the memorandum), the National Socialists, and the Socialists. He also said that in 'broad outlines' he had secured the consent for his plan of 'all middle-class parties of the nation at large and of the entire young generation'. He did, however, point out that opposition to his ideas was to be expected from the aristocracy and from the clericals. He also related to his friend a talk he had had with the Governor of Bohemia, in which Masaryk had said that 'all Czech parties without exception have the Slav programme and Slav sentiments. The nation is Russophil and Serbophil, and this fact cannot be changed'. The information Masaryk gave Seton-Watson was highly misleading: the author of the memorandum did nothing to clarify certain points during their conversations. Firstly, both the radical Young Czechs and National Socialists would have regarded Masaryk, at this stage of the war, not only as an unsuitable representative of their parties, but also as a man who was pursuing aims different from theirs. Even the names of the other parties Masaryk claimed to have represented became, probably owing to language difficulties, rather

[19] R. W. Seton-Watson, *Masaryk in England*, pages 40–47, Cambridge 1943.

garbled. By 'Socialists' Masaryk probably meant Stránský's People's party: he had not had contacts with the Social Democrats, and their policy was sharply opposed to his. After the description of the political conditions in the Czech lands, the second part of Seton-Watson's memorandum was devoted to Masaryk's plans for the future. Unlike Kramář, whose heart was set on a Slav confederation, Masaryk demanded an independent state. At this time he was not yet a republican:

> The new state could only be a kingdom, not a republic; a decided majority of the nation would favour this. In the interest of its future, and above all in the interest of the future Russo-Bohemian relations —this he [i.e. Masaryk] strongly emphasized—it would be wiser not to place a Russian Grand Duke on the throne, but rather a western prince, preferably a Dane or a Belgian. He is of the opinion that in the event the intimacy with Russia is more likely to subsist—paradoxical as it may seem at first sight—than in the event of direct Russian sovereignty, which would tend merely to bring out the differences of outlook. As to the shape of the future state, Masaryk said: 'Without a decisive defeat of Germany there can be no independent Bohemia; but, Germany once defeated, it can be created on maximum lines. In that case the proper course would be to restore the historical Bohemia–Moravia–Silesia, and to add to this the Slovak districts of Hungary.'

Seton-Watson's memorandum clearly brought out the difficulties of Masaryk's position, while it recorded, for the first time, his bold plans for the future. What Svatkovski, the Russian, was for Kramář, Seton-Watson was for Masaryk: a confidential listener and recorder of, in 1914, rather visionary ambitions. Masaryk's enthusiasm for his future action, and his conviction that the Czechs would have to work against Austria–Hungary in the Entente countries, made him blur the distinction between political fact and fiction. In order to improve his own position and the case for radicalism he attempted to make the credentials he had collected in Prague into something weightier than they really were; at the same time, he did not hesitate somewhat to enlarge the scope of the pro-Russian movement and feeling in his country. Nevertheless, he did not completely abandon his pre-war 'western' standpoint and his unwillingness to get too involved with Tsarist

Russia: he indicated to Seton-Watson that a direct contact between the Czechs and Russian sovereignty would prove a difficult experiment with unfortunate results.

After his return from Holland at the end of October, Masaryk spent his last six weeks in Prague before his return, four years later, as the first President of the Czechoslovak Republic. His plans, as recorded in the Rotterdam memorandum, underwent some change during this time, especially under the influence of the *Sokol* leader, Scheiner. Masaryk valued his contacts with Scheiner: he expected the *Sokols* to form the backbone of the future Czech army. Scheiner, who had been an enthusiastic Russophile before the war, told Masaryk at the end of November about his disappointment with Russia and her military achievements. At the same time he introduced Masaryk to a new idea, which seems to have originated among the Young Czech radicals: it was proposed that after the war the agricultural South Slav territories should be connected by a corridor with the industrial Czech lands. Masaryk was not very enthusiastic about the suggestion, but he put a high value on Scheiner's co-operation, and agreed. Shortly before he left for Rome, Masaryk saw Hajn, a deputy of the Progressive party, in order to find out what were the territorial demands of his party. Hajn had ideas similar to those of Scheiner: he not only included Slovakia in the future state, but extended its frontiers southwards into the Hungarian provinces of Sopron and Moson, to form a corridor between the Slovaks and the South Slavs.

On 18 December Masaryk left for Rome and permanent exile. Shortly after his arrival in the Italian capital he met Svatkovski for the first time. It was from the Russian agent that Masaryk learned about Kramář's plan for a Slav confederation. He may have been taken by surprise but he did not voice his disapproval, confining himself to the remark that 'this is a question that would depend on the political and military strength of Russia at the time of the conclusion of hostilities'.[20] The progress of the war justified, in the long run, Masaryk's western sympathies; at the time of their meeting in Rome, however, Svatkovski had already set out

[20] *M.O. III.*, vol. 6, part 2, Document No. 696.

on the road that ended in his seeking the favours of the German Minister to Switzerland three years later. He was becoming pessimistic about the internal situation in Russia: he no longer saw any prospects for the plans of Kramář and other Czech Russophils. Svatkovski's appreciation of Russia's internal problems brought him nearer to the position of Masaryk, and it eased the relationship between the two men.

Before Masaryk left for Rome he had made provisions for his successor as the Realist party's chairman; Přemysl Šámal, a young lawyer, took over the leadership of the party at the end of December. He came to play an important role in the anti-Habsburg movement. He began to work for a closer co-operation among the groups that were pursuing a clandestine radical policy, but pre-war animosities continued to hamper Šámal's effort. With great patience, he removed some of the difficulties; his task was facilitated by the fact that he was a young and unknown man who had not, like Masaryk, taken part in the arguments with Kramář before the war. Šámal's good works resulted in the formation of a loosely knit secret society, which came to be known as the Mafie; it was to become an effective instrument in the struggle of the radicals against the Habsburg state. Šámal was introduced to the chairman of the Young Czechs by Scheiner, who had told him that Kramář was looking for a place where the meetings of a secret society could be held; Šámal offered his office and flat in the centre of Prague for this purpose. Originally—this was early in 1915—the hard core of the Mafie consisted of Kramář, Scheiner, Rašín, Šámal, and Eduard Beneš. Shortly after the outbreak of the war Masaryk told Beneš about his plan for an action against the Habsburg monarchy with which the younger man wholeheartedly agreed. He was a practical, ambitious, and hard-working person: for him, perhaps more than for Masaryk, the idea of an independent state had an additional attraction—such a state would have its own representation abroad, its own civil service, and an army with its own officers' corps. These prospects appealed to Beneš, who preferred the chance, however remote, of the first place in Prague to the uncertainty of a second in Vienna.

At the beginning of 1915, Beneš went abroad for the first time:

he returned to Prague from Switzerland, where he had seen Masaryk and Svatkovski, at the end of February 1915. It was mainly due to the fact that he had met Kramář's friend that he was acceptable to the leader of the Young Czechs as a member of the secret society. In Beneš, the Mafie acquired one of its most useful and active members. He began organizing contacts with Masaryk and other Czechs abroad: it was by his services as a messenger and a link with the exiles that Beneš was able to win the confidence of his prominent fellow members of the secret society. He brought with him a message from Svatkovski, urging Kramář to come abroad, and another from Masaryk, who also insisted on the necessity of having more men to help him.

The question of who should go abroad was discussed at one of the meetings of the Mafie early in the spring. Scheiner, who was one of the conspirators' choices, could not get a passport; Kramář still maintained that his place was at home. At the same time, he revealed his plan for a Slav federation to the members of the Mafie. Though neither Šámal nor Beneš shared his opinions, they did not feel in a strong enough position to oppose the leader of the Young Czechs on a question of vital importance. In the early stages of the work of the secret society, Šámal and Beneš not only tried to prevent giving offence to its Young Czech members, but they also did their best to compensate for their own political insignificance. This they did by dedicated work and absolute openness towards their colleagues. Whereas Kramář and Rašín never told their fellow-conspirators about their connexions with Sofia,[21] Beneš reported everything he knew about the activities of Masaryk in Switzerland.

Sometime in March, the Mafie succeeded in persuading Dürich, an Agrarian deputy, to go into exile. Dürich was a bad choice. Temperamentally he was unfit for such activity, which demanded both a good deal of toughness and an elasticity of mind that Dürich did not possess; he was an epitome of Czech provincialism. He was, however, selected not for what he was, but for what he represented. He was a member of the Agrarian party, and the Mafie was very interested in creating connexions

[21] See above, page 74.

with the strongest political party in the Czech lands, and in drawing at least some of its members into the anti-Habsburg action. According to Dürich's evidence,[22] Švehla, the Agrarian leader, knew about his decision to leave the monarchy; there was no reason why he should have disapproved, as he was pursuing the policy of 'two irons': he was convinced of the necessity of maintaining good relations with Vienna, and at the same time, having some connexions with the Entente countries. Another argument in favour of Dürich's selection was his attitude towards Russia. He was a convinced Russophil, and as such he was acceptable to Kramář and other Young Czech radicals who regarded the fact that their nation was represented abroad by Masaryk, who was in their eyes an anti-Russian, as regrettable.

These considerations also helped to smooth Dürich's way abroad financially. Before he left Prague he received a grant of 30,000 crowns from the reserve fund of the National Committee, a non-party organization for the protection of Czech interests. Masaryk, on the other hand, in spite of the fact that he was a member of the committee's financial board, had received no contribution, before his departure, to his expenses. Although Masaryk left Prague with about the same amount of money as Dürich, it all came from private sources. Some of it was his own; Beneš and Šámal each made a small contribution, and Scheiner gave Masaryk 10,000 crowns. In one of his first messages from exile to Prague, dated 21 March 1915, Masaryk included a budget of the costs for his action abroad.[23] He estimated that he would need, till the end of 1915, 200,000 Swiss francs for propaganda purposes. Considering the small resources at Masaryk's disposal, this was an ambitious budget. There were times, in the early months of his exile, when he did not even have enough money to live on. The Czechs at home were either unwilling or unable to invest large sums of money in an enterprise fraught with risks; in the spring of 1915 Beneš sent Masaryk some more money and Scheiner and Šámal

[22] J. Dürich, *V českých službách*. Klášter nad Jizerou, 1921.

[23] E. Beneš, *Světová válka a naše revoluce*, vol. 3, page 23 et seq., Prague 1935. This, the last volume of the Czech edition of Beneš's memoirs, is a collection of documents relating to the action of the Czech exiles between 1914 and 1918. It will be referred to in these pages as *Dokumenty*.

contributed an additional 11,000 crowns from their own pockets. Later in the war, Masaryk's revolutionary activities came to be financed by the Czech immigrants in the United States; in this respect, Vojta Beneš, Eduard's brother, was to be of great service to the revolutionary cause.

The desire to sound the international situation was not confined to the Young Czechs and the Progressives. In the spring of 1915 some of the leading Social Democrats in Prague considered the idea of sending one of their members to Switzerland to report on the world abroad. Deputy Habrman was asked to make the trip. In Geneva, Habrman arranged to see Masaryk: the meeting took place in Masaryk's hotel room. The first thing the socialist emissary noticed was a large map of the future Czechoslovak state displayed on the wall; it was connected by a corridor with another new state, Jugoslavia. Habrman was amazed by the change which had come over Masaryk; he could not understand the transformation of a sober deputy in the *Reichsrat* into a passionate antagonist of the Habsburg monarchy. For a long time Habrman listened to Masaryk's impassioned talk; in the end he seems to have given his private approval to the revolutionary action. Nevertheless, the mood inspired in Habrman by Masaryk soon left him. When he arrived in Zürich and read the news from the battle fronts, which he had no reason to suspect of bias in favour of the Central Powers, the socialist deputy soon sobered up. When, back in Prague, he reported to his comrades, Šmeral, on hearing that Habrman had visited Masaryk in Switzerland, angrily walked out of the meeting.

Habrman was the last Czech politician to have left the monarchy on an exploratory visit; the Austrian authorities were soon to put a stop to the liberal issue of passports. The government in Vienna began taking a more active interest in the exiles, especially those in Switzerland; it had an adequate source of information in Colonel von Einem, the Military Attaché in Berne. As a result of an increase in the watchfulness of the military and civil authorities, the activities of the Prague Mafie were becoming more and more restricted: Kramář and Scheiner were arrested in March 1915. Because of lack of evidence, Scheiner was released soon afterwards; the offices of the Young Czech daily newspaper were thoroughly searched in June; in the following month, Rašín joined Kramář in prison. The work of the conspirators became still more difficult when, in August, Beneš was placed under police supervision; he decided to flee the country at the earliest opportunity. Before his departure he made another attempt to persuade a few politicians, preferably Social Democrats, to go into exile: but the war situation did not look very promising for the radical plans. On 3 September 1915 Beneš left the monarchy, carrying a forged passport.

After Beneš's departure, the Czech radicals were to go through a critical period. Their leaders were either abroad or in prison; the state authorities had intensified their efforts to stamp out treason. The military and the police co-operated in tracing dangerous elements among the population; they were very much better informed than at the beginning of the war, and the conflict between the military and civil administration was also abating. By the end of 1915 they were agreed on the treatment of treason. These were the darkest months of the war for the radicals; they carried on their work against the monarchy without many hopes for the future; their only driving force was their desire to protect the nation against the intensified ambitions of the Germans.

Šámal did his best to carry on the work of the Mafie; he was helped by Kvapil, a poet and a producer at the National Theatre in Prague, by Hajšman, a clerk in the office of Masaryk's party newspaper, and by Professor Bělehrádek and a few others. The collection of intelligence and contact with the exiles, the activities Šámal and his friends regarded as the proper task of their society, were becoming increasingly difficult: the first concern of the conspirators was to avoid arrest and interrogation. Their activities became confined almost exclusively to combating the threat of German ambitions. The Austrian Germans, and especially those who lived on the ethnical and linguistic borderlines that divided them from the Slavs, were quick in appreciating the opportunities that the war and the alliance with Germany opened up for them; they set out to exploit them in full. For the first time since the Hungarian compromise of 1867 they had a good chance of reversing the subsequent political developments that had undermined their position as the dominant nationality in the Austrian part of the monarchy. In 1915, the *Deutscher Nationalverband*—a parliamentary club that did not embrace either the German clericals or the Social Democrats—demanded a closer alliance between Germany and Austria–Hungary; a new constitution that would strengthen the hegemony of the Germans in Austria by granting complete autonomy to Galicia and thus eliminating the Poles from the *Reichsrat*, and finally, the introduction of German as the official language, and the maintenance of a non-parliamentary régime throughout the war. Similar demands were incorporated in the so-called Easter Programme of 1916; it was these plans, together with Victor Neumann's best-selling *Mitteleuropa*, which appeared early in October 1915, that Šámal and other members of the mutilated Mafie spread among the Czechs to demonstrate the dangers threatening them from the German side.

Since the belief was widespread in Austria–Hungary that the war would bring about far-reaching changes in the organization of central and eastern Europe, it was only natural that men of the most extreme views expected it to fulfil their hopes. Extreme nationalist, socialist, and even anarchist doctrines found a suitable breeding-ground in war-time Austria–Hungary: the theory that the hegemony of the Germans in the Habsburg monarchy could be established within a wider framework of reorganized central Europe belonged to the same category of extreme doctrines as the plans of the Czech radicals. However, at the end of 1915, the prospects of the Germans for the realization of their ambitions appeared much brighter than those of the Czechs or, for that matter, any of the Habsburg Slavs. In spite of overwhelming difficulties, the members of the Mafie succeeded in preserving their small clandestine organization for employment in more propitious circumstances: indeed, Prague was the only town in the Habsburg monarchy where such an organization existed.

Beneš's departure in September—he was the last man to go into exile—marked the completion of the split of the Czech anti-Habsburg movement: from now on, the politicians at home and the exiles were to go their own separate ways. Nevertheless, during the early months of their exile, Masaryk and his friends did not recognize their isolation: they continued to insist that they represented not only the radicals organized in the Mafie, but the 'whole nation'; since they had no such support behind them as the South Slav exiles had in the Serbian government, the Czechs were over-concerned with the repercussions their action might have at home, and especially with the danger of being disavowed by the politicians in Prague. This was one of the reasons why the advancement of the plans of Masaryk and his friends was slow compared with the quick progress of the South Slavs. At the same time, the Czech immigrants in the Entente countries, and in Russia in particular, proved difficult to organize around a central authority consisting of recent political exiles; there was also the chronic lack of funds.

Šmeral had been right when he warned Beneš that there was no interest in the Czech problem in the Entente countries:[24] Masaryk and other exiles had to work hard to remedy this state of affairs. In May 1915 Professor Denis of the Sorbonne, one of Masaryk's pre-war academic friends, began to publish the periodical *La Nation Tcheque*; three months later *Československá Samostatnost* began to appear in Annemasse in France, edited by Leo Sychrava, the first Czech political exile. The *New Europe*, edited by R. W. Seton-Watson, was added to these publications in October 1916: they were the three main instruments of Czech publicity in the Entente countries. They all pursued the campaign against the Habsburg monarchy vigorously, although at times with a remarkable lack of scruple. The *New Europe*, for instance, often claimed that, in England, groups of financiers and 'society people', the Catholic church and the Jews had the most direct vested interest in the preservation of the Habsburg monarchy. This was not the case. There is no evidence that the bankers influenced the government in the monarchy's favour; apart from having no desire to undertake unnecessary obligations as to far-reaching reforms in central and eastern Europe, neither the British nor the French government could be said, in the early years of the war, to have

[24] See above, page 46.

had a policy towards the Danubian monarchy. Although the Catholic church in France and the *Action Française* were in favour of the monarchy, the Catholics in England, under the influence of Hilaire Belloc and G. K. Chesterton and their anti-Semitic weekly *The New Witness*, were anti-Habsburg and remained so throughout the war. Opposition to the break-up of the monarchy came from rather unexpected quarters in England; a group of radicals and socialists like Henry Brailsford and Charles and Noel Buxton, who had taken an interest in this part of Europe before the war, argued against the dissolution of the Habsburg Empire, mainly on economic grounds.[25]

There was no firm political organization behind the periodicals that began to appear in France in the summer of 1915. After protracted and often difficult negotiations between Masaryk and the pre-war immigrants in the Entente countries, agreement was achieved, at the end of the autumn, that made the first political step possible. On 14 November the 'Czech Committee Abroad' published a manifesto that amounted to a declaration of war on Austria–Hungary. It was signed by the representatives of the Czech immigrants in Russia, England, France, and the United States, by Masaryk and Dürich, the Russophil emissary abroad sponsored by Kramář. Beneš did not sign the manifesto because he knew that his was not a very well-known name and because he 'wanted to give an example of political restraint to our immigrants'.[26]

The November declaration bore every mark of a hasty compromise in which Masaryk and Beneš had been forced to make heavy concessions to the Russophils. It concentrated on the developments on the eastern front:

> We are entering the political arena at a moment when the withdrawal of the victorious Russian army from the enemy is being exploited against Russia and her allies. . . . We are forced to take this step [the publication of the manifesto] by an acute feeling of Slav reciprocity; we would like to express deep sympathies with our

[25] H. Hanák, *The British Press and Austria–Hungary, 1914–1918*. M.A. Thesis, London University.

[26] Beneš, *Světová válka*, vol. 1, page 100.

brothers the Serbs and the Russians, as well as with the Poles, who all are subjected to so much suffering by the war.

This was the first and the last declaration signed jointly by Masaryk and Dürich. In 1916 the differences between them led to a breach which, had it not been for subsequent internal developments in Russia, might have caused a serious division of the anti-Habsburg movement abroad. In fact, the conflict between Dürich and Masaryk was a continuation of the pre-war differences of Masaryk and Kramář on the question of the attitude of the Czechs to Russia.

Dürich arrived in Switzerland at the end of May 1915; although in his messages to Prague, Masaryk had frequently asked for reinforcements, the arrival of the Agrarian deputy proved disappointing. In his memoirs, Masaryk wrote about him:

> He was quite a good parliamentarian, speaking French and Russian, but not strong enough politically for the new situation now facing us. He came saying that Dr. Kramář had selected him specially to represent our nation in Russia. To this I had no objection as long as we were agreed on a programme. He was for the Tsar and for the Orthodox church, like so many of our Russophiles who awaited salvation from Russia.[27]

Having surveyed the activities of Masaryk and Beneš in the West and having come to disapprove of them, Dürich settled down to a quiet existence in Berne, punctuated by frequent visits to the Russian Embassy. He made little attempt to help the 'westerners' to further their plans; on the contrary, he got in touch with several conservative, pro-Russian members of the Czech colony in Paris. Discussing the formation of the representative Czech body in exile, Masaryk wrote that 'In Switzerland, Holland and England there was no opposition; but in Paris the ambitions of the sundry bibulous aspirants to the future Russian Satrapy of Bohemia gave a little trouble.'

While in Switzerland, Dürich was waiting for an invitation from the Russian government, which was long in coming: it was only in the summer of 1916 that he finally arrived in St. Peters-

[27] *The Making of a State*, pages 55–56.

burg. Masaryk and Beneš viewed his departure with some apprehension; Beneš referred to the trouble ahead:

> Serious complications began only when, at the beginning of July 1916, deputy Dürich arrived in Russia. Since the spring of this year he has been regarded, by the Russian government, as a suitable person to lead the Czech revolutionary movement in Russia, a counter-balance to Professor Masaryk.[28]

In order to keep Dürich in line, the exiles in Paris decided to send to Russia a young Slovak, Milan Štefánik. Štefánik had been drawn into Masaryk's circle in the spring of 1916; he was an astronomer, a naturalized Frenchman, and an acquaintance of Masaryk from Prague. His mission to Russia was intended to bring about an understanding between the Agrarian deputy and the Paris committee; in August, an agreement was in fact concluded in Kiev. Although its text has not been published, Beneš maintains in his memoirs that Dürich and the society of the Czech immigrants in Kiev (these were pro-Dürich; a similar society in St. Petersburg was largely inclined to recognize the leadership of Masaryk) acknowledged the leading position of the Czechoslovak National Council in Paris. Nevertheless, there are several reasons for questioning the reliability of Beneš's information. There are conflicting statements by the exiles themselves as to the date of the establishment of the National Council, the successor of the 'Czech Committee Abroad': its origins are lost in the obscurity of the early activities and struggles of the exiles. Whereas Beneš wrote that it had already been instituted in February of 1916,[29] Masaryk gave us a different date for the origin of the institution. According to him, the name was used for the first time by Štefánik in the draft of the agreement with Dürich in Kiev; the composition of the Council was first announced in the organ of the exiles, the *Československá Samostatnost*, as late as 1 November 1916. Dürich was still included in this announcement: he and Štefánik were the two vice-presidents; Masaryk its president, and Beneš the secretary-general.

Nevertheless, in the autumn of 1916, the conflict between the

[28] *Světová válka*, vol. 1, page 128. [29] Idem, vol. 1 ,page 117

western and the pro-Russian faction among the Czech exiles began in earnest. The reasons for the flare-up of the crisis were doubtless the weak position of Dürich on the National Council, his desire to play the leading role in the politics of the exiles, and the change in the policy of the Tsarist government itself. Originally, the men in the Foreign Ministry had not been interested in the encouragement of the national movements in the Habsburg monarchy: they had no desire to disturb the dynastic *status quo*, nor did they want to jeopardize the chances for a separate peace with Germany and Austria–Hungary, which, on several occasions during the years 1915 and 1916, looked remarkably promising. Nevertheless, after a long period of indifference—even of hostility—the Russian Foreign Ministry began to take an active interest, in the autumn of 1916, in the Czech anti-Habsburg movement. The desertions of the Czech troops[30] could not have failed to attract the Foreign Ministry's attention to the advantages of encouraging the anti-Habsburg movement; also, the Russians resented the concentration of the political exiles in the West. This is in fact the explanation Masaryk gave for the awakening of Russian interest:

> In the autumn of 1916, the Russian Foreign Ministry began to pay more attention to the Czechoslovak movement which it decided to direct and control. In this it was inspired by a spirit of opposition to the West and by dislike of the favour shown to us by England and France.[31]

Although Masaryk was right in recognizing the hidden rivalries and suspicions that existed between Russia and the western Allies, he overestimated the success his movement had achieved in England and France. In fact, during the first two years of the war, the Czech revolutionary action in Russia had resulted in more concrete achievements than that of Masaryk in the West. At this point it is necessary to return to the very beginning of the war. While Masaryk was still in Prague, uncertain as to what action to take against the Habsburg monarchy, the Czechs in Russia were presenting their plans and demands on the highest levels of Russian

[30] See above, page 55. [31] *The Making of a State*, page 153.

government. On 20 August, and again on 24 September 1914, representatives of the societies of the immigrants presented themselves to the Tsar; during the second audience Nicholas II showed a great interest in Slovakia and he asked the delegation for a memorandum on the subject. These audiences were followed by many others; the Tsar also alluded to the 'Czech problem' in a number of public speeches. All these occasions took place in an atmosphere of enthusiastic Pan-Slavism: the brief address delivered by the Czechs to the Tsar at their first audience in August, for instance, concluded with the sentence: 'Let the free and independent crown of St. Wenceslas reflect the rays of the crown of the Romanovs.'[32]

On the military side, the Czechs in Russia had also achieved a considerable success shortly after the outbreak of the war: on 4 August, a day before the declaration of war by Austria–Hungary on Russia, the Czechs in Moscow put a plan for their own unit in the Russian army before the Tsarist government. Permission to form a unit was soon granted: at the end of October, the *Družina*, a unit of about 800 men, left for the front. As it consisted entirely of Czech immigrants who had become Russian subjects, its approval by the government had presented no difficulties: the later proposal to recruit among the Czech prisoners of war did not have such an easy passage. The government demanded that the prisoners should apply for Russian nationality, and that at least one third of their officers should be Russian born.[33] The immigrants' societies, on their own account, started to carry out missionary activities among the prisoners of war, trying to convert them to the Orthodox faith. Under such conditions, the recruitment drive was not very successful: as late as January 1916 the original unit was expanded into a regiment; four months later the formation of a brigade was announced. The leaders of the League of Czech Societies in Russia were, however, content with having achieved this much: they regarded the unit as a symbol of the pro-Russian feelings of the Czechs.

Indeed, most of the Czech immigrants in Russia, perhaps without the Tsarist government fully realizing it at first, shared

[32] *Dokumenty*, page 554. [33] Masaryk, *The Making of a State*, page 148.

Kramář's views on the reorganization of Slav Europe after the war; when Dürich finally arrived in St. Petersburg in July 1916 this movement received a political leader who sympathized with such plans. Masaryk and Beneš, on the other hand, had to bide their time during the first two years of the war. Before it became clear that Tsarist Russia could not survive the strain imposed on it by the war, the Russophil policy was not only more successful in practice than that of Beneš and Masaryk in the West, but it was also a logical continuation of the pro-Russian sympathies of the Czechs. The movement in Russia caused a profound concern in Vienna. The Austro–Hungarian government was naturally suspicious of Russian ambitions as far as its own Slavs were concerned; the Ministries of the Interior in Vienna and Budapest knew from long and first-hand experience the dangers presented by the Russophil movement to the territorial integrity of the Habsburg monarchy. In comparison, the activities of the exiles in the West appeared harmless for the time being: Masaryk could be regarded as an aged university professor indulging, together with a few friends, his academic fancies.

IV

DEATH OF THE EMPEROR

The stage for the second, crucial stage of the war was set in the last months of 1916. The governments of the belligerent Powers and the alliances they had created came under severe strains. It became clear that the war had run into a blind alley, and the devastation on a vast scale had either to be justified, or better still, concluded; if this could not be done, the way had to be cleared for a decisive victory. While the war machines were being overhauled and tightened on both sides, peace and war aims came under discussion. The mood of this period of the war, the mood of growing bewilderment, was perhaps best expressed in an inscription by an anonymous German fatalistic philosopher, hoisted up in a town near the western front: 'Do not be angry, only wonder.' Men felt that they were gripped in a process they could neither understand nor control: they paused for a while, watching in amazement. The days of wrath were yet to come.

On the surface, the fortunes of war seemed to have run in favour of the Central Powers; the battle fronts, in the West as much as in the East, cut deep into the territory of their enemies. But neither the German nor the Austro-Hungarian leaders were optimistic about the situation. Since the plan for a quick and decisive victory in the West had misfired at the beginning of the war, the German war-lords at once set out to reduce the struggle to a one-front engagement by diplomatic means. Two years later their objective was still dismally distant. In December 1916 Ludendorff expressed his opinion that unless one of the Allies collapsed in the near future Germany would lose the war.

The internal situation of the Habsburg monarchy was fast becoming critical: this only increased the doubts of the men in Berlin whether their ally was able to look after its own affairs. At the end of September, von Tschirschky, the well-informed German Ambassador in Vienna, reported on the situation in the monarchy:[1]

> The longer the war lasts, the more strongly the simple question whether Austria–Hungary will be able to carry on the fight, not only in the military but also in the economic field, comes to the foreground.

After having complained of the conditions at the Austro-Hungarian Supreme Command, the Ambassador continued:

> The reserves of troops are nearly exhausted, and we should expect that next spring Austria–Hungary will reach the limit of its military potential, though perhaps not in the sphere of production of armaments and ammunition, where surprising progress has been made under our leadership. The mood of depression here is increased—unfortunately not without justification—by the economic situation. This and the political measures concerning economy are simply impossible. There is no organization; when attempts were made to organize after our example, they ran into difficulties because of the local proclivity for 'muddling through', and because of an economy based on protection. No systematic work in this respect has been done, regulations were made without expert knowledge, and usually for one province at a time: such practices have led to a completely unjust distribution of provisions. The people in the suburbs of Vienna are starving; they are driven to despair by long queueing, which often brings no results. . . . The situation has become still more serious since the poor results of this year's harvest in Austria and in Hungary, and also by the unsatisfactory economic relations between the two countries, which should, and this goes especially for Hungary, support each other loyally with food supplies. The Hungarian government, led by Count Tisza, pursues a Hungarian policy; in spite of high-minded phrases, it has no understanding of common needs and aims. Here, too, there is no personality that could dictate a policy which would safeguard common interests.

Although the German Ambassador disapproved of the men in the Austrian government and argued that a change of personalities might improve the monarchy's war effort, he singled out the Hungarians, and Count Tisza in particular, for blame. Further on in his report, he returned to the question of relations between

[1] *AA*, a report in the series *Oesterreich 95 sec*, of 28 September 1916.

Austria and Hungary once again, but he qualified his criticism of the Hungarians in the following manner:

I would like to point out that during the war, the relations between the two parts of the monarchy have deteriorated considerably. Although the feeling of common interest had seemed, at the beginning of the war, to have been strengthened by common danger, some time later exactly the opposite happened. Hungary is trying to loosen its ties with Austria more than ever before. Hungarian chauvinism is flourishing and one must admit that this is mainly Austria's fault. The many mistakes made by the Supreme Command—which is exclusively in Austrian hands—has embittered the Hungarians. The sins of Vienna's internal policy, committed during several decades, which have made the treason of the Czechs possible and for which many Hungarians have died, have also had their effect on the people in Hungary. . . . Magyar regiments are stationed in Bohemia in order to prevent unrest there, instead of being able to defend their fatherland. Recently, an Austrian politician has told me: 'Bohemia is in fact occupied by the Hungarians.' Nobody in Austria is prepared to introduce a new policy in the Czech lands: this was further illustrated when both the Czech members of the cabinet, who are ministers not because of their qualifications but because they represent their people, were elevated to the rank of baron.

On the financial situation of the monarchy, von Tschirschky had the following observations to make:

A similar [i.e. chaotic] situation can be observed in the financial field. Although the Minister of Finance has the best intentions of introducing order, he despairs because he cannot make the two Premiers introduce suitable measures. Germany pays its ally 100,000,000 marks every month, and apart from that it transfers to Austria regular subsidies for Bulgaria and Turkey; it is not impossible that the monarchy will present to us further bills in order to maintain the value of its currency.

The report ended on a pessimistic note:

I believe that we should make an attempt to stabilize the situation here. We are running the danger that the Habsburg monarchy will suddenly sicken, and that Germany will share in its downfall.

On 30 September Bethmann-Hollweg sent Tschirschky's communication to the Kaiser, agreeing that only personal changes on the highest level might help, and that the Kaiser should meet the Habsburg Crown Prince. He commented: 'Herr von Tschirschky paints the picture, I fear, in not too dark colours'.

Personal changes did, indeed, occur in the monarchy, though perhaps not entirely to the liking of the Germans. On 21 October, Stürgkh, the Austrian Premier was assassinated; at the beginning of November Emperor Franz Josef fell ill. A fortnight later, the bronchial catarrh he suffered from took a turn for the worse: he lost appetite and started running a temperature. In spite of his illness, Franz Josef continued to get up and work at his table as usual. On Tuesday, 21 November, he asked for an armchair to be put at his desk; early in the evening he felt too weak and had to retire to bed. Two hours later, his two personal physicians could no longer help the Emperor and they sent for the court chaplain, who administered the extreme unction. At 9 p.m., Franz Josef I died a gentle death. A special edition of the *Wiener Zeitung*, announcing the ruler's demise, was soon being sold in the streets of Vienna, but in the middle of the war, and in the middle of a depressing, grey winter, the news somehow failed to move the inhabitants of the capital. Late in the night, Josef Redlich recorded his impressions of these hours: 'The whole town is surrounded by a deep and intense tiredness; neither sorrow for the dead ruler, nor joy over his successor, can be felt.'

On 28 November Kaiser Wilhelm arrived from the German General Headquarters to pay the last respects to his departed ally; the Kaiser left Vienna on the same day, after a dinner with the new Emperor and Empress. Two days later the funeral procession set out from the castle chapel, and proceeded around the Ring to St. Stephan's Cathedral, where the members of the House of Habsburg were waiting, to escort their former head to the family tomb at the Capuchin monastery a few hundred yards away. This was the last time that so much European royalty assembled in Vienna; the Kings of Bulgaria, Bavaria, and Saxony, the German Crown Prince, the successor to the Turkish throne, and the Crown Prince of Sweden all escorted the late Emperor on his last journey to the Habsburg family tomb at the Tegetthoff.

In Prague, Josef Pekař, the well-known historian and professor at the Czech Karl-Ferdinand University commemorated the Emperor's life in a public oration. He described the achievement, by his own nation, of political and cultural maturity during the reign of Franz Josef, and he tried to define the ruler's own contribution to the development. Pekař said:

> Emperor Franz Josef followed our progress with loving care; the first Imperial Minister of Education, Count Leo Thun, broke the German hegemony in secondary education and thus paved the way for the advance of the Czech language even in Slovakia; the first middle-class Czech who was made a member of the Upper House, in 1861, was František Palacký, who had reconstructed our past for us. Soon afterwards secondary schooling was made completely Czech; the technical university was divided [into Czech and German parts] and legislation was passed for far-reaching autonomy in our districts and provinces . . . which in so many respects stimulated our national development. In the period which began with the entry of the Czechs into the *Reichsrat*—after 1879—the development followed of our secondary schools, the division of the university, the foundation of the Academy of Sciences—which bears the name of His Majesty, the foundation of the Academy of Arts, of the technical university in Brno. . . . Our national endeavours were thus provided with all the aids and institutes necessary for a higher cultural life, which a strong and conscious nation should possess if it wants to take an honourable place in the work of human progress.[2]

But at the same time the Czech historian said that the ruler had lived through many difficult trials and that he had often been forced to disregard his ideals. He added:

> When a historian shall look for a formula which might describe and sum up Franz Josef's reign, he will find it in the conflict and the compromise between the dynastic principle and the principle of nationality.

Pekař's conclusion was clear-sighted: but for some time in the past, and especially after the death of Franz Josef, this struggle

[2] *Die Presse*, 18 January 1959.

was marked more often by unresolved conflicts rather than concluded by a compromise.

Although Franz Josef was able to console himself with the victorious advance of the armies of the Central Powers on the Rumanian front, the last weeks of his life did not remain unclouded. On 5 November 1916 the Manifesto by the two Emperors concerning the future of Poland was published; neither this, nor the relations between Austria–Hungary and Germany, a problem that was again brought to the forefront by the attempt to solve the Polish question, could have put the Emperor's mind at ease. The war had brought with it the possibility of solving the whole Polish problem by one of the sides engaged in the struggle on the eastern front: since most of the territory of the Russian part of Poland was under the occupation of the armies of the Central Powers by the end of autumn in 1915, the initiative was theirs. The front-line in the north-east looked permanent enough: there was little hope that the Russians could regain control of their former Polish territories and the commanders of the armies of the Central Powers were aware of this. Yet the German and Austrian leaders hesitated for more than a year to decide on a final settlement. One of the difficulties that made progress slow was the fluctuation of the hopes of a separate peace with Russia: this concerned Germany more than Austria; the Germans were engaged in the years 1915 and 1916 in putting out frequent feelers to the Tsarist government, and they feared that a solution involving the detachment of Polish territory from Russia might jeopardize their chances for a separate peace. The Austrians knew little about the German–Russian negotiations, and since they entertained high hopes as far as Poland was concerned they soon became suspicious. The men in Vienna hopefully envisaged Galicia united with Russian Poland and attached to Austria by ties as close as those binding Croatia to Hungary. Indeed, the plan for the incorporation of Poland was regarded by many Austrians as one of their unofficial war aims. They were not only after a territorial acquisition; they hoped that such a solution, by establishing a parliament in Poland and excluding the Poles from the *Reichsrat*, would strengthen the position of the Austrian Germans. They also argued that it would deprive the

Russians of their interest in Poland, which, as they knew from their pre-war experience, did not stop at the frontiers between Austria–Hungary and Russia. Nevertheless, the negotiations between Germany and Austria–Hungary on the Polish question put the alliance between the two countries to a severe test; the differences between Berlin and Vienna did much to alienate the two countries during a crucial stage of the war, when victory and defeat were in the balance.

At this point it is necessary to retrace the negotiations between Vienna and Berlin which resulted in the ill-fated Two Emperors' Manifesto of 5 November 1916. On the German side the initiative came from General Falkenhayn.[3] In a telegram of 4 August 1915 to the Chancellor, the General declared that the deliberations of the *Duma* in St. Petersburg had clearly shown that an official peace offer by Germany would be out of place; at the same time, he enquired whether the endeavours aimed at detaching Polish territories from Russia should be supported and if so, whether the Chancellor was thinking in terms of an independent Poland or of its annexation to Austria–Hungary or Germany. Bethmann-Hollweg replied on the same day; he telegraphed to the General Headquarters:[4]

If Russia should decide for a separate peace, although the prospects at the present moment are poor, we would be forced to give her a peace at a cheaper price, which would leave Poland to her after certain strategic correction of the frontier. There is no doubt that in this case Russia would grant Poland a far-reaching autonomy. If the war should end differently, in the event of Russia's collapse, there are two possibilities: either an autonomous Poland would be created, connected with us and with Austria–Hungary by an alliance and a military convention, or the greater part of Congress Poland would form a state, together with Galicia, under Austrian rule. In this event, our frontier claims would perhaps have to be greater, but not of such nature that they would mean the fourth partition of the country: this has to be

[3] *AA*, No. 262 in the series *Weltkrieg 20c sec.* The documents on German–Austrian negotiations concerning Poland can be found in this series, entitled *Zukunft der besetzen Gebieten: Polen.*

[4] Telegram No. 965, the Chancellor to Treutler, the Foreign Ministry's liaison officer at the GHQ.

avoided. It is difficult to say which combination would be the less inconvenient for us. As far as we are concerned, there is no solution of the Polish problem that would be completely safe; in any event, it is in our interest not to make the Poles into our enemies. Russia would use an autonomous Poland under her domination to pursue irredentist aims on our territory. Such endeavours would be successful to the degree to which the Poles would entertain bitterness and hatred against us after the war. A Poland detached from Russia in one form or another would become an effective protection against the Pan-Slav threat only at such a time as we are regarded by the Poles as their good friends.

After the initial exchanges, conducted in general terms, more detailed suggestions started coming in. On 8 September General Falkenhayn commented on the value of the Poles as allies; he expressed the hope that Polish recruits could be trained during the winter and employed on the eastern front early in 1916, but he did hasten to point out, however, that such a programme would be practicable only if an early decision was made about the future of Poland. In his reply, Bethmann-Hollweg enclosed a long memorandum on the problem by Jagow, the State Secretary in the Foreign Ministry. Jagow was the first German political leader to analyse the question in detail. His ideas were to influence the German attitude to this problem for a long time to come: it was also for the first time that the Austro-Hungarian solution was strongly advocated in Berlin.

Jagow, like his Chancellor, was pessimistic about the possibility of finding a 'wholly satisfactory solution' as far as Germany was concerned. Although he introduced his thesis by arguing that, in a number of respects, it would be best if Russia retained its Polish territories, he reasoned against this solution in the following manner:

The giant state of Russia, with its vast human resources and its opportunities for economic growth, has weighed heavily on western Europe. In spite of superficial western civilization, introduced by Peter the Great and the German dynasty, it is divided from Latin civilization by its basically Byzantine–Oriental culture; the Russian people, a Slav-Mongoloid race, is foreign to the German-Romance peoples of the West. These differences were bound to grow with the spread of Pan-Slav ideas and with the alienation of the Russian dynasty from Germany. The so-called 'traditional friendship' between Russia and Prussia mainly relied on personal and blood ties between the two ruling houses.

After having discussed the course of German–Russian relations during the nineteenth century, Jagow got down to analysing the Polish problem; he remarked that 'Although the Poles are a Slav race, they are without the Mongoloid admixture of the Russians; their Catholic and Protestant creeds also differentiate them from the Russians.'

Further, the State Secretary pointed out that the incision into Prussia by Congress Poland would always remain a threat to the Prussian and Silesian provinces, especially when Russia completed building strategic railways and when there were more Russian troops stationed in Poland. It would also be impossible, Jagow argued, to detach the province of Kurland from Russia as long as Poland was a part of the Tsarist Empire. To reinforce his argument, Jagow turned his attention into the enemy camp:

> In view of present internal developments we can expect, after the war at the latest, a revolution in Russia; its outcomes are now impossible to foresee. Because of the Russian nature, which often falls from one extreme into another, a complete change of internal conditions, leading to the fall of the dynasty, cannot be ruled out. . . . In a parliamentary or constitutional Russia, Pan-Slav tendencies would come into the foreground still more strongly. . . . [The creation of] an autonomous Russian Poland would result in lively irredentist activities in other parts of Poland, which would be attracted and supported by a country hostile to us. As soon as Russia stops suppressing its Poles, it will start exploiting the irredentist movement against us.

Having dismissed the possibility of Russia's retaining its Polish territory, Herr von Jagow began to consider other solutions. A completely independent Poland seemed to him impracticable because, in his view, the Poles were not yet 'ripe' for it; he criticized the idea of the incorporation of this area into Germany, since an 'increase in the number of Polish and Jewish subjects would be a national disaster'; neither did he like the idea of dividing Congress

Poland between Germany and Austria–Hungary: the Poles would certainly view another partition with disfavour. The remaining possibility, i.e. the incorporation of an autonomous Poland into Austria–Hungary had a number of attractions, the State Secretary argued. He knew that the ruling circles in Vienna wanted it; he was of the opinion that it would be difficult to find another territorial 'reward for victory' for Germany's ally. He wrote:

> Vienna is thinking about the annexation of Poland in terms of 'subdualism', i.e. the unification of the six million Galician Poles with the twelve million of their compatriots in Congress Poland in a kingdom, which would have a similar relation to Austria as Croatia does with Hungary. This would be followed by the grant of certain autonomous rights to the Poles, and their elimination from the Austrian Parliament, where they would send only a delegation for the discussion of problems common with Austria. Poland would become financially independent; it would not be financed, as Galicia has been hitherto, by Austria. This would have the advantage of strengthening the German element in Austria. Irredentist movements might also come into being, but they would not be strong; our Poles would be economically more powerful than their compatriots under Austrian rule. We could, by pressure on Vienna, defend ourselves more easily against such tendencies.

Nevertheless, Jagow indicated that a number of objections could be raised against the Austro-Hungarian solution of the Polish problem; firstly, trade routes with Russia would be cut off —the question of the right of transit would have to be raised with the Austrians; secondly, it might be objected that the Habsburg monarchy would become a more powerful state and an awkward ally who might turn against Germany. On the second point, Jagow wrote:

> Because of the peculiar characteristics of the Habsburg monarchy, this acquisition would not mean an internal strengthening of the state. The Germans in Austria would in any event be reinforced by the foundation of a kingdom of Poland, and their influence on the policy of the monarchy would increase. Their sympathies will be with us in the future, unless they have suicidal tendencies. It is true that there are many people among the Viennese aristocracy, clergy and senior army

officers who have not yet forgotten 1866 and who cannot reconcile themselves to the fact that the Prussian upstart has superseded the old Empire. But they are dying out and the younger generation have learned to think differently. Most Germans in Austria are now convinced that only their strong reliance on Germany can save their country.

Jagow was of the opinion that, apart from strengthening the Germans in Austria, the detachment of Congress Poland from the Tsarist Empire would make it easier for Germany to stake its territorial claims in the Russian Baltic provinces. In this connexion he mentioned the 'sentimental arguments that speak for the annexation of the former territories of the Teutonic Order'.

In his letter to Falkenhayn of 11 August 1915 which accompanied Jagow's memorandum, Bethmann-Hollweg expressed himself strongly in favour of the solution suggested by the State Secretary in the Foreign Ministry. In fact, for several months to come, this was the official German policy. Count Burian, the Austro-Hungarian Foreign Minister was assured, during the talks in Berlin on 11 and 12 November, that the German government favoured no other solution. Several notes and memoranda from Vienna to Berlin, written at the end of 1915 and during the first half of 1916, show that the Austrians regarded the matter as settled and their solution of the Polish problem as final.

The first indications of a change in the German attitude can be traced to the beginning of 1916; it was at this time that new ideas began to germinate in Berlin. They were first expressed in the dispatches of von Mutius from Warsaw, but they were unlikely to have been entirely his own. Mutius was the Foreign Ministry's liaison officer with the military administration of the German-occupied territories in Poland; he was in constant touch with General von Beseler, the Governor-General. The army administrators of Poland, who used von Mutius as a channel for their ideas, originated the new policy. It was suggested that the creation of an independent state with close ties with Germany would be the best solution. The first time the idea was expressed was in a letter from the State Secretary to the Ambassador in Vienna on 6 April 1916. Several days after this communication had reached the German Embassy, Count Burian came to consult his colleagues in Berlin once more. On this occasion, open conflict between the allies was unavoidable: indeed, Burian defended his former standpoint and refused even to consider the new German proposals. On 22 April von Beseler, in a letter from Warsaw to the Chancellor, expressed his regret that no agreement with Vienna could be reached:

Since I place high value on an agreement with Austria–Hungary on the Polish problem *before* peace negotiations, I can only regret the fact that no satisfactory basis for a settlement has been found. The Austrian demand that the whole of Congress Poland should be incorporated into the Habsburg monarchy is naturally unacceptable to us; on the other hand, the suggestion by Your Excellency that an autonomous Poland should be created, under all guarantees necessary for the safety of Germany, is preferable, in spite of serious drawbacks, to all other arrangements.

General Beseler did not argue in his letter against the objections of Count Burian that the creation of such a state would in fact mean another partition of Poland, the most unwise solution of the whole problem; he merely restated the ideas which he had already expressed in a letter to Jagow on 23 January; firstly, that the German eastern marches should be protected against Russia, and secondly, that the Polish question should be eliminated from the number of outstanding European problems once and for all.

It took the Austrians several months to come to terms with the change of the German attitude and it was not until the negotiations in Vienna on 11 and 12 August that they reluctantly accepted the new approach. One day after the conclusion of the discussions a joint memorandum was drafted:

An agreement has been reached that an independent kingdom of Poland, with a hereditary dynasty and a constitution, should be established. An early announcement of the intention to found a national state should be made by the two allied monarchs, although the establishment of the state itself would have to be postponed to a later date—preferably after the end of the war. As long as hostilities continue, Poland will have to remain an occupied territory. The wish was expressed that the customs and transit barriers which are now dividing the German and Austrian zones of occupation should be abolished.

Further, the memorandum pointed out that the Polish state should extend as far eastwards as possible; it should have its own administration but it could not pursue an independent foreign policy: the nature of Poland's foreign representation would have to be discussed by Germany and Austria–Hungary in the future and the new state would be allowed to enter only into approved alliances. It would have its own army organized by a mixed military commission: Burian agreed that the high command of this army should have a unitary character and that it should be run by Germany. The Chancellor also argued at the Vienna meeting that Poland should be drawn into the German economic sphere. It was only at this point that the Austro-Hungarian Foreign Minister objected, and it was agreed that the question should be examined by experts. Finally, the allies gave an undertaking which they hoped would later be embodied in a formal treaty, namely that no part of their own Polish territory was to be taken over by the newly established state.

The settlement of the Polish problem was, of course, unpopular in Vienna; a change of government further complicated its reception. At his first audience with the Emperor, von Koerber, the new Premier, found Franz Josef in an extremely excited state. The Polish solution was the cause; he implored von Koerber to accept it. However, the government in Vienna made an attempt to counteract the German solution of the Polish problem. Indeed, one day before the publication of the Two Emperors' Manifesto on 5 November, Franz Josef himself wrote to the Prime Minister:[5]

It is my will to confer on the province of Galicia, as soon as the new state is created, the right to decide, in full measure but within the demands of the unity of the state, the way in which the province will be run and thus to create the basis for its political and economic development.

[5] *Politische Chronik*, November 1916.

The underlying assumption of the joint memorandum of 13 August was that the establishment of a Polish state should in no way affect the situation either in the German or the Austrian part of Poland. Vienna's decision to confer a higher degree of autonomy was regarded, especially by the German military leaders, as a breach of agreement; they profoundly resented Austria's unilateral action. On 7 November Hindenburg telegraphed to the Chancellor:[6]

> Your Excellency is of the opinion that the increase in the autonomy of Galicia is an Austrian internal measure to which we should raise no objections. I see in it also a step of great significance for foreign policy; Austria–Hungary is seeking to make our position in Poland difficult and to achieve, through Galicia, a higher degree of influence there for itself. It can achieve this under the mask of autonomy sooner than if Poland were a member of the Austrian state. Because of these measures, the security of Prussia will require a different adjustment of frontiers from that which I have demanded so far. Further, I see in the attitude of Austria not only discourtesy, but a sign of underestimation of our power and determination, which causes me a grave concern for the future.

Bethmann-Hollweg replied to Hindenburg in a telegram on 10 November:[7] he agreed that the Austrian proposal had a certain significance for foreign policy, and added that he had never disputed this. But he was not as certain as the Field-Marshal about the ultimate effects of the Austrian action:

> It is impossible to tell as yet what effect this step will have on us and on our relations with Poland. It is also impossible to tell whether it will win a higher degree of influence for Austria or whether it will speed up the secession of Galicia from the Austrian state and with that, the exclusion of some six to eight million badly governed, but politically influential Slavs.

The Two Emperors' Manifesto on the future of occupied territories in Poland was published two days before the exchange of telegrams between Bethmann-Hollweg and Hindenburg began. The declaration was based on the ideas expressed in the memorandum of 13 August; it was by no means a compromise between

[6] Telegram No. 910 in the series *Weltkrieg sec.* [7] No. 1373 in *Weltkrieg sec.*

the views of Vienna and those of Berlin: the Austrians had been forced to accept the German solution of the Polish problem. The way in which the future of Poland was settled by the central European allies demonstrated their inability and unwillingness to deal with national problems. The solution they produced, after long negotiations, was short-sighted and contradictory, and it did not take into consideration the views of the Poles themselves. Although Poland was to remain partitioned, the creation of a Polish state was certain to affect the Poles in Austria–Hungary and Germany. Berlin, at any rate, expected too much from the settlement: apart from hoping that the establishment of an independent Poland would, somehow, strengthen the hand of the Austrian Germans, they thought that the promise of an independent state would impress the Poles to such extent that they would prove themselves faithful allies of the Central Powers and that they would gladly provide troops for the eastern front. Indeed, the official St. Petersburg Telegraph Agency commented, on 16 November, on the Manifesto:

> The German and the Austro-Hungarian governments have exploited the temporary occupation of a part of Russian territory to detach Polish provinces from the Russian Empire. Our enemies are clearly aiming to replenish their armed forces by recruits from Russian Poland.

The fact that the Austrians had agreed to the publication of the Manifesto on the one hand, and that on the other they hoped to weaken its effects by their pronouncement on Galician autonomy, marked the beginning of a crisis in the relations between the Habsburg monarchy and Germany. The announcement of the Two Emperors' Manifesto was a heavy blow to the prestige and self-confidence of the Austro-Hungarian government. Although in the past there had been a number of occasions when Austria–Hungary had pursued a policy independent of Berlin, it became clear as the war wore on that, whenever Germany decided to take a tough line on any major issue, the government in Vienna could do no more than state its objections. Indeed, the visible evidence of the increasing predominance of Germany in the councils of the

Central Powers could not fail to make a powerful impression on the Slav politicians in the monarchy. Although neither the Emperor nor the government had taken any action since the beginning of the war to strengthen the position of the Germans in Austria—such as, for instance, settling the national dispute between the Czechs and the Germans in Bohemia in their favour—the increase of Berlin's influence naturally aroused the fears and suspicions of the Habsburg Slavs.

In Berlin there were many advocates of German interference in Austro-Hungarian internal affairs: they were convinced that it was their duty to 'stabilize' the conditions in the monarchy. The exchange of telegrams between the Chancellor and Hindenburg in November 1916[8] did not concern only the Austrian reactions to the solution of the Polish question: in it the fundamental differences among the German leaders on the subject of their country's relations with Austria were discussed. In the telegram to the Chancellor, on 7 November, Hindenburg argued:

> Non-interference in the internal affairs of Austria–Hungary, before and during the war, has made the conduct of the hostilities extremely difficult for us. If we continue this policy, even when our interests are directly concerned, we can give up all hopes for the strengthening of the monarchy: the question can be then raised why we fight for Austria at all.

Hindenburg's rhetoric question roused Bethmann-Hollweg, who answered it in the following manner:

> We are not justified in interfering in the internal policies of Austria–Hungary: nor do we possess any means of imposing our will on the government in Vienna. The criticism that our unwillingness to interfere makes the conduct of the war difficult and that it presents us with the question of why we are fighting for Austria, lacks therefore any foundation. I have to reject this objection against my conduct of policy, with which His Majesty the Emperor entrusted me, and for which I alone am responsible. If the burdens that we incur through the alliance entitle us in practice to make certain demands that are not based on international or national law—enough use is being made of such

[8] See above, page 108.

opportunities as it is—abuse of our position would bring its own penalty. At the peace negotiations, the monarchy may be in an advantageous position because its relations with France and England have not been seriously disturbed by the war; this, because of the ill-will they bear against us, may become an important factor in the way peace will be concluded, and for the future of international relations.

After stating that the Kaiser had issued clear directives concerning Germany's relations with the Habsburg monarchy, the Chancellor concluded:

> I regard as politically impracticable and harmful attempts to reduce the sovereignty of the Danube monarchy in such a manner as to enable us to interfere directly in the formulation of its policy. I hope that we shall be able to clear up the misunderstandings between us at our next meeting.

Bethmann-Hollweg took a strong stand against Hindenburg and his military friends when they began to advocate a tight control from Berlin of their Austro-Hungarian ally. He pointed to the directives of the Kaiser for the regulation of Germany's relations with the Habsburg monarchy, although they did not quite reinforce the point he was trying to make. (The German Emperor desired 'stabilization of the existing political alliance, its deepening by a military convention and by a guarantee of our economic relations'.) The Kaiser's directives were, of course, very loose; they could have been used to force Vienna into a greater dependence on Germany. But for the time being the Austro-Hungarian leaders were permitted to muddle through; the generals, the advocates of direct control by Germany of Austro-Hungarian internal affairs, had to wait for a more suitable opportunity to renew their efforts.

It was at the end of 1916 that the thoughts of men responsible for the destinies of nations turned to problems of peace and peace conferences, or at least a definition of war aims that would justify the wholesale destruction. On the occasion of his accession to the throne, Emperor Karl had promised an early peace to his subjects and soon he began to do his best to fulfil the promise. His brother-in-law, Prince Sixtus of Parma, then serving in the Belgian army, had influential contacts in France: through him the young Emperor approached the French Prime Minister and his government. He committed grave errors during the secret negotiations and for these he was to pay dearly later in terms of a higher degree of subservience to Berlin. He did not give Count Czernin, his new Foreign Minister, sufficient information about his intentions; while Czernin was under the impression that the Emperor had put out private feelers as to the chances of a general peace, Karl had in fact become involved in negotiations of a separate peace for Austria–Hungary. He also underestimated the loyalty to Germany of his Foreign Minister; while he, in his efforts to save the Habsburg state sank deeper and deeper into duplicity, Czernin was trying to bring about a meeting between his Emperor and the Kaiser, and with it a *rapprochement* between the two countries.

Emperor Karl may have been justified in trying to extricate his country from the war; but he was unsuccessful, and his activities, when made public, appeared treacherous. In a conversation with a German diplomat,[9] Czernin compared the situation in Germany with that in the monarchy in this manner: whereas in Germany, because of the existence of a peace party and a war party, the government could afford to play a waiting game, the Austrian leaders were in a different position; in Austria–Hungary, there existed a peace party only, and the government would run grave risks if it ignored this fact.

Because of the complex nature of the internal problems of the Habsburg monarchy, its leaders were more susceptible to panic than those of Germany: but Emperor Karl was by no means alone in exploring the possibilities for a speedy conclusion of peace. On 12 December the German Chancellor disclosed to the world a peace offer by his government and those of Austria–Hungary, Turkey, and Bulgaria. This move was marred by the condescending tone of the offer; Germany and its allies appeared to have had no doubts as to which was the victorious party. The Entente countries made no reply until the end of December.

Six days after the offer by the Central Powers President Wilson addressed an enquiry to all the belligerents, asking what aims they

[9] *AA*, memorandum dated 29 April 1917, in *Oesterreich 95 sec.*

were pursuing in the war. The Allies' reply reached Washington on 11 January.[10] The Entente governments desired

> . . . the restoration of Belgium, of Serbia, and of Montenegro, and the indemnities which are due to them; the evacuation of the invaded territories of France, of Russia and of Rumania, with just reparation; the reorganization of Europe, guaranteed by a stable régime and founded as much upon respect for nationalities and full security and liberty, economic development, which all nations, great or small, possess, as upon territorial conventions and international agreements suitable to guarantee territorial and maritime frontiers against unjustified attacks; the restitution of provinces and territories wrested in the past from the Allies by force or against the will of their populations, the liberation of Italians, of Slavs, of Rumanians and Czecho-Slovaks from foreign domination; the enfranchisement of populations subject to the bloody tyranny of the Turks; the expulsion from Europe of the Ottoman Empire, decidedly foreign to western civilization. The intentions of His Majesty the Emperor of Russia regarding Poland have been clearly indicated in a proclamation which he has just addressed to his armies.

The tone of the Allied reply to President Wilson appeared to be quite radical—although it could have been interpreted in a number of different ways—on the subject of the Habsburg monarchy. Apart from the direct reference to the 'liberation' of some of the Habsburg peoples, *obiter dicta* to 'respect for nationalities', although they were originally calculated to appear to President Wilson, indicated the lines on which the discussions of the future of the Habsburg monarchy, as well as the anti-dynastic ideology of the war, were to move.

At the end of 1916, the political exiles working in the Entente countries for the destruction of Austria–Hungary watched the stirrings of the desire for peace with apprehension: they feared the conclusion of peace before they had achieved their aims. It was at this time that Masaryk revealed to Beneš his anxiety that, in the event of an early cessation of hostilities, he would have to continue his work in exile. After the publication of the Allied reply the political emigrés, and the Czechs in particular, were

[10] *U.S.F.R.*, 1917, Supplement I, page 8.

jubilant. The reference to the 'Czecho-Slovaks' was the first concrete achievement of the Czechs in exile: it was included in the note after Beneš's concentrated effort in Paris and at the French Foreign Ministry. Indeed—in spite of the fact that Beneš was told at the Quai d'Orsay that the final attitude of the Allies to the Habsburg state would depend on the success of the Entente in the war—the emigrés interpreted the reply to President Wilson as a demand, for the first time in the war, for a complete disruption of the Habsburg state. The Entente countries, however, had by no means committed themselves to such an extent: their reply was consistent with the reorganization of the monarchy on a federal basis.

The exiles erred on the side of optimism when they misread the true meaning of the Allied reply to President Wilson; they did not, on the other hand, realize what effect the reference to the 'Czecho-Slovaks' would have on the politicians in Prague. Masaryk wrote in his memoirs:[11]

> I did not and could not expect that our success in the Allied reply to President Wilson, a success won by intense effort on our part and by the exceptional friendliness of France, would bring about what I so greatly feared—that our members of Parliament at home might disavow us.

At this time, as at the beginning of his activities abroad, Masaryk was still concerned with the attitude of the politicians at home: but soon even he stopped looking over his shoulder in the direction of Prague. Since the contact with their friends had become difficult in the autumn of 1915, after the interception, by the Austrian police, of one of the first messages to Prague, the Czech exiles began to understand that too much concern with the developments at home would only obstruct the progress of their revolutionary action abroad. As soon as they began to feel that they were achieving a certain measure of success in the Allied countries, they began to act completely independently.

The Czech emigrés never missed an opportunity of exploiting the propaganda value of acts of oppression by the Austrian

[11] *The Making of a State*, page 129.

authorities: Masaryk wrote 'we made the most of the persecution of our people by the Austrians',[12] but when the politicians in Prague made a pronouncement—and this happened often enough—disapproving of the plans of the exiles, they simply dismissed it on the grounds that it had been made under some kind of pressure. In most cases this was not so. While Masaryk and his friends were working for the destruction of the Habsburg monarchy, political life in the Czech lands was moving on different lines.

Under the impression of the closing of the ranks of the German political parties, accompanied by several threatening declarations which demanded more protection of the German interest in the Austrian part of the monarchy, the Czechs also began to think in terms of a united national front. The pre-war animosities were on their way out in Czech politics; the manifold threats to their national life, brought about by the war, convinced the Czechs in 1916 of the necessity to form a united front. The initiative came, at the beginning of the year, from the middle-class parties; their original idea was to found a 'national party', in which all Czech political bodies would participate. This plan did not make much progress: the difficulties of attracting working-class parties to a middle-class movement soon became apparent; the events in the autumn of 1916, to which every party reacted in its own way, did not make the process of unification any easier.

However, the knowledge that the parliament was to meet—this was the programme of the short-lived government of Koerber which was intended to ease the growing national tensions in Austria—soon gave fresh impetus to the Czech politicians' plans for the formation of a national front. Although they had abandoned the idea of a 'national party', their plans were carried through, in view of the new situation, very quickly indeed. By the middle of November, two united bodies had been established: the National Committee and the National Union. The latter was a purely parliamentary club: it took the place of the pre-war 'Czech circle', an association of Czech deputies in the Viennese parliament. Both bodies were joined by all

[12] op. cit., page 129.

political parties, except the Progressives, who were represented in the *Reichsrat* by two deputies only and who, before the war, had already taken a decided anti-Habsburg stand, and the Realists, whose only deputy, Masaryk, was abroad. On 18 November the National Committee published its first declaration:

> Contemporary events force the Czech parties to take up a common attitude to a number of questions. Changes are indicated in the near future, which might affect the foundations of our state and its constitution; a one-sided solution would not be in the interest of the state or of our nation. . . . Since we express the will of all our people, who now more than ever strive for unity, and at the same time act in the interests of the monarchy and of the great historical mission of the Empire, which rest first of all on the unity and indivisibility of its kingdoms and lands, and also on the complete equality of all its nations, we have united all our deputies in the *Reichsrat* in one body, the Czech Union. Apart from this Union, the aim of which is a common attitude to political and constitutional questions, the National Committee has been founded, which will support all undertakings of the Union and at the same time will be the highest moral authority in those fields of political life that are outside the sphere of activity of the deputies. The formation of both the bodies was approved unanimously at a meeting of the representatives yesterday.

The creation of the national front and the subsequent declaration was the result of free deliberations by the Czech politicians: it clearly showed that their concerns differed widely from those of the exiles. The men in Prague did not question the continued existence of the Habsburg monarchy; they sought, first of all, to protect their nation against the ambitions of the Germans and against unwelcome administrative reforms, such as the proposed division of the Czech lands into Czech and German administrative units, and with it, the disruption of the administrative and historical unity of the 'crownlands'. Only the two Progressive deputies and Šámal, the leader of Masaryk's Realist party and the moving force behind the Mafie took no interest in the formaation of the united front. This small group of men, whose hopes were aimed at the establishment of an independent Czech state, regarded the dangers that motivated the actions of most of their compatriots as immaterial: in fact, they had transcended the traditional considerations of Czech politics. The radicals knew that the best plan for them would be to keep out of any united body: in it, they would have represented an insignificant minority. They made some attempts to influence other politicians: Šámal, for instance, tried to convince Stránský, Masaryk's pre-war friend and political associate, not to join, with his Moravian People's party, the national front. When Stránský and his party entered the newly created bodies, and Šámal reproached him for it, Stránský argued that the Progressives and the Realists could well afford to take up a negative attitude, but that his party, supported by an influential section of political opinion in Moravia (it sent four deputies to the *Reichsrat*), had to be aware of its responsibilities.[13] This was the situation when the Allied reply to President Wilson reached Prague on 12 January 1917. The text of the reply was supplied by the official Austro-Hungarian press agency: it was printed in full; only the reference to the Czecho-Slovaks in the original was mistranslated and read 'Czechs and Slovenes'. Comment in the press was unanimous in rejecting such 'embarrassing attention to our nation', and was interspersed by attacks on Masaryk. Although most of the material was supplied to the press by Ballhausplatz, the letter from the Czech Union to the Foreign Minister left no doubt as to the attitude of the politicians to the Allied reply. The committee of the Union met on 21 January; the result of the consultation was the following communication to Czernin:

> Your Excellency, with regard to the Entente reply to President Wilson, in which the countries at war with the monarchy gave, apart from other aims, 'the liberation of the Czechs from foreign rule' as one of the war aims, which they intend to achieve by force of arms, the committee of the Czech Union rejects this insinuation, based entirely on wrong premises. It declares that the Czech nation will, as it has done in the past, continue to look for the proper conditions for its development only under the rule of the house of Habsburg in the future.[14]

[13] J. Hajšman, op. cit., vol. 2, page 236.
[14] *Politische Chronik*, January 1917, pages 73–74.

The letter, and the visit of the leading representatives of the Union to the Foreign Minister at the end of January, showed the wide gap between the positions of the Czech politicians at home and abroad: the action of the united parliamentary body confirmed Masaryk's worst fears when it denounced his work abroad. Although the isolation of the exiles from the politicians at home was strikingly illustrated at the beginning of 1917, time, and the course the war began to take, were working in favour of the exiles. Even the anti-Masaryk press campaign, after the publication of the Allied reply in the monarchy, did not have a completely adverse effect on the cause of the radicals: bad publicity was better than none. It informed the public of what the exiles were doing abroad, and that there was an alternative policy to that of the moderate politicians in Prague. Not only Vienna, but the Entente countries as well, were aware that a Czech question existed. At the end of 1916, Germany and Austria–Hungary had demonstrated their inability to deal with national problems by their settlement of the future of the occupied territories; the Austrian Poles did not take long to learn their lesson. The Czechs, too, came to understand that if Vienna were not prepared to come to an agreement with the moderate politicians at home, or if these did not have a policy to suit the needs of the moment, they had a second string to their bow: the radicals abroad would drive a very much harder bargain on their behalf.

V

REVOLUTION IN THE EAST

The principal members of both alliances were by no means equally fitted to take the strain of the exhausting war: after two years these differences were becoming apparent. In both belligerent camps, the problem of the weaker allies had to be faced. Just as the Germans were concerned about the instability of the Habsburg monarchy, the British and French leaders knew that there were limits to the endurance of Russia. But the overall situation on the battlefields, and the relative strength of the two alliances, were finely balanced at the beginning of 1917; although both the Russian and the Austro-Hungarian rulers had made attempts to withdraw from the war in order to preserve their dominions and their systems of government intact, they were too deeply committed not only to the prospect of a final military success, but also to their stronger allies. They were trapped in a maze of their past mistakes and obligations, unable to take a decisive action on their own accord.

Although, at this time of the war, the Russian revolutionaries in exile, including Lenin, did not regard the situation as ripe for action, the first intimation of troubles ahead in Russia had come in December 1916, when Rasputin was murdered by a group of right-wing conspirators at the court. The melodramatic plot and assassination did not, as its organizers had hoped, clear the way for internal reforms that would ensure the survival of the Tsarist régime. By the middle of February a revolution in Russia was expected in well-informed circles not only in London and Paris, but in Berlin as well. Although it surprised no one when it finally came in March, the revolution made a profound impression in Austria–Hungary. The spectre of revolution began to haunt the rulers of the Danube monarchy: the stunned pessimism of

Czernin, when he wrote to his Emperor, was characteristic of their mood:

> . . . the amazing facility with which the strongest monarchy in the world was overthrown, contributes to our anxiety and calls to memory the saying *exemplae trahunt*. . . . The Russian revolution affects our Slavs more than the Germans, and the responsibility for the continuation of the war is a far greater one for a monarch whose country is only united through the dynasty than for one where the people themselves are fighting for their national ideals.[1]

The men in Vienna were amazed at the ease with which the Tsarist régime gave way to popular pressure; under the threat of national and social unrest they began to look for ways and means in which to canalize it. The summoning of the *Reichsrat* was clearly the first step in this direction: the government of Koerber had contemplated it and after the revolution in Russia it came to be regarded by many Austrian politicians as essential for the survival of the monarchy. But there was strong opposition to the reopening of the parliament, and it came from various quarters. The German nationalists opposed it because they suspected that some of the Slav deputies would use it as a platform for declarations against the state. The military authorities were afraid that they might be called to task over the measures they had taken when the parliament was in recess and that the resuscitation of constitutional life in Austria might impinge on the rights they had acquired during the war. Nor were the exiles enthusiastic about the idea: they were aware of the advantages to their cause of the withdrawal of the Czech and other Slav politicians to their respective provinces.[2] They feared that once the Czechs returned to the Austrian capital they would come under the influence of moderate politicians of other nationalities; they knew that the give and take of parliamentary life in Vienna, in spite of the dramatic clashes between the nationalities, might cement the unity of the monarchy. But most of all the exiles abhorred the prospect of national concessions to the Slavs reconciling them with the Empire, and making them less inclined

[1] Ottokar Czernin, *In the World War* ,page 146 ,London 1919.
[2] See above ,page 41.

to work for a clean break with it. Their concern was clearly expressed in a message Masaryk and Beneš sent to the Czech politicians in April 1917:

We draw your attention to the success we have achieved here. . ., Austria is doing her best to save herself. We are relying only on your resistance. The present situation urgently requires the settling of the question of who should negotiate in the name of the Austrian nationalities, whether the dynasty and the diplomats or the nationalities themselves. You have to speak clearly and openly. Now, at the time of the summoning of the parliament, you have an opportunity to do so . . . we ask you to agree unconditionally: (1) Not to approve of the war, or the budget, or the army . . . not to allow anything that would facilitate the conduct of the war [for Austria–Hungary]. (2) To ask for the release of all imprisoned deputies, freedom of speech for them, no more political trials, freedom of the press. (3) To prevent the disavowal of our action at any price. (4) To demand Czech historical rights, without jeopardizing either the annexation of Slovakia or the disruption of the monarchy. (5) To demand that some of our politicians come to consult us abroad, in a neutral country. . . . (6) Under no circumstances must all our deputies go back to the *Reichsrat*. At least the Czech and the Moravian radicals [i.e. the Progressives and Stránský's People's party] must stay away. (7) Finally: you have to make every use of the Czech state rights. That means that for us, the December constitution does not exist; therefore you must take no part in the Emperor's oath to the constitution; keep away from the *Reichsrat*. We shall see to it that it makes a proper impression here. . . . Remember there is a revolution in Russia and that they will have a republic there.[3]

The message reached Prague at the end of April, and it stimulated the radicals connected with the Mafie to intensified efforts; it had, however, no immediate effect on the policies of the parties in the Czech Union. They supported the reopening of the *Reichsrat* because they regarded the parliament as a guarantee against the dictatorship of the military authorities, and as a means of protecting and advancing the national rights of the Czechs. But the example of the Russian revolution, the entry of the United States

[3] *Dokumenty*, pages 121–123.

into the war and President Wilson's principle of national self-determination, had a profound effect on the members of the Union: they raised their sights from the defensive to the political offensive. In April of 1917, the deputies were of the opinion that the revolution in Russia made a basic reorganization of the monarchy inevitable. On 14 April the Union declared itself for democracy, for government by parliament, and the revision of the constitution from the point of view of self-determination of nations. It maintained that the needs of the nationalities were the 'most important and burning problems'. Although it was at this time of the war that the Czechs relinquished the positions of timid defence which they had maintained throughout the war and began to rally their ranks for attack, they were not yet aiming at complete independence of their country from Vienna. The policy of a clean break with the monarchy was then preached only by the two deputies of the Progressive party, who maintained that the Czechs should in no circumstances join the parliament and that the Union should demand the summoning of the Czech Diet instead; they used the traditional pre-war slogan 'without a Czech Diet, there will be no Czechs in the *Reichsrat*'. But everybody knew, possibly even the Progressive deputies themselves, that such a programme was impracticable. Since the Diet was run on the 'estates' basis, its composition bore no relation to contemporary political realities: the conservative elements, the landowners and the German bourgeoisie commanded the majority there; the representation in the Diet of parties which had begun to grow only after the introduction of general suffrage, and of the Social Democrats in particular, was completely out of proportion to their real strength.

Nevertheless, the spring of 1917 saw the first public success of the radicals. They knew their weakness in the field of conventional party politics, but they were anxious not to let a unique opportunity created by the revolution in Russia pass by. The action of the radicals in May took the form of the 'Manifesto of Czech Authors', addressed to professional politicians. The organizer of this missive was Kvapil, a producer at the National Theatre who was associated with the Mafie. In his fifties, Kvapil was a forceful and highly impulsive personality. The action was well stage-managed; it was taken entirely independently of the newly established National Committee and it was launched at the right time, when the imagination of the people was stirred by the events in Russia. It was Kvapil's idea to goad the writers, 'the heart and the mind of the nation', into making a political pronouncement; he first told Šámal about it in April. The fact that Kvapil did not count many writers among his friends was no insuperable obstacle to him; in the end, 222 of them signed the Manifesto. Kvapil did, however, know Jirásek, the immensely popular author of historical novels; Jirásek was the first to sign, and it was doubtless in response to his signature that so many followed.

To the utmost surprise of its organizers the Manifesto was passed by the censor, and appeared in the press in the middle of May. It began by exhorting the deputies to insist on 'Czech rights', which were not specified further, on freedom of expression in the parliament, and for a general amnesty for political prisoners; although no Slovak signed the declaration, it made the first passing reference to the 'Czechoslovak nation'. The Manifesto concluded:

> A democratic Europe, consisting of autonomous and free states, is the Europe of the future. The nation demands, gentlemen, that you [i.e. the deputies] should rise to this historic occasion and that you act as free and independent men, without any regard to personal advantages, men of supreme moral and national conscience. If you cannot act according to the demands of the nation . . . give up your mandates before you enter the *Reichsrat*.[4]

The Manifesto was received with mixed feelings; press comment varied from enthusiastic approval to downright condemnation. In an editorial of 19 May, the Social Democrat daily *Právo Lidu* condemned Kvapil's action: 'Anyone who can harangue the deputies at this time in such a manner must be either irresponsible or politically naïve.' A writer who had not signed the Manifesto

[4] J. Kvapil, *Projev Českých spisovatelů*, 1917, Prague 1924.

remarked about it: 'That was not the voice of Czech authors, it was the voice of the Prague coffee-houses.'[5]

Whatever the reaction, the declaration caused a stir that lasted throughout the summer: as late as 7 October, 'national and cultural workers and also the representatives of all Czech societies' in Silesia gave it their support. To some organizations it appeared incomplete; steel workers organized in the National Socialist party sent a supplement to the National Committee demanding a new Bohemian Diet, based on the principle of general suffrage. They also suggested that an immediate amnesty should be granted to all political prisoners, especially to their leader Klofáč, and that all censorship should be abolished. The Authors' Manifesto was directed against the circumspect policy of the Union and of the National Committee: in making a demand for a radical policy, its organizers were launching a sharp attack on the professional politicians. In questioning their ability to conduct the nation's affairs, and by implying that the politicians had lost touch with the people, the Manifesto indicated, for the first time, the shape of politics to come. Although it incorporated the advice of the exiles, and it had been drawn up and organized by men who thought in terms of absolute independence, its programme left room for different interpretations. The 'autonomous states' of the manifesto could have existed either in a federation, or completely independent of each other.

The Manifesto was published at a time when the politicians were in the middle of their deliberations on parliamentary policy: it had the effect of a bomb-shell. It was customary for the parties represented in the *Reichsrat* to publish their programme at the beginning of every parliamentary term; since the formation of the Czech Union, the deputies had to work out a joint programme. They were in agreement on the attitude to the parliament: they intended to give up the pre-war practice of 'obstruction'—they simply walked out when they felt that the debate was taking an unfavourable turn, or that the government had made the wrong decision—and to adopt a more positive approach to parliamentary work. But agreement on common policy was much more difficult

[5] J. Hajšman, *Česká Mafie*, vol. 3, page 68, Prague 1934.

to achieve; this discussion was concluded only at the end of May, a few days before the opening of the parliament. The deputies were on the whole agreed that they should insist on the traditional 'state-rights'; that they should demand the establishment of a parliamentary committee to revise the constitution, an official enquiry into the treatment of the Czechs during the war, and amnesty for their political prisoners. But the radical programme, as expressed in the Manifesto, provided the topics for the most heated discussion. Švehla, the leader of the Agrarians, a partisan of the opportunist policy of 'two irons in the fire', and one of the most powerful men in the Union, believed that the radical iron was becoming hotter: the final draft of the programme of the Czech deputies owed a lot to his influence. During the frequent meetings of the Union in May, where the parliamentary programme was discussed, the traditional differences between the parties were further complicated by the impression the radical demands had made: at the end of the negotiations, four National Socialist deputies and one Agrarian found themselves unable to support a programme based on the belief in the possibility of the continued existence of the Habsburg monarchy. The most passionately disputed question, at these meetings, was whether a reference to the Slovaks should be made in the declaration. The majority of the deputies first opposed the suggestion: they argued that the Slovaks, being devout Catholics, were incompatible with the Czechs and that, at any rate, Tisza and his Budapest government were strong enough to frustrate such a plan. But Švehla, who had originally sided with the majority, met the Slovak politician Vavro Šrobár—he was one of the Protestants who favoured a union with the Czechs—who convinced the Agrarian leader that a reference to the Slovaks should be made. Švehla used all his influence to persuade his colleagues in the Union that this was a good idea, and in the end he succeeded. The Czech deputies realized that their case for a constitutional reform would be strengthened by such a reference and that without it, their attack on dualism would lack in substance. On 29 May the deputies approved the final draft; on the following day, it was read to the opening meeting of the *Reichsrat*:

The representatives of the Czech nation are deeply convinced that the present dualist form of government has produced the emergence of ruling and subject nationalities, detrimental to the interests of the whole. The transformation of the Habsburg monarchy into a federal state consisting of free and equal national states is necessary if all national privileges are to be done away with and if the general development of nationalities in the interest of the Empire is to be secured. Relying at this historic moment on the natural rights of nations, on self-determination and free development, reinforced in our case by inalienable historical rights, we shall demand the unification of all the branches of the Czechoslovak nation in one democratic state; we must not forget the Slovak branch, which forms a close historical unity with the Czech lands.[6]

This direct attack on the dualist system caused consternation in the parliament, and on the government benches in particular. The Germans had expected the usual defence, in great detail, of the Czech historical rights; they were not prepared for the switch of emphasis to 'natural rights of nations' and for the far-reaching demands that the Czechs deduced from them. Clam-Martinitz, the Austrian Premier, asked the chairman of the Union to withdraw the declaration, which he maintained amounted to an open admission that the 'gossip' spread about the monarchy abroad was true. Tusar, the Social Democrat secretary of the Union, turned down the Prime Minister's request: he argued that foreign opinion was better informed about the conditions in Austria–Hungary than was commonly conceded and he added that it was in the interest of the state that the new arrangements of its affairs should be openly discussed.

While the declaration of the Union stole all the limelight, the programme of the two Progressive deputies, who had dissociated themselves from the united body, virtually passed unnoticed. Even in Czech political circles they were regarded as belonging to the lunatic fringe; when they had approached the only dissenting Agrarian deputy and asked him to support their programme, he turned them down. Kalina impassionately delivered his party's

[6] *Stenographische Protokolle über die Sitzungen des Hauses der Abgeordneten des österreichischen Reichsrats im Jahre 1917*. Session XXII, vol. 1, page 34.

Bildarchiv d. Ost. Nationalbibliothek.

The funeral of the Emperor Franz Josef, 30 November 1916. The cortege is turning into the Ringstrasse in front of the Imperial residence

Bildarchiv d. Ost. Nationalbibliothek.

The coronation of the Emperor Karl I as King of Hungary in Budapest, 30 December 1916

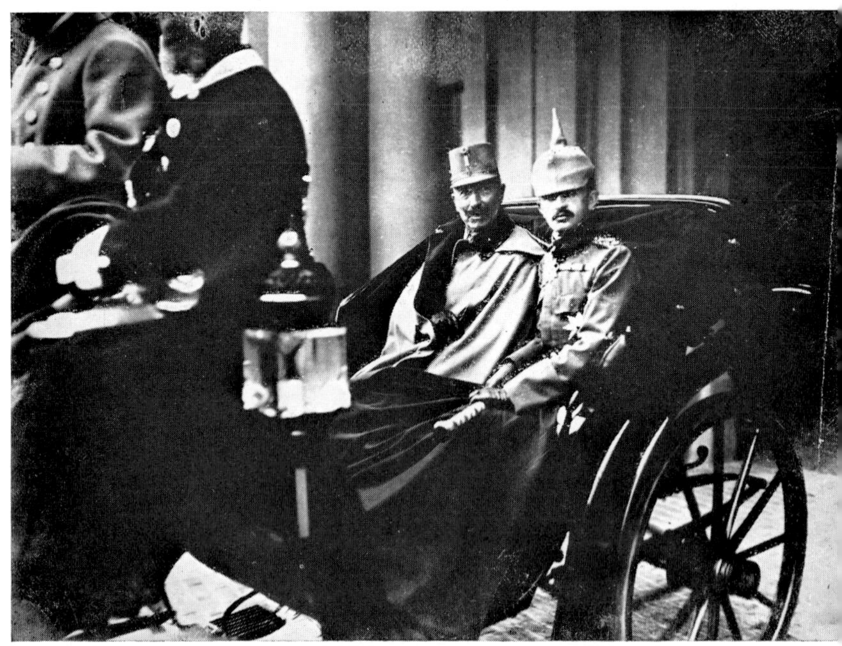

Bildarchiv d. Ost. Nationalbibliothek.

The German Emperor's visit to Laxenburg in July 1917. Emperor Wilhelm is wearing an Austro-Hungarian and Emperor Karl a Prussian uniform—a courtesy observed at the Imperial meetings during the war

programme to a half-deserted house; this was the first statement, in public, of the radical aims. The declaration of the Progressive party attributed the responsibility for the war to the Central Powers, and it went on to express its sympathy with the work of the exiles; it demanded that 'representatives of the Czechoslovak nation, who would have full powers to negotiate the questions concerning the establishment and existence of the new Czechoslovak state, should take part in the peace conference'.[7]

The declaration of the Union at the opening meeting of the parliament was subtly ambiguous. It made sufficient concessions to the political climate of the time: it attacked the dualist system, and it proposed to do away with it. But it was as unacceptable to the Czech radicals as to the government in Vienna. Like many Austrian politicians, Clam-Martinitz was no supporter of the federal reform of the monarchy: he knew that, especially as long as Tisza remained in control of the government in Budapest, federalist plans affecting the whole of the monarchy were well outside the realm of political possibility. The declaration of the two Progressive deputies on the other hand contradicted the programme of the Union: the Progressives had associated themselves, without reservations, with the revolutionary action abroad. Masaryk and Beneš made good use of this: they treated the Progressive declaration as the true expression of the nation's will, and as complementary to that of the Union; they argued that the demand for a federal state was a tactical necessity, largely intended to ward off persecution. *Československá Samostatnost*, the organ of the exiles, commented: 'The programme of the Progressives... is not contrary to the declaration of the Czech Union; it is complementary to it. It is an interpretation of the Union's declaration, which must have been agreed upon with the rest of the deputies.'

All the other Austrian peoples had undergone the same process as the Czechs; they presented a united front when the *Reichsrat* reopened. As early as March 1917, the South Slav deputies to the parliament in Vienna had agreed with the Czech Union on a common attitude to constitutional problems—this parliamentary

[7] *Stenographische Protokolle* 1917, vol. 1, page 35.

alliance was to last till the very end of the war. On 30 May the Slovene deputy Korošec presented a programme that, like the Czech demands, struck at the very roots of the Austro-Hungarian dualism. On behalf of his South Slav colleagues, Korošec said:

On the basis of the principle of nationality and of the Croat state-rights, we demand the unification of all the lands inhabited by the Slovenes, Croats and Serbs of the monarchy in one autonomous state, free from all foreign domination, ruled in a democratic manner and under the sceptre of the Habsburg dynasty. We shall work for the realization of these demands of the united nation with all our strength.[8]

The declaration of the Ruthene deputies followed that of the Czech Progressives; in it, all the pre-war differences between the Old Ruthenes and the Ukrainian party were merged in their common concern over the proposed changes by the late Emperor[9] in the status of Galicia. The Ruthene deputies asserted that the 'present crownland of Galicia is an artificially administrative unit, in opposition to historical and national rights'. They demanded that the Ukrainian provinces should form one state unit, separate from the Polish provinces, and including those territories inhabited by the Ukrainians in the Russian part of Poland and in the western provinces of Russia. They added:

The Ukrainians of Austria heartily welcome the endeavour of the Ukrainians of Russia for the achievement of the right of self-determination and declare that they will not give up their fight until the great Ukrainian nation acquires its full rights in the whole of its national territory.

The Poles, on the other hand, still irritated by the unsatisfactory solution contained in the Two Emperors' Manifesto of November 1916, were content to declare that their club would comment, in due course, on national problems in the light of the unanimous agreement made in Cracow on 28 May 1917 concerning the united and independent Poland. Pacher, a Christian Socialist deputy, read the programme of the united German

[8] *Parliamentarische Chronik*, May 1917, pages 86–87. All the subsequent quotations from speeches made on the opening day of the *Reichsrat* come from the same source.
[9] See above, page 107.

parties; it criticized the Czechs for exaggerated insistence on their state rights which 'would force millions of Germans in the Sudeten territories into a union in a new state against their will', and Herr Pacher added: 'the endeavours of the South Slavs will also be resolutely opposed by the Germans of Austria'. The Prime Minister had no comment to make on these national demands at the opening session of the parliament; he said that the government would have to deliberate, and that it would state its position shortly after the customary speech from the throne.

One day later, Emperor Karl made a solemn promise to the *Reichsrat* that he would rule constitutionally; his speech amounted to a plea to his peoples for moderation, at least as long as the war lasted. It was not until 12 June that Clam-Martinitz had his speech to the parliament ready; unfortunately, the deliberations of his government served no good purpose. This was due to the Prime Minister's political short-sightedness, his tendency to underrate the gravity of the situation, and to the fact that, while the parliament had been adjourned for more than three years, Vienna had lost touch with the politicians in the provinces. Far-reaching constitutional reforms could hardly have been indulged in during the war: but the Prime Minister held out no hopes to the peoples of Austria either that they would receive a different treatment after the conclusion of peace, or that peace was within sight. 'It is clear at the first glance,' Clam-Martinitz remarked, 'that the programmes we have listened to are not practicable because they cut across each other and because they are mutually exclusive.' He knew the explanation for this phenomenon: 'the special ethnic conditions in which the nations and national minorities live in this very centre of Europe and which have of necessity led to the formation of our state . . .', and he suggested that the government was in a position to offer the nationalities a programme different from their contradictory declarations: 'The programme of my government is Austria. An Austria that has grown up through splendid historical development.' Such a pronouncement gave nobody any hope. By a sleight of hand, the Prime Minister dismissed the Czech, South Slav, and Polish demands. He had no intention of regarding them as the considered opinion of the majority of the Slav politicians, whose sympathy Vienna could retain only by giving their programmes serious consideration. Clam-Martinitz was, of course, right in saying that the demands 'cut across each other': but the proper task of his government was to look for a balanced solution as many Austrian cabinets had successfully done in the past. The government's policy was based on a misapprehension; like the majority of the German politicians in Austria, the Prime Minister believed that in their declarations the Slavs—the Czechs and the South Slavs in particular—had taken the side of the Entente and that it was therefore futile to take their demands seriously.

Apart from its powerful impact inside the Habsburg monarchy, the March revolution had important repercussions on the Czech movement in Russia. It made it possible for the Czechs to complete building up their own army unit; it also eased Masaryk's way to gaining effective control of the Czech colony and prisoners of war. A few days after the revolution, on 18 March, Masaryk telegraphed Milyukov, the first Foreign Minister in the provisional government and an academic acquaintance of his from pre-war days; he congratulated the Russian on the success of the revolution, and expressed his conviction that the

> . . . solution of Slav questions is now guaranteed. Free Russia has every right to liberate the Slavs from the German, the Magyar and the Turkish yoke. . . . United Poland, connected with free Russia, the unification of the Russians in Galicia and those in Hungary with Russia, the unification of the Serbo-Croats with the Slovenes, and the liberation of Bohemia, together with Slovakia, will be realized by rejuvenated Russia.[10]

At the same time, the leader of the Czech exiles decided that the moment was propitious for a visit to Russia. The new régime in St. Petersburg suited his political sympathies: '. . . knowing that the Russian reactionaries liked neither me nor the Allies, I did not hasten to Russia during the Tsarist régime', Masaryk wrote in his memoirs.[11] Dürich, the Agrarian deputy who had been elected in September 1916 as the 'only and absolute leader' of the Czechs

[10] *Dokumenty*, page 615. [11] op. cit., p. 133.

in Russia, had had too strong ties with the former government; Masaryk now knew that he was himself in a better position to take over the leadership of the Czechs. Finally, by the end of 1916, there were between 210,000 and 250,000 of his compatriots in the prisoner-of-war camps in Russia, a source of military manpower hitherto untapped.[12]

In the middle of April, Masaryk left London for St. Petersburg, carrying a British passport. The ground for his visit had been prepared, shortly before the March revolution, by the expulsion of deputy Dürich from the National Council. In January the government in St. Petersburg had begun to support an independent Czecho-Slovak committee and to grant it regular subsidies; the ministers' council decided that:

> . . . a committee should be established with a branch in Kiev, which would counter the Czecho-Slovak movement harmful to Russia. The existence of this committee depends on government subsidy. The proposal of the Foreign Ministry, supported by the Ministry of War, was approved by the Council of Ministers; a subsidy of 8,000 roubles for November and 25,000 for December last year were referred to. Financial help for the committee has been fixed at 4,500 roubles and for its newspaper at 3,500 roubles per month.[13]

Soon afterwards, Dürich declared his independence of Masaryk and his council in the Russian press. Štefánik, the Slovak member of the National Council, then on his second visit to Russia, suggested to his colleagues in Paris that Dürich should be expelled from the council; the suggestion was approved on 18 February. However, Dürich's expulsion was proved to have been unnecessary; his position depended on the support of a government that was swept away by the revolution.

Masaryk arrived in St. Petersburg at an unpropitious moment early in May. Milyukov had left the Foreign Ministry a few days before; the situation concerning the Czech troops—Masaryk's

[12] The most exact figures on the number of Czech and Slovak prisoners-of-war in Russia are contained in a report on recruitment by the Russian branch of the Czecho-Slovak National Council, printed in *Za Svobodu*, vol. 3, page 692. The estimate gives the minimum figure as 210,000 men; of these about 30,000 were Slovaks.

[13] *Dokumenty*, page 599; cf. J. Papoušek, *Carské Rusko a naše osvobození*, page 169.

main interest in Russia—was far from satisfactory. The revolutionary government, and Guchkov, the Minister of War in particular, shared, with its Tsarist predecessors, a certain unwillingness to do too much for the Czechs: indeed, in the spring of 1917 the danger existed that the already existing Czech units might be dissolved. In spite of the vacillations of the revolutionary governments, Masaryk met with more understanding among the soldiers; at the same time, with the help of a branch of the National Council in Russia, he succeeded in taking over the control of the Czech movement from Dürich. At the end of August General Brusilov, the Supreme Commander, agreed to the formation of a Czech army corps; the proposal was formally approved, at the beginning of October, by General Dukhonin, the last Supreme Commander of the Russian army prior to Bolshevik revolution. Before the recognition of the corps, Masaryk and his friends had spent several months recruiting volunteers in the prisoner of war camps: but Masaryk did not believe that they could be successfully employed in Russia. At the beginning of June he had reached an agreement with Albert Thomas, the French Minister of Munitions, then visiting Russia, on the transfer of 30,000 Czech volunteers to France. Although, in the months before the Bolshevik revolution, some 30,000 volunteers joined the Czech army (the recruitment figures, given by Beneš [13a] were 21,760 for May to September 1917, and 9,780 for October to December), Masaryk had to work hard to win over the prisoners of war to the cause of national revolution. At any rate, only about twelve per cent of the total number of prisoners of Czech and Slovak origin entered the revolutionary army; in view of this, the argument of both the Austrian military authorities and of the Czech exiles, that the large majority of these prisoners of war in Russia were traitors who had deserted because of the opposition to the existence of the Habsburg state, lacks conviction.

Masaryk's western orientation and his confidence in the power of the western Allies clearly affected his attitude towards the Czech revolutionary army in Russia: he settled the transfer of his troops to France as soon as an opportunity presented itself. Never-

[13a] *Paměti*, volume 1, page 335.

theless, he did not make the decision on the spur of the moment under the impression of the Russian internal situation: in his memoirs, the Czech revolutionary leader himself informs us that the plan had been discussed for the first time a year before its final approval in June 1917.[14] Both the Russian military and civil authorities agreed to the transfer; although Russian and Czech were the language of command, and a National Council representative was attached to the Russian General Headquarters, the western character of this army was symbolized by the introduction of the French disciplinary code. Finally, Masaryk and the Russians agreed that the corps could be employed only against an external enemy. Thus at the time of the Bolshevik revolution in November 1917, there was a Czech corps in the Russian army consisting of some 39,000 troops (the original *Družina* had amounted to about 8,000 troops at the time of Masaryk's arrival in Russia), concentrated in the Kiev area and committed to transfer to France and to non-interference in Russian internal affairs.

In central Europe, the winter of 1917–18 was very severe: by the end of December, Vienna was covered by a layer of snow several feet thick. The events on the battle-fields, reported in the press as if by the force of habit, no longer appeared absorbing: everybody's attention was concentrated on the opening moves in the peace negotiations at Brest-Litovsk, the seat of the German Headquarters in the East, between the Central Powers and the Soviet government. But the peace talks long remained inconclusive; on his frequent visits to Brest, Trotsky skilfully used the negotiations for spreading Bolshevik revolutionary slogans westward of the now stationary battle-line. In the Habsburg monarchy the Bolshevik demand for peace, with its undertones of social revolution, fell on fertile ground. Throughout the year 1917 the food-supply in the monarchy was steadily decreasing, and the harvest that year fell below the most pessimistic expectations. At the beginning of 1918 the government was faced with a severe food crisis. Desperate reports from the provinces began to reach the recently established War Office of Food Supplies

[14] Masaryk, op. cit., page 162.

(*Kriegsernährungamt*); on 11 January Count Coudenhove, the Governor of Bohemia, wrote to his friend Czernin, who led the Austro-Hungarian delegation in Brest-Litovsk:

I do not doubt that you have already been informed by the Austrian government about the serious situation of our corn reserves until the next harvest. But judging by impressions I got in Vienna I doubt that you know the whole truth, that we are faced with a catastrophe that will hit us during the next few weeks, unless at the last moment we receive foreign help. At best, the reserves in Bohemia will last until the middle of April, but only if Bohemia does not have to supply other lands. In other crown-lands the situation is much worse; there, starvation has already begun. Also there are already the beginnings of unrest in Bohemia, because sufficient corn for the rations is difficult to procure even in small amounts. During the last few days in Vienna I had an opportunity of convincing myself of the desperate situation in the whole of the monarchy. As early as September and October, I had requested the lowering of the flour ration; the government refused this, because it wanted to avoid giving the impression that our economic situation demanded such measures. But now the sad truth will out. Austria gets only a small amount from Hungary. From Rumania it should still get 10,000 railway wagons of maize: that means 30,000 wagons less than planned, without which it will go under. As soon as I discovered what the real situation was, I went to see the Premier. I asked him whether he knew that this will mean that in a few weeks the war industry and railways will come to a standstill; the supply of the army will become more difficult and the army will collapse, and that such a catastrophe will mean the end of not only Austria, but Hungary as well. To all these questions the reply was yes, he knew about it, and he told me that everything was being done to bring about an improvement, especially as far as supplies from Hungary were concerned. Nobody, not even the Emperor, has so far succeeded in achieving anything in this respect. He can only hope that some *deus ex machina* will, at the last moment, save the monarchy from the worst.[15]

On 14 January the flour ration was reduced, in the Austrian part of the monarchy, from 200 to 165 grams per day; one day later the Minister of Food Supply telephoned the Foreign Minis-

[15] J. Opočenský, *Konec monarchie rakousko-uherské*, pages 85–86, Prague 1928.

try informing them that unrest among workers in the industrial districts around Vienna had assumed a revolutionary tone. Indeed, as soon as the cut was announced, about 10,000 workers from the Daimler factory, among them members of the armed forces, made a demonstration. They were already suspicious of their government's conduct of the peace negotiations at Brest-Litovsk; the demonstration was set off by the announcement of the reduction of food rations. The town hall in Wiener Neustadt was attacked and shouts for the election of Soviets could be overheard. The spontaneous demonstrations developed into a mass strike movement, which spread outward from the industrial environs of Vienna leaving, however, the centre of the town comparatively unaffected. During the following two days, some 95,000 men came out on strike in Lower Austria; soon it spread to Styria, Upper Austria, Tyrol, and to the industrial suburbs of Brno, the Moravian capital. The Ministry of War issued an order to the commanders of factories under military control to exhort their men to return to work by printed announcements: apart from a strike in the printing industry, they achieved nothing. On 18 January the movement spread to Budapest and a large part of Hungarian industry came to a standstill. Here, the strike was both more widespread and more radical than in Austria: it affected, and completely paralysed, Hungarian railways; workers' Soviets were elected at a number of factories. Leaflets were spread among troops stationed in the country, advising them to free themselves, after the example of the Bolsheviks in Russia, and asking them to render the German militarists no help on the western front.

The strike movement did not, however, affect all the districts of the monarchy with the same force. In spite of the call to strike from the representatives of the workers in Lower Austria—who sent a mission to Kladno, the centre of left-wing Social Democrat miners in a district north-west of Prague—the majority of the workers in Bohemia did not join the movement. Here, the cut in the flour ration led to a protest by the urban council of Prague and to a number of demonstrations by housewives. In Pilsen, Social Democrat deputy Pik declared to the workers in the Škoda factory that the decisive moment had not yet arrived, but that the workers should be prepared for it. Only the miners in Kladno declared themselves willing to strike; workers in Brno industrial districts, because of the strength of the Social Democrat centralists there, who advocated co-operation with their comrades in Austria, joined the strike at its very beginning. In Bohemia, the leadership of Social Democracy decided, on 8 January, to organize a one-day token strike, but only if the strike in Austria lasted at least until 21 January. The strike was declared on 22 January; some 122,000 workers took part. However, in Austria the tide of revolutionary unrest had begun to ebb the day before the Czech demonstration of solidarity: workers started to return to the factories, in some places under the compulsion of the military, in others under the threat of it. The situation was similar in Hungarian industry; the strike had been broken by the army, who took over the control of the railways.

The mass movements in Austria and in Hungary were in sharp contrast with the orderly one-day strike in Bohemia. The Czech Social Democrat leaders were able to control their workers: although Šmeral, the party's chairman, continued to pay lip-service to the monarchy and the dynasty, the swing towards radicalism inside the party's executive had begun soon after the March revolution in Russia; it gathered fresh momentum after the visit of the Czech Social Democrat leaders to the socialist conference in Stockholm in the summer of 1917, where they met representatives of the Czech radicals in Russia. The Austrian and Hungarian socialist leaders, on the other hand, having no such alternative radical policy as the Czechs had to fall back on, found it more difficult to contain popular unrest.

Before the January events, the leadership of the Austrian party was still giving qualified support to the government; in October 1917 a party congress accepted the programme of Renner, which regarded a 'democratic administrative reform' as the first step towards the transformation of Austria into a federation of nationalities. But at the October meeting, the demands of the left-wing Social Democrats were already being put forward. They argued against Renner's programme:

In the same way that the social problem cannot be solved merely by administrative work but by the proletarian capture of political power, so the national problem cannot be solved by a couple of administrative laws but by the full victory of democracy. The creation of national assemblies, and not the reform of district administration should be our solution of the fight for national autonomy; each assembly would decide the constitution and administrative organization of its nation in a sovereign manner, and it would agree on the management of its affairs in common with other nations.[16]

The principal author of the left-wing programme was Otto Bauer, who had witnessed the revolutionary events in Russia; he had returned to Vienna in September 1917. The programme incorporated the demands the Slav deputies had made at the opening of the *Reichsrat* in May;[17] nevertheless, in October 1917, only a minority of the Austrian Social Democrats thought on those lines. It was a revolutionary programme: it regarded national and social revolution as compatible. Whereas the October congress showed the lines on which the struggle inside the leadership of the party was to develop, the January strikes demonstrated the wide gap between the leaders and the party's rank and file. The workers were by no means concerned with their bread and butter only; the strike movement was inspired by political motives and it had articulate political aims. The sympathy of the strikers with the first socialist state in the world was combined with their concern for the conduct of the negotiations in Brest-Litovsk, their distaste for the behaviour of the German army negotiators, whom they suspected of wanting to sabotage the conclusion of peace while grabbing as much territory as they could. Speakers frequently reminded the strikers that there was no need to fear the machine-guns the military authorities might turn against them; the soldiers manning the guns were their comrades and shared their views. Leaflets distributed among the strikers also propagated Bolshevik ideas: the masses of Austrian workers demand peace at any price; their hopes are pinned to Lenin and Trotsky, not to Kühlmann and Czernin; the revolution in Russia has to be

[16] O. Bauer, *Österreichische Revolution*, page 62, Vienna 1923.

[17] See above, page 128.

protected from the guile of the German and Austro-Hungarian negotiators. This was the beginning of the world revolution the Russian Bolshevik leaders were hoping for; in their view, socialism could not survive confined to one country. In January high hopes were raised in Moscow. On the 22nd *Pravda* brought news of the strikes and the formation of workers' committees in Austria–Hungary. The report was headlined *On the Eve of the Austrian Revolution.* On the same day von Hempel, the Austrian representative in Petrograd, informed his government that '... the men in power here are reckoning with a revolution on the Bolshevik lines in our country in the spring'.[18]

Later developments in Austria did, however, disappoint the hopes of the Bolsheviks. As early as 16 January, two days after the outbreak of the mass-strikes in Lower Austria, the Viennese *Arbeiter Zeitung* carried a declaration by Social Democrat deputies which announced that the people did not want to

> ....continue the war on Russia, in order that the Emperor of Austria may be elected the King of Poland and the King of Prussia acquire economic and military domination over Kurland and Lithuania.... Therefore we ask you, workers, [the declaration concluded] to raise your voices again and again, and demand with us: the earliest possible end of the war. Peace, without open or veiled annexations. Peace, on the basis of genuine self-determination of peoples.

The party executive not only passed this declaration: it also advised the Premier against censoring it. At the same time, it adopted Bauer's programme and the left-wing dissenters were drawn back into the party. The differences that had threatened socialist unity at the October congress disappeared; the January strikes drew both wings together. They were agreed that the time for a revolution was not ripe: the army was still strong; there also existed the possibility of a German intervention. The Austrian Social Democrats had no doubts that, at Brest-Litovsk, two parties of unequal strength were negotiating: the Bolsheviks, the heirs of Russian defeat on the one hand, and on the other the German and the Austro-Hungarian politicians, the engineers of

[18] *HHuSA*, PA I., 808, Krieg 10.

this defeat. Both the German and the Austro-Hungarian armies appeared, at the beginning of 1918, to be at the zenith of their power. The war had, at last, been reduced to a one-front engagement; German divisions were released to deal the decisive blow in the West. Indeed, the Austro-Hungarian army were able to move considerable forces from the eastern front—seven full strength combat divisions—into the affected industrial areas; the mere threat of military intervention was often sufficient to break the strike. The Austrian Social Democrat leaders also knew that their position was made no stronger by the reserved attitude of the Czechs: in these circumstances, they decided to call an early end to the strike. The workers' council, elected at the early meetings of the strikers, agreed with the party leadership on certain demands to be made on the government; on 19 January the Premier handed to the representative of the workers' council a declaration by Czernin. The Foreign Minister solemnly promised not to let the peace negotiations be hampered by territorial demands; he recognized the self-determination of Poland, and promised a reform of the laws and regulations on military control of the armament factories and food rationing. On the same day, the party executive suggested to the workers' council that the strike should be called off, and that the workers should return to their factories on Monday, 21 January. After stormy debates in the council, the suggestion was approved. But at the same time, a new socialist splinter group came into prominence; the call to end the strike was violently opposed by the 'left-radical' group led by Franz Koritschoner, which had emerged in the summer of 1917 and which was later to develop into the communist party of Austria. Radicalism thus became confined to a small group, and the authority of the Social Democrat executive was reasserted.

But there was more trouble to come. The end of the mid-January strike movement was by no means the end of the social unrest, which during the last months of the war continued to tax the resources of the army and the resourcefulness of the administration of the Habsburg monarchy. Later in the month the strikes in Germany spread as far as Moravská Ostrava, the mining district in north-east Moravia. Here again the army, now encouraged by its earlier success in Austria and in Hungary, and also by the strike-breaking achievement of its German ally, was soon successful in putting a stop to the movement and in driving labour back to work. Nevertheless, the armed forces were not to remain immune for long. Social unrest soon began corroding their discipline and depriving the Habsburg state of its last reliable organ.

On 1 February the fifth fleet of the Austro-Hungarian navy, concentrated in the Gulf of Kotor, mutinied. Admiral Hansa commanded one battleship, three cruisers, and a number of smaller ships, forty in all, manned by 6,000 sailors. At noon, a shot from the admiral's flag-ship resounded through the gulf; a red flag was hoisted; the band, which usually played in the officers' mess at lunch-time, struck up the *Marseillaise*. Soon afterwards, all the ships of the fifth fleet were flying red flags. Although there had been plenty of complaints by the sailors about the food-supplies and about the disparity between the ratings' and the officers' rations, this was, like the January strikes, not a mere hunger demonstration: the mutiny had been well prepared.

The Allied blockade had forced the Austrian navy into inactivity; in the massed fleet at Kotor opportunities for the sailors to meet and discuss the current events in the monarchy, about which they were well-informed, were plentiful. At one of the meetings on the mainland, about 20 January, the sailors decided to demonstrate for peace; one of their leaders was František Raš, a member of the Czech Social Democrat party, who, on 1 February, took over the command of the flag-ship, while another Czech, Gustav Stonavský, became the chairman of a 'central council of sailors' to which all the ships of the fifth fleet sent their representatives. In spite of the fact that the mutiny was well organized and that the sailors took over the command of the fleet without any difficulty, the rising was short-lived. The sailors had to rely on their own ranks to provide their leaders; unlike the officers' corps of the army, which contained a large number of Slav reservists, naval officers were almost exclusively German and Hungarian professionals. The omission of the sailors to capture, at the beginning of the rising, the fleet's system of communications brought a bloody vengeance upon their heads. The sailors' knowledge of the mechanics of revolution was not as marked as their interest in politics; on the first day of the mutiny they drafted telegrams to Victor Adler, a deputy to the *Reichsrat*, and to deputy Karolyi in Budapest, expressing their desire to negotiate with Austro-Hungarian politicians on how to conclude peace as soon as possible and how to put self-determination of peoples into practice. But the messages were never transmitted: instead, Admiral Hansa sent out pleas for help. On the second day of the mutiny, when the sailors began showing interest in the telegraphic installations of the ships, the officers turned off the dynamos. The coastal batteries were trained on the ships; on 3 February the third fleet of the Austro-Hungarian navy arrived in the Gulf of Kotor. Gradually, the sailors withdrew their support from their revolutionary council; the leaders of the mutiny were arrested and court-martialled. Of the forty defendants, seven were Czechs; the rest of them were Germans, Italians, South Slavs, and Poles. Five sailors, František Raš among them, were sentenced to death. The naval mutiny in the Gulf of Kotor was the first serious disturbance among the Austro-Hungarian armed forces, but it was also the last rebellion that was quelled without great difficulty. Although the mutiny's failure was mainly due to the technical mistakes committed by the sailors, their vacillating political aims—a mixture of Bolshevik slogans and the programmes of the political exiles—soon deprived the sailors' council of support by some national groups, and of the Germans and the Hungarians in particular.

In spite of the fact that in March 1918 the government finally plucked up enough courage to carry out intensive requisitioning of food in Hungary, and that the decision was energetically carried out under Prince Windischgrätz's supervision, the food situation in the monarchy reached the nadir of hopelessness. By the time the needs of the army were satisfied there was little left for distribution among the civilians; there were insufficient supplies in the government stores even for the meagre rations. The people had to rely on their own efforts to provide enough provisions to live on; black market flourished; and townspeople had to make frequent expeditions to the country to buy food from the peasants direct, usually on a barter basis. Such self-help was described as 'rucksack economy' at the time. It gradually deteriorated into plunder by working-class urban population, usually connected with unrest and strikes in the industry, which sporadically swept the countryside; starving town masses pilfered landed estates, farms, goods in transit on the railways, and Jewish-kept stores. In their economic misery, all nationalities of the monarchy were equal; the incipient opposition of the Germans and the Hungarians to the Habsburg state dates from the beginnings of the economic breakdown. Indeed, the intensity of social unrest in Austria–Hungary during the last months of the war reached the same revolutionary pitch as it had done in Russia by March 1917.

It was into such a situation that, at the end of March, prisoners of war started returning from Russia. Most of them had witnessed both the revolutions and also knew something of the activities of the national revolutionaries, and of the Czechs in particular; some of them returned as confirmed Bolsheviks.[19] The Austro-Hungarian authorities, both civil and military, began making their last effort to prevent the spread of revolutionary doctrines, Bolshevik in particular, by the returning prisoners of war and on 1 April a special department for propaganda was set up at the General Headquarters. As soon as the prisoners crossed the frontiers of the monarchy they were directed to camps where they were thoroughly screened; the concept of 'politically unreliable' men was introduced and employed so often that the Ministry of War had to explain to the camp commanders that it should be applied only when a concrete proof of unreliability could be introduced. Nevertheless, the screening established the fact that the Bolshevik government had spared no effort to convert the prisoners of war to its ideas. Propaganda literature had been distributed in the camps; revolutionary agitators had been trained, prisoner of war councils had been established, and the members of Bolshevik organizations among the prisoners had been granted certain privileges, such as opportunities to buy cheap food. It also became apparent that the Bolsheviks had concentrated on the German and the Hungarian prisoners, the two of the

[19] *VA*, 15297 MI ex 1918.

Radio Times Hulton Picture Library.

Charitable distribution of bread in Vienna, late 1917

Masaryk and Colonel Stepanov, Commanding Officer of the 1st Rifle Regiment. Russia 1917

Defenestration of the Imperial insignia in Prague, October 1918

Habsburg peoples least susceptible to the attraction of an exclusively national fight against Vienna; Bolshevik ideas had even affected the Hungarian officers in the camps. Some of the returned prisoners became deserters: they formed into small bands and began roaming the countryside, relying on charity and theft for their subsistence. Most of them, after a short leave, rejoined the army, where they produced a corrosive effect on discipline. The first serious mutiny in the army took place at Judenburg in Styria on 12 May. A platoon of the 17th Infantry Battalion revolted and captured the barracks and the munition dump; then it plundered food stores and the railway station and destroyed the telephone and telegraph lines. The platoon was largely Slovene; when attacking the barracks the rebels shouted:

> Let us go home comrades, this is not only for us but also for our friends on the fronts. The war must be ended now, whoever is a Slovene, join us. We are going home; they should give us more to eat and end the war; up with the Bolsheviks, long live bread, down with the war.[20]

As soon as this mutiny was suppressed and six men executed, a unit of the 7th Jaegers rebelled at Murau on 14 May. The investigation proved that here, too, the troops had been incensed by insufficient supplies of food and by the agitation of the returned prisoners of war, who had maintained that Russia was economically much better off than Austria–Hungary. Six days later, a part of the Ruthene 58th battalion revolted at Ljubljana and again the former prisoners played an important role; they also complained about the shortness of the leave after their return. On the same day, a largely Serbian unit mutinied at Fünfkirchen and a serious fight developed between them and the Hungarian Honveds; after their defeat most of the rebels dispersed into the neighbouring woods. On 21 May Czech troops mutinied at Rumburg. A part of the 7th Rifle Battalion refused to go to the front until they received the money due to them for the time they had spent as prisoners of war. The rebels, who were well armed, occupied the town—they received some support from the civilian population

[20] J. Opočenský, op. cit., page 146.

—and threatened to move, via Česká Lípa, to Prague and Pilsen, where they intended to persuade the 18th battalion to join them. Indeed, some of the rebels left for the capital by train, to 'put an end to the war' there, but they were soon intercepted and disarmed. A martial court sentenced ten men to death and 560 to varying terms of imprisonment.

From Prague, the Governor reported on this latest, and so far most serious, mutiny.[21]

The events were mostly of a military nature, but since they also affected civilians, they were of grave concern to the administration as well. First of all, the connexion with the Russian social revolution and the military and internal political situation in the monarchy has become clearer. I need not go into the frightful danger of such happenings, and especially on Czech soil. I am convinced that the military authorities have done and are doing everything in their power in order to anticipate and prevent a catastrophe. Naturally, they will find support and co-operation from the political administration. In order, however, that this preventive activity and co-operation may be successful, I regard a special, painstaking, and precise supervision and screening of the prisoners of war returning from Russia as essential.

After having advised the Minister that the ex-prisoners should receive either no home leave or a very short one; that they should be dispersed, and not concentrated in large groups in the army as was the case in Rumburg, and that they should not be armed before their reliability was established, the Governor continued:

As far as the events of 21 May are concerned, it is perhaps superfluous to point at the great danger that they mean to us. It was only because of the lack of organization and leadership among the rebels on the one hand, and on the other because of the immediate, powerful and well-directed intervention by the military and political organs and the gendarmes that the mutiny was suppressed in a few hours without losses on our side. Had the rebels succeeded in advancing southwards and had they found support—and this was by no means impossible—among the civilians in these regions, we might have by now faced a regular revolution in several parts of Bohemia.

[21] Report from Coudenhove to the Minister of Interior, of 24 May 1918, quoted by Opočenský, pages 774–776. Cf. *VA*, Situation Report from the Military Command in Przemysl of 17 May 1918. 15297 MI ex 1918.

The similarities between the events in Russia and Austria-Hungary during the year 1917 were striking; for a short time, especially at the beginning of 1918, it seemed that the political development of the Habsburg monarchy was heading in the same direction. The March revolution was followed by the reopening of the *Reichsrat* in Vienna; the Bolshevik revolution marked the beginning of a period of intense social unrest in the monarchy. In Russia, constitutional reform proved inadequate to allay the revolutionary situation; in Austria, the opening discussions in the parliament only demonstrated the wide gap that separated the government from the majority of the politicians; social unrest, the result of economic privations, was given an added impetus by the Bolshevik revolution and culminated in the ominous mass strikes of January 1918.

Indeed, from the beginning of 1918 until the end of the war, strikes, mutinies in the armed forces, and hunger demonstrations followed each other in tragic succession. While corroding the political structure of the Habsburg monarchy, social unrest speeded up the radicalization of political life among the Slavs; it did not, however—as we shall see in the concluding chapters—alter the essentially national character of the revolutions of the Habsburg nations against their state. The struggle for independence from Vienna became the most immediate concern of the Slav politicians: it was a revolutionary programme in itself. National divisions went much deeper than social differences. Working-class leaders, wherever they had a revolutionary national programme to fall back on, did so; only among the Germans and the Hungarians—because of the absence of such a programme—did the revolution begin taking a more pronounced social turn. The national movements, on the other hand, were largely led by the middle-class parties: they were also social revolutions in the sense that they were directed against the hegemony, in the state, of the upper classes with a vested interest in the survival of the monarchy. Indeed, social revolution and the fight for national independence went hand in hand. The doctrine of self-determination of nations, preached by the Bolsheviks, met more than half-way the demands of radical nationalism in

Austria–Hungary; in the slogans of the strikers and the army rebels social and national demands were inextricably mixed. It was at this time, at the beginning of 1918, that the rulers of Austria–Hungary began losing their ability to discriminate between the various dangers to the state. Bolshevism appeared to them the graver threat: while dealing with it, they lost sight of the progress radical nationalism was making. But while strikes and mutinies could still be put down by the force of arms, the radical politicians were able to bide their time and strike at an opportune moment.

VI

THE VICTORY OF THE RADICALS

The fall of the Tsarist régime and the entry of the United States into the war added a new dimension to the struggle in Europe: it could now be regarded as a conflict between the authoritarian, aristocratic systems of the Central Powers on the one hand, and an alliance of middle-class, democratically-organized states on the other. Indeed, this was the way many Slav politicians in the Habsburg monarchy came to look upon the war: the new simplification substituted their former view of the war as a 'struggle between the Teutons and the Slavs'. Demands for democratic institutions, autonomy, and self-determination of nations became the order of the day; however, for some time after the opening of the parliament in May 1917 it was sometimes impossible to tell whether the Slav politicians intended to put these principles into practice inside Austria–Hungary, or whether they regarded the Habsburg state and these demands as incompatible. During the last months of the war in 1918 such uncertainties disappeared: the radicalization of Slav political life was concluded against the background of popular revolutionary unrest and the increasing dependence of Austria–Hungary on Germany.

From the beginning of their activities, the exiles had made a concentrated effort to convince the public and the governments of the Entente countries that Austria–Hungary was completely dependent on Germany and committed beyond redemption to the expansionist plans of Berlin. There was, however, a marked discrepancy between such propaganda and the real situation. Throughout the war, the relations between the two central European partners were unsettled; occasional storms broke out. The rulers of Austria–Hungary were highly sensitive to any semblance of interference from Berlin in the internal affairs of their country; although there were, especially at the German General Headquarters, men who had strong views on the conduct of the monarchy's internal affairs, their suggestions for improvement were contested not only in Vienna, but by the *Wilhelmstrasse* itself.

Of course the Germans watched with displeasure the developments in Austria–Hungary; in a memorandum of 28 December 1917 Diego von Bergen, a Minister in the German Foreign Office, touched the core of the problem:

> In a note of 13 November 1915 to the Austro-Hungarian Embassy here, we suggested that our alliance with the Habsburg monarchy rested on the idea of Magyar supremacy in Hungary and that of the Germans in Austria. Whereas in Hungary this principle could be put into practice and further developed, in Austria it has, in the course of the years, suffered numerous setbacks. Because of the increase in the political power of other nationalities, in the lands of the Austrian crown, a development has taken place that has partly deprived the German element of the leadership we had planned for it. . . . We have repeatedly stressed to Vienna the fact that we are greatly interested in the strengthening of the German element in Austria and in its freedom from the increasing Slav pressure. In private conversations I have pointed out that our wish does not mean interference in the internal affairs of Austria; satisfaction of the Austrian Germans is in Vienna's own interests; the neglect of this element, faithful to the Emperor, in favour of the disruptive Slav nationalities would of necessity create a German *irredenta* in Austria; the Germans, whose national consciousness has been strengthened by the war, would not tolerate the increasing suppression of their Austrian compatriots; they would in the end force their government to come to the aid of the Austrian Germans in a form which would far exceed our present academic interest in the subject.[1]

The Austrian government had indeed taken a number of measures that invited the displeasure of the Germans: the opening of the *Reichsrat* in May 1917 provided the Slav dissenters with a political platform; the amnesty to political prisoners in July caused a good deal of irritation in Berlin. The generosity of the

[1] *AA*, WK 20c sec.

government in Vienna did not appear to affect the Germans as much as the Slavs. Nevertheless, the reverses in domestic and foreign affairs that repeatedly shattered the self-confidence of the Austro-Hungarian leadership did not only force the government in Vienna to make half-hearted concessions to the Slavs: they also propelled the rulers of the Habsburg monarchy—and this point von Bergen did not appreciate—in the direction of a greater dependence on Germany. Count Czernin, the Austro-Hungarian Foreign Minister, did much to tighten his country's ties with Berlin; he regarded this policy, without giving much thought to its consequences, as one of loyalty to the ally and he tried to implement it in the face of open opposition and the secret activities of his Emperor for a separate peace. Again, the key to Austria's relations with Germany were the differences between the Allies on certain problems of foreign policy, and on the Polish question in particular.[2]

Very few men in Vienna regarded the Two Emperors' Manifesto as the final solution of the Polish problem. The joint German and Austro-Hungarian plan had undermined the confidence of the Poles in Austria; when the revolution in Russia had cleared the field of dangerous competition, a number of German politicians and diplomats started giving the problem more thought. Tschirschky, the Ambassador to Vienna had been replaced by Wedel soon after the publication of the Manifesto in November 1916; the new Ambassador's reports did much to impress on Berlin the fact that there had been a considerable turn of opinion against Germany and that this had been largely caused by the treatment of the Polish question. In a report of 22 July 1917[3] the Ambassador described the unease in the monarchy at the time of his arrival; Imperial Germany was regarded, by the Germans and the Hungarians alike, as the saviour of the Habsburg monarchy. The Czechs and the South Slavs were lying low, while only the Poles were dissatisfied and anti-German. But:

after the revolution in Russia, the feeling against Germany began to rise here. The turn of opinion started slowly; by now it has assumed

[2] See above, page 100.

[3] *AA*, Wedel to the Chancellor, *Oesterreich 70 sec.*

the proportions of an avalanche. One cannot speak of friendliness any longer: hatred and bitterness are the keynote.

It was the Ambassador's considered opinion in July 1917 that, if a plebiscite was taken in Austria—but not in Hungary—the majority would vote in favour of an attack against Germany on the side of the Entente. Since the upheaval in Russia, Wedel reported, the creation of a Polish state was assured. If the Poles received their state from the Entente, they would get the German part of their territory as well and with it access to the sea; if the Central Powers granted them a state, they would have to be satisfied with less. The Poles still had some sympathies for Austria—although, in their heart of hearts, they had already dissolved the monarchy—but none whatever for Germany. Even the Austrian Germans, the Ambassador complained, had started being influenced by considerations unfavourable to Berlin.

In the German lands of Austria we have determined friends and determined enemies. The Germans in Bohemia are the only reliable people in Austria. Fürstenberg, Clam-Martinitz, Czernin, Nostiz, in fact the whole of the Bohemian German aristocracy are the pillars of the alliance between Austria–Hungary and Germany. That is two and a half million people on whom we can rely. Fortunately they are, and the aristocracy especially, very influential.

The mood in Hungary was, according to the Ambassador, better though not completely satisfactory. The Czech aspirations to Slovakia, the amnesty to political prisoners, and the failure of the Russian summer offensive, had all corrected the situation in Germany's favour. But again, Wedel regarded the 230,000 Saxons of Transylvania, like the Bohemian Germans in Austria, as the only absolutely reliable people in Hungary.

Wedel was in no doubt that the coolness in the monarchy's attitude towards Germany was a direct result of the Two Emperors' Manifesto:

The Poles in Galicia were the first to oppose this solution; they lost no time in starting a keen agitation against it. Their principal aim was the amalgamation of Galicia with Congress Poland, and the question whether this should be done under German, Austrian or Russian auspices is of secondary importance to them.

The Poles in the *Reichsrat* also lost much of their interest in supporting the government, which had to turn for help to the Czechs, but without success. 'Internal chaos is the result of the Polish question,' Wedel remarked, and proceeded to stress, on familiar lines, the importance of Galicia to the Habsburgs, and the difficulties the dynasty would be faced with if any part of Poland were to remain under Russian rule. At this point, the Ambassador lapsed into distortion: it was not Berlin but Tisza and Burian who now got all the blame for the rejection of the Austro-Polish solution, because they regarded it as a threat to the dualist system. Wedel saw only one way out of an impossible situation, in which 'relations between Austria–Hungary and Germany were being poisoned by the Poles', and that was the adoption of the Austro-Polish solution. But such a settlement 'would be acceptable to us only in very special circumstances. We can, in exchange, demand a military convention and the creation of a common German, Austro-Hungarian, and Polish economic area'.

These were stiff conditions; in this direction lay greater dependence of Austria–Hungary on Germany. Nevertheless, the impression of an atmosphere hostile to Germany was soon reinforced from other sources. Grünau, who was at the time the Foreign Ministry liaison officer at the German Imperial court, reported that Czernin had warned the Kaiser that an opposition majority, consisting of the Poles who were supported by other Habsburg Slavs, the Social Democrats, and the Karolyi party in Hungary was being formed in the monarchy, and that this opposition would take a decisive stand against the policy of alliance with Germany at the forthcoming meeting in September of the delegations of the Austrian and Hungarian parliaments.[4] Goldmann, the representative of the Viennese *Neue Freie Presse* in Berlin, who spent August and September in Vienna, also reported to *Wilhelmstrasse* that 'the old enemies of the alliance, especially the clericals, are at work again, but other influences are making themselves felt, at the

[4] *AA*, Grünau's telegram to the Foreign Ministry of 25 July, 1917. *WK 2 sec.*

court in particular'. But Goldmann had a cheering anecdote to tell: 'The Austrians are made of a softer material than we; they have no staying power and they are irresolute. An Austrian friend told me, "There are many people in high places who would like to make a clean break with Germany. But, as with everything, we would be too weak to carry out such an intention." '[5]

At the beginning of October, the Germans began seriously to consider the plan outlined in Wedel's report. In a private letter to Kühlmann, the State Secretary in the Foreign Ministry, the Ambassador in Vienna warned the head of his office that Emperor Karl was opposed to the idea of a military convention with Germany, and that the temptation, to which the German army leaders were particularly open, that is, to annex large tracts of Polish territory and to leave the remainder to Vienna, would have to be resisted.[6] Three days later, Michaelis, the Imperial Chancellor, informed Grünau at the General Headquarters about his long conversation with Ludendorff and Hindenburg on the Austro-Polish solution; as in 1916, the Generals opposed the plan. The attitude of the Supreme Command did not, however, prevent Kühlmann from concluding on 22 October an important and highly secret agreement with the Austro-Hungarian Minister of Foreign Affairs.[7] Although the agreement was not binding, it set down the lines on which future discussions and the development of relations between Germany and Austria–Hungary were to move. Under the first paragraph of the directives, Austria–Hungary undertook to sign a military convention with Germany, binding for twenty years, which would provide for the co-ordination of armaments, common treatment of all 'measures necessary for war': in fact, all the military lessons the two countries learned during the war were to be put into practice and the Supreme Commands were to work out the details. Further, the agreement provided for a new settlement of economic relations between Austria–Hungary and Germany: a customs union was envisaged, and everything was to be done to achieve a closer co-operation in the economic field. These

[5] *AA*, Goldmann's report from Vienna, dated 1 October 1917, *Oesterreich 70 sec.*

[6] *AA*, Wedel to Kühlmann, 6 October 1917, *WK 20c sec.*

[7] *AA*, a memorandum dated 25 October 1917, *Oesterreich 70 sec.*

measures worked out as concessions to Germany; both Kühlmann and Czernin were aware of this. Germany on the other hand was prepared to concede, under conditions to be agreed upon, a personal union between the Habsburgs and Poland: the kingdom of Poland, however, was to maintain close economic and military ties not only with Vienna but with Berlin as well. But there were more concessions from Czernin to come. He agreed to a closer union between Germany and Rumania; Germany was to have the right of transit through the monarchy for its Rumanian trade. Yet Czernin and Kühlmann did not want to create the impression that they were settling the future of these two peoples over their heads:

> Both the Polish and the Rumanian questions can be solved in the above-mentioned manner only if the solutions come from the two countries first; therefore Germany and Austria–Hungary undertake to start preparing the ground now.

Soon after the preliminary agreement between the Austro-Hungarian Foreign Minister and the German State Secretary, negotiations between the two countries started on government level, exactly one year after the publication of the Two Emperors' Manifesto. At the meeting on 6 November,[8] Kühlmann described the purpose of the conference as an attempt to ascertain whether either party desired a revision of the secret 'Kreuznach convention', which had put Poland into the German sphere of influence and Rumania into that of Austria–Hungary. Although the State Secretary did his best to act as a peace-maker, the views of Ludendorff and Czernin developed into a sharp clash. Ludendorff held that the German–Polish solution had put the defence of the eastern frontier into Germany's hands, but now it was proposed that the Habsburg monarchy should be entrusted with it. 'It is desirable to have the defence of the frontier in one's own hands rather than in those of one's best friend,' Ludendorff remarked; later he added, rather acidly, that the war had taught the Germans to rely on themselves. Ludendorff knew what was coming; he forestalled Czernin's argument by casting doubt on the

[8] *AA*, record of the meeting between the German and the Austro-Hungarian military nd Foreign Ministry representatives, 6 November 1917. *WK 15 sec.*

suggestion that the Austro-Polish solution would strengthen the alliance between Berlin and Vienna. The Austro-Hungarian Foreign Minister, on the other hand, was convinced that the revision of the Kreuznach directives was essential; indeed he argued that since a close alliance between Germany and his country after the war was highly desirable, the only way of achieving it was to rid the *Reichsrat* in Vienna of the deputies from Galicia. The policy of a close alliance with Germany would be unacceptable to an Austria with a Slav majority: if a German majority was to be achieved, the deputies from Galicia would have to be excluded from the parliament:

> The advantage of this solution would be that a German majority would carry the alliance of Austria–Hungary with Germany. The German solution of the Polish problem would mean a partition, because Galicia would remain in the monarchy.

The differences between the allies were sharply defined: there was no obvious way out of the impasse. But soon, these problems were to be overshadowed by the events in Russia, and shelved. While Ludendorff and Czernin were arguing about the future of Poland, the Bolsheviks began taking over power in Petrograd: peace negotiations were to begin soon between the new régime in Russia and the governments of the Central Powers. From December onward, the protagonists in the discussions between the representatives of Austria–Hungary and Germany were fully occupied at Brest-Litovsk. But while negotiating with the Bolsheviks, the Central Powers were also attempting to bring about peace with Rumania and the Ukraine. Indeed, it was the Ukrainian treaty, signed on 10 February, that profoundly affected the political developments in Poland. The Germans had, since the beginning of the war, given support to the Ukrainian separatist movement, as a part of their policy of weakening the Tsarist régime through national and social revolutions. The Austro-Hungarian leaders, on the other hand, had had to be more careful: whereas the Ukrainian question was completely extraneous as far as Berlin was concerned, they faced the problem on their own territory, in eastern Galicia, Bukovina, and Carpathian Russia. Although Vienna had also favoured the Ukrainian party in Galicia, it did so in order to counteract the pro-Russian Ruthene movement;[9] it could not afford to discriminate too much in favour of the Ukrainians at the expense of the Poles. Nevertheless, during the peace negotiations for a separate Ukrainian state, Czernin was pushed, by his allies, into a position which made it inevitable for him to favour, or appear to favour from the point of view of the Poles, the Ukrainian cause. Indeed, the Ukrainian peace and the subsequent developments in Poland were the highest price the Austro-Hungarian government had to pay for its alliance with Germany. There were other factors that influenced the Austro-Hungarian Foreign Minister: the pressure of social unrest at home, and his belief that the Ukrainian corn supplies would considerably alleviate the food shortage in the monarchy, made Czernin keen to achieve concrete results on the peace front as soon as possible; finally, the Ukrainians were proving themselves more pliable than the Bolsheviks. On 6 February 1918 Hertling, the new German Secretary of State, reported to the Kaiser on the results of a meeting of German departmental chiefs with Ludendorff and Czernin at Brest-Litovsk:[10]

As far as the developments at Brest-Litovisk are concerned, everybody agreed that peace with the Ukraine should be concluded as soon as possible, and after that the negotiations with Trotsky, no matter whether successful or not.

Later in the telegram, Hertling turned to an aspect of the negotiations that concerned Austria–Hungary in particular:

When the Austro-Polish solution was discussed, it became clear that the objections against it had considerably gained in weight. The planned cession to the Ukraine of the Kholm district and the corresponding grant of autonomy to eastern Galicia, lessens the value of the future kingdom of Poland to such a degree that it cannot but bring serious discontent among the Poles.

But he thought that:

. . .an early solution [of the Polish question] cannot be expected. It is not, however, very urgent, as long as we succeed in concluding peace

[9] See above, page 4.

[10] *AA*, Hertling's telegram to Grünau at the GHQ, *WK 15 sec.*

with the Ukraine and with Rumania, and if we clear up our relations with the Bolsheviks.

Hertling was right in his prediction of the effects on the Poles of the Ukrainian peace, although he overestimated their patience. Until January 1918, the deputies concentrated in the Polish Circle, the united parliamentary club, supported the government of Seidler and the foreign policy of Czernin: in spite of the dissenting left-wing—the Social Democrats, led by Moraczewski and Daszyński, and Glabiński's People's party—the conservative nobility was successful in directing the policy of the Polish Circle on pro-Austrian lines. But the provisions of the peace with the Ukraine showed the Poles that they could expect nothing from the Central Powers in the way of furthering their national cause. They were to lose Kholm and Podlasie to the Ukrainians; eastern Galicia and Bukovina (though not Carpathian Russia in Hungary) were to be amalgamated into a separate crown-land, with its own administration; at the same time, it was becoming clear that Berlin intended to make further inroads into Polish territory: in the West, the frontier was to be redrawn in favour of Prussia, while a new satellite principality of Lithuania, ruled by a German prince, was to infringe on Poland in the north.

In Warsaw, as soon as the provisions of the February peace became known, Kucharzewski's government resigned; Prince Lubomirski broke off relations, in the name of the Regents Council, with the Austro-Hungarian representative in occupied Poland. The reaction in Galicia to the Ukrainian peace was still more violent. Immediately after its conclusion, on 11 February, some 3,000 people demonstrated in front of the German consulate in Cracow; popular unrest spread from the capital and lasted until the end of the month. Large posters with the slogan 'Down with Germany and Austria–Hungary' appeared in the Cracow streets and Habsburg insignia were torn down from official buildings. On 18 February a day of national mourning was declared: in Cracow, Lwow and in the Boryslaw industrial district, the Poles demonstrated against the concessions to the Ukraine and for an independent state. In the processions of that day, dogs wore the Austrian military medals with which the men of Pilsudski's Legion had been decorated. On the front, the remnants of the Polish Legion mutinied; the rebels, under General Haller's command, deserted their positions on the eastern front.[11] The Governor of Galicia, Count Huyn, informed Vienna at the end of February that the rebellion had gripped the whole country, and that since Polish officials could no longer be relied upon, the administration of the crown-land was becoming increasingly difficult.[12]

In the *Reichsrat*, the Polish Circle protested against the government's agreement with the Ukrainians; it requested two of its members, Ministers in Seidler's cabinet, to resign: the Emperor, however, refused to accept their resignation. Dazsyński told the parliament that the interests of Poland were no longer compatible with those of Austria–Hungary, and that for his compatriots the 'Habsburg star' had definitely gone down. In the division following the budget debate only the conservative deputies backed the government. The Social Democrats, the All-Polish group led by Glabiński and Witos's Peasant party, entered into opposition and left the Circle. The final breach between the Polish politicians and the monarchy began. Only the conservatives remained devoted to the idea of the Austro-Polish solution; but in supporting the government they also protected their class interests. The estrangement with the Habsburg state meant that the leadership of the national movement passed into the hands of the middle and lower middle-class intelligentsia and the mass organizations that emerged after the introduction, three years before the war, of general suffrage: the political situation in Galicia thus came closely to resemble that in the Czech lands.

The government in Vienna, however, refused to draw the obvious conclusions from the events in Galicia: it continued to regard the Austro-Polish solution as a practicable possibility. For several weeks after the conclusion of peace with the Ukraine, the Austrian Foreign Minister had no opportunity of discussing the problem with the Germans; relations between the two countries

[11] See below, page 198.

[12] Opočenský, op. cit., page 169; *VA*, 5083, 13437, 66321 MI ex 1918.

were strained to breaking point by their differences on the treatment of the Bolsheviks. Whereas the Germans were inclined to take a tough line with the régime in Moscow and to issue an ultimatum, Czernin, largely because he feared the effects of such a policy on the socialists in his own country, insisted on the continuation of the negotiations. Soon similar differences arose between the allies on the question of peace with Rumania, and high-level discussions on Poland had to be postponed until the problems of peace with Russia and Rumania had been dealt with. On 16 March, in a telegram to the Chancellor, Kühlmann expressed his concern over the future of Poland.[13] Kaiser Wilhelm, according to the State Secretary in the Foreign Ministry, had given support to the Austro-Polish solution, now came under the influence of the Supreme Command, who opposed it; the Poles themselves, in Kühlmann's view, wanted first to gain independence from Austria with German help, in order to be able to turn later against Germany on the side of the western Allies.

Nevertheless, the revival of interest in Poland did not last long: the attitude of the Austro-Hungarian leaders towards Rumania convinced the Germans that they were not only under no obligation to make concessions to their partners, but that there was little point in discussing the problem at all. On 7 April Hindenburg informed the Chancellor of his ideas, 'on the order of the Kaiser':

> After the conclusion of the Bucharest peace treaty the Austro-Polish solution is unacceptable to us. We supposed that Austria would take no further interest in Rumania. But the territorial and economic gains by the monarchy, her continued influence on the occupation of the country and on the dynastic question, all constitute a deep penetration by Austria–Hungary into the German sphere of interest. Emperor Karl's defence of the present royal house against a Prussian or other German prince, who would further German interests on the Lower Danube, is yet another move in the Habsburg struggle against the House of Hohenzollern. The adoption of the Austro-Polish solution would mean another success for the Habsburgs.[14]

[13] *AA*, a telegram dispatched from Bucharest; in *WK 20 sec.*

[14] Telegram from Lersner, the Foreign Ministry liaison officer at the Supreme Command, to the Chancellor; *WK 20c sec.*

While German opposition to the Austro-Polish solution was on the increase, the relations between Vienna and Berlin were to go through their final and most violent crisis. Czernin's indiscreet speech to the City Council of Vienna on 2 April, in which the Foreign Minister made a reference to French peace-feelers, embarrassed and enraged Clemenceau; it was followed by a slanging-match from which the Austrians, and the Emperor in particular, emerged thoroughly discredited. The letter in which Emperor Karl's promised support to the 'just claims of France to Alsace Lorraine', was published with momentous consequences. The German leaders did not hesitate to exploit the opportunities presented to them by this evidence of the Austrian Emperor's duplicity; they realized that now was the moment to tighten the alliance. Their task was facilitated by the effect of the scandal in Austria–Hungary itself. Wedel reported on the change of political atmosphere from Vienna on 22 April:

> Anyone who has spent the last months in Austria cannot but wonder at the effect on public opinion here by the Sixtus affair. Before, criticism of the German ally was plentiful, our troops and transports met with unfriendliness and chicanery of every kind, one could believe that there was a strong desire to break away from Germany. Now, however, when the alliance is in danger, protests against such policy have been raised throughout the country. It becomes clear how little there is behind the critical and often negative attitude of our ally.[15]

Soon, Wedel began preparing the ground for the strengthening of the alliance. One day after the dispatch of his report to the Chancellor, he discussed the problem with Burian, Czernin's successor in the Foreign Ministry.[16] He told Burian that although he was convinced that Austria–Hungary would remain faithful to the alliance, he was not quite certain how the relations between the two countries would develop later; he then added that since Germany's confidence in its ally had recently come in for some severe buffeting, his government had to demand a clear and binding answer. Burian replied that he regarded the strengthening of the

[15] *AA*, Report from the Ambassador to the Chancellor, 22 April, *Oesterreich 95 sec.*

[16] *AA*, Report from the Ambassador to the Chancellor, 24 April, *Oesterreich 95 sec.*

M

alliance as his 'first and most important task', and that he would do his utmost to bring it about and to win over the Emperor in its favour. Concluding his report, Wedel remarked: 'It may sound odd, but I have the feeling that pressure from our side would not be unwelcome at present, since it would help to overcome their own vacillation.'

As soon as the third and final peace settlement in the East—between the Central Powers and Rumania—was concluded on 7 May, German leaders turned their attention to the problem of their relations with Austria–Hungary. The date for Emperor Karl's visit to the German General Headquarters at Spa—where the Kaiser and his court lived—was fixed; the Germans discussed the question of the relations with their ally at a number of high-level meetings in Berlin. At a last-minute conference at Spa, the German Chancellor, the State Secretary in the Foreign Ministry, Field-Marshal Hindenburg, and General Ludendorff, settled the main outlines of the agreement which was duly signed by the two Emperors the following day. It read:

His Majesty the German Emperor, the King of Prussia, and His Majesty the Emperor of Austria, the Apostolic King of Hungary, wishing to build up and strengthen the alliance between their two countries, which had proved true in peace-time and then was forged by brotherhood in arms, which is to serve the welfare of the nations and the needs of future generations, and which is to guarantee the inviolability of their states, to hold their glorious armies in a close connexion, and to further and merge, as far as possible, the economic interests of their countries, are agreed and they undertake to instruct their governments to work out and conclude agreements, as speedily as possible, which would put into practice the following aims:

I. The conclusion of a long-term and close political alliance between the two Empires, for their defence and security.

II. The formation of a military union.

III. The creation of a customs and economic union between Germany and Austria–Hungary, gradually and with the aim of creating a completely tariff-free traffic between the two signatory Powers.

The customs and trade agreements should not be directed against other states and they should not make friendly trade relations with these states any more difficult.

The contracting Powers are agreed that the final settlement of the questions under I–III depends on an understanding about the Polish problem.[17]

The agreement was signed at the German General Headquarters and provided with the seals of the two Emperors on 12 May 1918. At the same time, the 'Directives for a League of Arms' (*Waffenbund*), signed by Field-Marshal Hindenburg and General Arz, and originally drafted by General Cramon, were appended to the treaty. There were seven paragraphs:

1. Both allies undertake to employ their national resources exhaustively. (2) Every able-bodied man must do his national service. (3) The rules of organization, training and employment must be built on a uniform basis. (4) Equipment will have to be provided uniformly and in such a manner as to ensure that in a future war the troops would not have to rely for the supply of arms and ammunition on their home country, but that these could be provided in the speediest possible manner. (5) Exchange of officers seems to be indicated in order that they may learn the conditions in both armies. (6) All preparations for war are to be undertaken together. (7) The railway network is to be built up uniformly according to the experiences of the present war. The supplies of rolling stock and other materials will be provided by both countries together.

The agreement between the two Emperors promised seriously to circumscribe the independence of Austria–Hungary, clearly the weaker side in the partnership. At his Canossa in Spa, Emperor Karl put his signature, in contradiction to all his previous policies, to a document that bound his state to the German Empire more closely than ever before. The two Emperors' contract sanctioned the secret agreement between Czernin and Kühlmann of October 1917 and it fulfilled the demands the German nationalists in Austria had made early in the war.[18] But many politicians—quite apart from those in the Slav countries of the

[17] *AA*, Protokoll über die am 11 Mai 1918, nachmittags ½5 Uhr in Spa abgehaltene Sitzung. *Osterreich 95 sec.* It was printed, without the *Grundlagen für den Waffenbund*, in Opočenský, op. cit., page 769.

[18] See above, page 86.

Empire—bitterly disapproved of the agreement: Josef Redlich in Vienna, for instance, convinced that such a policy would result in Austria's complete dependence on Germany, described it as 'this form of abdication of the Habsburgs';[19] in Budapest, Count Karolyi poured his scorn on the agreement in an impassioned parliamentary speech. Since Seidler, the Prime Minister, had dismissed the Austrian parliament on 3 May the Slav deputies could not criticize the agreement in Vienna; it is doubtful, however, whether they would have availed themselves of the opportunity. Although the implementation of the Spa convention was made dependent on the satisfactory settlement of the Polish problem, the Austro-Polish solution had lost supporters not only in Germany, but in Galicia itself. The two Emperors had made a political deal without taking the nationalities into account; now the peoples began taking the initiative into their own hands.

The Ukrainian peace had estranged a large section of the Polish politicians from the Habsburg state; the early months of 1918 also witnessed a radical swing against the monarchy among the South Slavs and the Czechs. The reformist plans contained in the declarations submitted by the Slav deputies to the parliament on the occasion of its opening in May 1917 became a suitable basis for the programme of national revolution: the latter part of the demand for national self-determination within the confines of the Habsburg monarchy was simply dropped; self-determination and the Habsburg state appeared as two irreconcilable concepts.

After the naval mutiny at Kotor, and after the military rebellion at Mostar in Hercegovina the bands of deserters—the so-called 'green cadres'—that roamed the countryside in the South of the monarchy began to increase and to cause serious concern to Austro-Hungarian military authorities. On 11 February Field-Marshal Wucherer reported to the Supreme Headquarters from Bosnia:

> I am gaining the impression that a political and military revolution is on the way in the Balkans. The increasing number of deserters' bands in Montenegro and in the frontier territory of Hercegovina and the fact that Serbian officers are with these bands, that they are daily

[19] *Die Tagebücher*, vol. 2, entry for 17 May 1918.

receiving reinforcements and that some of them possess army rifles and hand grenades, all point to the fact that the Serbs are aiming to infiltrate into our ranks in Bulgaria and Albania and to penetrate to the north, and that we shall have to expect an increase in partisan activities and their spread into Serbia, at any rate in the territories south of Upper Morava.[20]

Overwhelmed by military problems, the southern commands of the army could no longer devote much time to political activities in the South Slav provinces; although some of the civil administrators continued to write long memoranda on the Balkan tangle, offering a variety of solutions, their activities were becoming an increasingly academic exercise. Whereas early in the war the Great Croat plan for the constitutional reform of the monarchy appeared acceptable to the majority of South Slav politicians, soon after the declaration in the *Reichsrat* at the end of May 1917, the political scene in the south of the Empire began subtly to change. There were two highroads for the advancement of radicalism here: apart from working for complete independence, the radicals had to aim at the achievement of a greater degree of unity among the Serbs, the Croats, and the Slovenes. While the first aim, that is complete independence, had to be pursued in secret, the second aim could be worked for overtly, with the knowledge of the Austro-Hungarian authorities. Indeed, it was imperative that the idea of South Slav unity, and the reconciliation between the Croats and the Serbs in particular, be revived after the setbacks it had suffered at the beginning of the war. This work was undertaken, like most of that conducted by the South Slav Committee abroad, by the Dalmatians: Angelinović and Bartulović, members of the Starčević group in the Party of Law, started to preach the idea of South Slav unity with great force and conviction in the *Hrvatska Država*, which began to appear on 1 September 1917. In the *Reichsrat* the South Slavs and the Czechs formed a working partnership: the alliance increased the self-confidence of the two national representations, while at the same time it contributed to speeding up their conversion to

[20] *AOK*, No. 1031/1, quoted by Paulová, *Diplomatická hra o Jihoslovany za světové války*, pages 120 and 121, Prague 1923.

thoroughgoing radicalism. Both the Czechs and the South Slavs used the same tactics in the parliament; they presented the government with a number of enquiries on the treatment of their peoples by the military, especially in the early stages of the war, and they voted together against the measures proposed by the government. But during the last year of the war the transformation of the parliamentary opposition to the government into an opposition to the very existence of the state was merely a question of time; the speed of the transformation varied in individual cases. Among the South Slavs, the Slovene clerical deputy Korošec was the first to question, in public, the right of the Habsburg state to rule the Slav peoples: he did so during the budget debate in the *Reichsrat* in November 1917.[21]

Under the impression of unrest in South Slav territories and of the militant tactics of the deputies in Vienna, the South Slav question once again came to be discussed in Austrian political and military circles. But the negotiations in Brest-Litovsk, the uncertainties as to the settlement of the Polish question, and the attitude of the Hungarian Premier to the solution of the national problems in the south, all combined to preserve the *status quo*. In December 1917 Clam-Martinitz, then the Military Governor of Montenegro, outlined in a letter to Czernin his plan: the unification of the South Slavs, under the auspices of a new form of sub-dualism; Austro-Polish on the one hand and Hungarian–South Slav on the other. On 26 December the Foreign Minister wrote to Clam-Martinitz from Brest-Litovsk:

> I have to oppose decidedly any radical solution of the whole problem, as you suggest it, now, when the monarchy is fighting the battle for its existence: your solution would not satisfy anyone. . . . You see the salvation of the monarchy in sub-dualism: Austria–Poland and Hungary–Jugoslavia. Apart from the fact that Poland is unlikely, at the present point, to be satisfied with this solution, it seems to me unacceptable to the South Slavs as well. Croatia–Slavonia already has a certain sub-dualist relation with Hungary, which does not suit these countries very well. But apart from the Hungarians, the Czechs would

[21] *Parliamentarische Chronik*, November 1917.

also protest against the increase of the South Slav territories under the crown of St. Stephen.[22]

After he received Czernin's letter, Clam-Martinitz was forced radically to revise his views. As soon as he became convinced, after the Ukrainian peace was concluded in February, that the Austro-Polish solution was no longer practicable, he worked out a new plan: wishing to avoid infringing on the dualist system, the Governor of Montenegro suggested the unification of his province with Serbia, Bosnia and Hercegovina, and Dalmatia under the rule of Austria; Croatia and Slavonia were to remain, for the time being, linked up with the Hungarian part of the monarchy. In the middle of May, the Military Governors of Serbia and Bosnia met Clam-Martinitz in Sarajevo to discuss his latest proposals; although they were all agreed that the solution of the South Slav problem was essential for the preservation of the Habsburg monarchy, they could do little to advance it in official quarters, or to make it acceptable to the Jugoslavs themselves.

The tightening of the alliance between Austria–Hungary and Germany encouraged those diehards who had advocated a tougher attitude towards the Slav peoples in the monarchy; the Austrian government itself began proving more receptive to their ideas. It was in the South Slav territories that the policy of repression was, for the second time in the war, put to the test. At the end of May, the government in Vienna advised its administrators in the south to prevent any public political action demanding the formation of a Jugoslav state; censorship became more severe, and a 'rectification' campaign among teachers, civil servants, and the clergy was launched. On 9 June a public meeting in Ljubljana, the Slovene capital, was banned and in territories with mixed German–Slovene population, where the Ministry of the Interior feared bloodshed, the ban on public meetings was strictly enforced.

Whereas Wekerle's government in Budapest remained comparatively undisturbed by the situation in Croatia—it merely replaced the Governor in Zagreb—both the Austrian cabinet and

[22] Private letter from Czernin to Clam-Martinitz, quoted by M. Paulová, *Tajná diplomatická hra o Jihoslovany*, pages 115–118.

the military authorities were, at the end of the spring of 1918, profoundly concerned and puzzled by the lapses of some Slovene politicians from loyalty to the monarchy. The clericals, who dominated the local political life, had always had a reputation for being devoted to the dynasty. The concentration of political power in one party did, however, facilitate the task of the Slovene radicals. Šusteršić was the leader of the loyalists; Korošec, on the other hand, became an exponent of radicalism. As the situation on the battle-fields and inside the monarchy steadily deteriorated, and connexions with other radical politicians, especially among the Czechs, were established, the power inside the clerical party was transferred, without difficulty, into the hands of its radical wing. The Austro-Hungarian authorities found it hard to understand this sudden and unexpected change of face: in order to rectify the situation an audience of the Slovene bishops with the Emperor was contemplated, but never took place.

A similar transformation in Croat politics also occurred in the spring and summer of 1918. The propaganda for national unity had prepared the ground for the advance of radicalism: but it was not the Croat–Serb Coalition, but Starčević's party that came to play the most prominent role in the anti-Habsburg movement. The Coalition had suffered serious setbacks after the outbreak of the war; at the same time it was a 'government' party, heavily committed to the Croat–Hungarian sub-dualist compromise. Its leaders were incapable, until late in the summer, of raising their views above the traditional considerations of the relations between Zagreb and Budapest. Ivo Frank's Party of Law, on the other hand, had staked everything on their alliance with the military, whom they expected to help them carry out their trialist plans for the reform of the monarchy, and at the same time to unseat the Coalition from its position of power. Beyond a mild version of Great Croat ideas—it was not averse from co-operation with the Serbs—Starčević's group had no such commitments as the Coalition or Frank's Party of Law. It could therefore devote itself wholeheartedly to the cause of national revolution: its leaders were among the first politicians in Croatia to realize that the Kingdom of Serbia, in the event of the success of the Entente

Powers, would find itself on the victorious side, and that, if the South Slavs in the Habsburg monarchy were to derive any benefit from this situation, demands for a Greater Croatia would have to undergo a drastic revision. None of the South Slav politicians did, however, concern themselves very deeply with the question of their future relations with Serbia: this point was to be clarified after their immediate task—the destruction of the Habsburg monarchy—was accomplished.

The declaration of Starčević's party, published in Zagreb on 3 March, marked the beginning of a radical swing against the monarchy in Croatia. Although the declaration contained certain similarities to that of the South Slav deputies presented to the first session of the *Reichsrat* in May of the previous year, it no longer contained—and this is the crucial point—any reference to the Habsburg state:

> . . . we have agreed on the necessity to carry out the concentration of all political parties and groups that maintain the standpoint of national unity and that demand, on the basis of self-determination of nations, their national independence and a democratic state of the Slovenes, the Croats and the Serbs.[23]

Following the failure of the German spring offensive in the West, when the fortunes of the war turned decisively against the Central Powers, and in the midst of the increasing popular unrest, the South Slav radicals, in spite of the repressive measures taken by the Austrian government, found a responsive audience among the masses. In Slovenia, deputy Korošec was energetically agitating against the requisitions of food and against the war loans, and spreading the message 'a friend of the Habsburg is an enemy of his own nation'. In the atmosphere of the summer of 1918 the position of the politicians still loyal to the monarchy was fast becoming untenable; the majority of the Serbs, the Croats, and the Slovenes were united in awaiting the Empire's demise.

The Czechs, unlike the Poles or the South Slavs, never occupied a prominent position in the deliberations of the Austro-Hungarian statesmen. They were not taken into account when

[23] M. Paulová, idem, page 122.

the numerous plans, trialist and other, were discussed during the war; the suggestion that they should be united with the Slovaks was generally regarded as impracticable, and received no serious consideration. Nevertheless, the Czechs disposed of economic resources second only to those of the Austrian Germans; their geographical position was also strong. Whereas the loss of Galicia or of some South Slav territories would not have necessarily meant the complete disintegration of the Habsburg dominions—such losses had been contemplated in Vienna on several occasions—the monarchy could not survive the dissolution of the ties with the Czech lands. Like the political views of the other Slav peoples in the monarchy, those of the Czechs evolved against the background of revolutionary unrest, the increasing dependence of Vienna on Berlin, the incompetence of the government and, finally, the military successes of the Entente.

Whereas the existence of Serbia and Congress Poland as well as of German Poland lifted the national movement of the South Slavs and the Poles from a purely Habsburg to an international question, the situation of the Czechs was more difficult, as all the territories claimed by the radicals lay within the confines of the Habsburg monarchy. Their politics were more diversified but at the same time more tightly organized than those of the Slovenes, the Croats, or even of the Poles. There were parties based on solid middle-class and working-class support: although both socialist and non-socialist organizations became radically national during the last year of the war the struggle for power in the independent state of the future began before its foundation. It developed into essentially a class conflict, and it seriously disrupted the national front that had been formed at the end of 1916.

At the time of the opening of the *Reichsrat*, only one party—the Progressives—gave unqualified support to the revolutionary aims of the exiles. The leaders of other political parties desired reform, but within the framework of the Habsburg monarchy. They knew that the Entente Powers were not planning the dismemberment of the Austro-Hungarian state; their unwillingness to commit themselves was also strengthened by confidential information, received by several Czech politicians from the Emperor himself, that he was negotiating a separate peace, and that his efforts might soon bear fruit.[24] In Paris, Beneš realized the gravity of the situation; on 12 July 1917 he sent this message to Prague:

> On the whole, the military situation is good. In France there reigns a very bad mood, but the English and the Americans are our main hopes. The French are suffering a great deal, and therefore they would not hesitate to conclude a separate peace with Austria–Hungary in order to end the war sooner. The danger of a compromise with Austria–Hungary is greater than it appears. Only if you help us prove that it is impossible to preserve the monarchy will they continue to fight till the bitter end.[25]

In July, in spite of strong opposition from the military and the German nationalists, the Emperor granted amnesty to political prisoners: Kramář and Rašín, the two top Young Czechs, and Klofáč, the National Socialist leader, returned to Prague after a long absence. Their arrival, however, did not immediately strengthen the position of the radicals; on the contrary. Although the three men came back from prison as bitter enemies of the Empire, they found it difficult to come to terms with the changed political situation at home and abroad. The Union of the deputies and the National Committee had been set up in December 1916 [26] in order to protect Czech interests inside the Habsburg monarchy: in the summer of 1917 the two united bodies were still dominated by politicians loyal to the monarchy. From July 1917 until the end of the war, the Young Czechs and the National Socialists, together with the Progressives and the Realists, made repeated attempts to form a united radical party that would take over the leadership of Czech political life. Although on several occasions they came near to reaching agreement, they never succeeded in uniting their organizations.

Sharp differences on questions of social policy between the Young Czechs and the National Socialists emerged; although Kramář revised his ultra-conservative views on his return from prison, and his colleagues agreed at a meeting, on 21 October,

[24] Z. Tobolka, *Politické dějiny československého národa*, vol. 4, page 348, Prague 1936.
[25] *Dokumenty*, No. 36, page 135. [26] See above, page 115.

that after the war far-reaching social reforms would have to be put into practice, they could not keep up with the even more violent swing to the left of the National Socialists. Under the influence of the younger members of the executive committee, especially of Franke and Stříbrný, a new programme was worked out, and a new name, the 'Czechoslovak Socialist Party' was chosen. Although the programme took the creation of the Czechoslovak state for granted, it demanded far-reaching social reforms. It advocated nationalization of the means of production, partitioning of large landed property, and it acknowledged the existence of class struggle. The new style National Socialists also claimed membership of the International and offered to co-operate with the Social Democrats. The Young Czechs on the other hand formed, in February 1918, a united party with the smaller groups, the Progressives, the Moravian People's party, and the Realists: all hopes of an amalgamation with the National Socialists had been, by then, abandoned. The radicals did not come to control the Union of deputies and the National Committee through one powerful united party, as they had originally planned: their movement was split into a socialist and a non-socialist group.

Nevertheless, Klofáč had another criticism to make of the Young Czechs at the time when the question of amalgamation of the two parties began to be discussed. The National Socialists' chairman maintained that the Young Czechs were unable to put their own house in order: in the summer and autumn of 1917, their executive committee in Prague was dominated by the radicals, while most of their deputies were loyal to the monarchy. It took some time to tip the scales in favour of the radicals inside the party; Kramář achieved his first important success when, in October 1917, he dislodged the board, loyal to the monarchy, of his party's printing press. A few days later at a general meeting of the party, Kramář and Rašín welcomed the suggestion that loyalty to the monarchy would disqualify politicians from holding office in the future Czechoslovak state. The phrase 'nationally and politically unreliable' was used for the first time; the radicals frequently employed it against their rivals inside the party. In the end all Young Czech deputies, apart from Kramář, Rašín, and

Lukavský, were accused of being unreliable: in May 1918 the most prominent politicians among them, Fiedler, Maštálka, and Tobolka, started to publish their own newspaper. They argued that the political system envisaged by the radicals would weaken the middle class, by no means strong, and deprive it of its political power. The dissenting Young Czech deputies soon came to understand the futility of their efforts; ostracized inside their own party, some abandoned political life altogether while others sought admission to more accommodating political groups.

But all Czech parties were to go through a similar process to that of the Young Czechs. At the time of the reopening of the *Reichsrat* there were at least three radical deputies among the Social Democrats; nevertheless Šmeral, the party's chairman, still dominated the executive committee and, supported by Tusar, he was able to conduct the policy of his party on lines loyal to the Empire. In September 1917 Tusar went to Switzerland on a reconnaissance visit: he met Beneš there, and although, in Beneš's own words, he was 'careful and would not commit himself',[27] on his return to Prague Tusar threw in his lot with the radicals. Without his support Šmeral was unable to retain control of the executive of the party: at a general meeting of the Social Democrats at the end of September five radicals were elected to the committee. Šmeral resigned his chairmanship, and the party was free to pursue an anti-Habsburg policy.

Whereas the Young Czechs and the Social Democrats had to carry out drastic personal changes in order to radicalize their parties' policies, the Agrarians, and later the Catholics, suffered from no such upheavals. Švehla, the Agrarian leader, was a convinced opportunist: his policy of 'two irons in the fire' made it possible for him to be on good terms with both the radicals and the loyalists in Prague, while in Vienna, deputy Udržal maintained the party's connexions with the cabinet. Thus the political position of the Agrarians at any given time depended on Švehla's estimate of the respective temperature of the two irons; by the end of 1917 he was convinced that the Habsburg iron had become too hot to hold. After the Agrarians, the two clerical parties were

[27] Beneš, *Světová válka*, vol. 1, pages 475–476.

to travel on the same road. On 22 May 1918 the Christian Democrats, at their congress in Brno, demanded the 'transformation of the monarchy into a federal union of independent national states'.[28] The same view was held by the other clerical party, the National Catholics, and it was at this time that the two organizations decided to unite. Nevertheless, even the clericals came to understand that federalism was not a practicable policy and that it found little support in Vienna. On 10 September the executive committees of the two parties met to prepare the way for their unification: the new party, however, was expected to 'work in harmony with other Czech political organizations towards the creation of our own democratic Czechoslovak state, which would secure full freedom for the development of national, Christian, and also social justice'. On 29 September 1918 Šrámek, the chairman of the Christian Democrats, said at a meeting of the Union of deputies, that, in view of the attitude of the government, a loyal policy was out of the question, and that it was necessary to fight the government in an all-out effort, since the nation could not expect the fulfilment, by Vienna, of its demands for autonomy and independence.[29]

During the crucial period—from July 1917 until September 1918—the political attitudes of the Czechs largely depended on their relations with Vienna on the one hand, and on the other by the success or failure of the radicals working in exile. The government of Seidler, formed in August 1917 and dissolved a year later, did little to inspire the confidence of Slav politicians; its indifference to the national ferment among the peoples of the Habsburg monarchy was manifested on countless occasions. At a time when separate peace and federal reform held out the only hope for the survival of the Empire, Seidler kept alive the dualist system—the compromise of 1867 with the Hungarians was renewed, in December 1917, for another two years—and the alliance with Germany. The promise of constitutional reform 'on the basis of self-government and the preservation of the unity of the state' was the only concession the government made to the Austrian Slavs.

The first serious clash between Seidler's cabinet and the Czech

[28] *Hlas*, Brno, 24 May 1918. [29] Z. Tobolka, op. cit., vol. 4, page 297.

and the South Slav deputies occurred over the negotiations at Brest-Litovsk: the deputies demanded that the principle of national self-determination, contained in the Bolshevik offer of peace, should be recognized by the government and that representatives of the Habsburg peoples should take part in the negotiations with the Russians.[30] On 19 December Seidler turned down the latter demand; a few days later Czernin, the Foreign Minister, commented on the problem of self-determination:

> The question of citizenship of national groups that do not form an independent state, cannot be, from the point of view of the Central Powers, discussed on the international level. The question should be settled by each state with its nationalities in a constitutional manner.

The Foreign Minister's pronouncement became known in Prague on the same day as the news about the formation of a Czech army unit in France; the radicals were in no mood to take it lying down. The Union asked the speaker of the *Reichsrat* for a parliamentary discussion of the Foreign Minister's pronouncement; when he showed his unwillingness to allow the debate, the Union decided to publish an extra-parliamentary declaration. On 6 January the parliamentary deputies, together with a few delegates to the Czech, Moravian, and Silesian Diets met in Prague; whereas the radicals wanted a complete revision, in the parliamentary programme of May 1917, of those points that dealt with the relationship of the Czech state to the Habsburg dynasty, the loyalists insisted that the deputies declare their confidence in the monarchy and that a reference to the parliamentary programme of 1917 should be made. The resulting compromise favoured the radical demands; although the 'Epiphany declaration' contained a clause that stressed 'all the previous pronouncements at the *Reichsrat*', it censured the policy of the government:

> A lasting peace must rectify old injustices, abolish the brutal force of the supremacy of arms and the supremacy of states and nations over

[30] *Stenographische Protokolle des Hauses der Abgeordneten*, vol. 2, page 2395 46th meeting, 1917.

other nations. Only such a peace can safeguard the development of nations large and small; can liberate those peoples suffering under foreign rule. The right to a free national life and self-determination, whatever their size and irrespective of under whose rule the nations live, must become the basis of future international law, the guarantee of peace and friendly co-existence of nations.[31]

The declaration of the Union accepted the ideas of both the Bolsheviks and President Wilson on self-determination; it made no reference to the Habsburg state, and in this respect it was more radical than the international situation warranted. The Epiphany declaration appeared one day after the speech of Lloyd George on war aims, and two days before President Wilson announced his fourteen points;[32] although the American President made a reference to the 'principle of justice to all peoples and nationalities', neither his nor the British Prime Minister's address contained any plans for the dissolution of the Habsburg monarchy, an omission that seriously disturbed the radicals in Prague. Šámal, the Realist leader and the organizer of the Mafie, the secret radical society, sent an enquiry to Beneš in Paris, demanding an explanation as to what exactly was the official attitude of the Allies to the Austro-Hungarian monarchy, and whether they were intending to invite Czech representatives to the peace conference. In January 1918, however, Beneš was not in a position to give a satisfactory answer to the radicals in Prague; indeed, he was obliged to intensify his efforts to convince the Entente Powers that the Habsburg monarchy could no longer be saved.

Although the Epiphany declaration had left a back door open for use in the case of the survival of the Empire, and although Hruban, a Christian Democrat deputy, had made it abundantly clear in the *Reichsrat* that not all Czech representatives were enemies of the dynasty, Beneš and his friends in exile acclaimed the declaration of 6 January as an expression of the revolutionary situation in the Czech lands and as a recognition, by all the politicians at home, of the aims the radicals were pursuing abroad.

[31] Z. Tobolka, op. cit., vol. 4, page 316.

[32] See below, page 178.

Seidler, the Austrian Premier, took a similar view of the declaration to that of the exiles; on 22 January he described it as 'a fruit of war psychosis'.[33] Although Hruban informed Seidler that it had been drawn up on the basis of the programme of 30 May 1917,[34] the government did nothing to help the remaining loyal deputies, and continued to regard the Epiphany declaration as a radically anti-Habsburg act.

The Foreign Minister's indiscreet and impolitic speech to the Vienna city fathers on 2 April did not only elicit an explosive reply from Clemenceau, revealing the efforts of Emperor Karl to achieve a separate peace; it also convinced the remaining Czech loyalists that the government either did not know of their existence or was not interested in it. Czernin was convinced that the activities of Masaryk abroad and of the Czech politicians in the monarchy were complementary; he fired a salvo in the direction of Prague:

> Certain leaders of the nation, representatives of the people, try to undermine our alliance with Germany and issue resolutions which oppose the ideals of the state; they are unable to find a single word of condemnation for the Czech army, which criminally fights against its own country and her allies in arms; they also intend to steal parts of Hungary and they make speeches, protected by parliamentary immunity, which cannot be understood in any other way than as an appeal to the enemy states. . . . Again and again, in London, Rome and Paris they [the exiles] do their utmost to ensure that the fury of the war may continue. Poor, wretched Masaryk is not the only one of his kind: there are many such Masaryks inside the monarchy itself.[35]

Once again the Union of Czech deputies assembled to protest; but this time there were no dissenters, and the reply to Czernin of 13 April assumed the form of an impassioned national oath which took the foundation of a Czechoslovak state for granted. There were still no Slovak politicians present at the meeting which drafted the reply, but a number of South Slav deputies—Korošec,

[33] *Stenographische Protokolle*, vol. 3, page 2795.
[34] See above, page 124.
[35] *Hlas*, 5 April 1918.

Stefan Radić, Valerian Pribičević—witnessed the occasion. Although the military had no difficulty in suppressing unrest in the streets of Prague on the day of the publication of the reply, it made a deep impression on the Czechs and left them in no doubt that their political leaders had pronounced their final verdict on the Habsburg monarchy.

VII

THE TRIUMPH OF THE EXILES

The endeavour of the German General Headquarters to reduce the war to a one-front engagement was rewarded by a late, yet nevertheless spectacular, success in the spring of 1918. The Brest-Litovsk peace released the men and arms necessary for a forceful onslaught against the Allied lines: the *Kaiserschlacht*, as the Germans grandly called their offensive, was the largest operation hitherto mounted in the war. The balance of power on the western front was decidedly tipped in favour of Germany: the six divisions of the American Expeditionary Force, present in France, but not yet engaged in combat, could not counterbalance the forty German divisions transferred from the East. At 4.30 a.m. on 21 March 6,000 guns began to boom on the sector between Oise and Scarpe; the first thrust was directed against the weakest part of the British-held lines. In the next four months, the Germans were to retain the initiative on the western front; they launched four more attacks, took some 225,000 prisoners, and inflicted nearly a million casualties on the Allied armies. The offensive that brought Paris within the reach of the German guns and which, on several occasions, threatened to rend the English and French fronts asunder, made a profound impression in the war-weary capitals of Allied Europe. The possibilities of strengthening the front were explored and strategic concepts were hastily overhauled. Before the end of March, nearly a quarter of a million British reinforcements reached the battle-lines; Marshal Foch was put in charge of co-ordinating the action of the Allied armies on the western front. In the turbulent situation created by the *Kaiserschlacht*, the fate of the Habsburg monarchy was finally settled.

Before Germany's final bid for victory in the West, the Allied statesmen had neither decided on the break-up of the Habsburg

Empire nor given unqualified recognition to the aims of the exiles. Tsarist Russia alone had shown signs that it would not mourn the demise, or at least a radical decline in the power of the Danube monarchy. The western Allies, when they took over the problem from the Russians, pursued a policy of separate peace with Austria–Hungary; they were not practised in the new and complicated art of psychological warfare, and they did nothing to encourage the Habsburg peoples in opposition to their government. The two crucial pronouncements on the subject, which bore out the unwillingness of the western Allies to commit themselves, were made by Lloyd George on 5 January and by President Wilson three days later. In his address to the Trade Union Conference in London, the British Premier announced that:

> . . . though we agree with President Wilson that a break-up of Austria–Hungary is no part of our war aims, we feel that unless genuine self-government on true democratic principles is granted to these Austro-Hungarian nationalities who have long desired it, it is impossible to hope for the removal of those causes of unrest in that part of Europe which have so long threatened the general peace.[1]

The American President, in the tenth of his famous 'fourteen points', outlined a similar policy:

> The peoples of Austria–Hungary, whose place among the nations we wish to see safeguarded and assured, should be accorded the freest opportunity for autonomous development.[2]

The memorandum on war aims, adopted by the Inter-Allied Labour and Socialist conference a month before the launching of the German offensive in the West, shared the attitude of the two official pronouncements towards the survival of the Habsburg monarchy; it was, however, more encouraging to the exiles in pointing out that the

> . . . conference cannot admit that the claim of independence made by the Czecho-Slovaks and the Jugoslavs must be regarded merely as questions for internal decisions. National independence ought to be accorded, according to the rules to be laid down by the League of Nations, to such peoples as demand it, and these communities ought

[1] *USFR*, 1918, Supplement 1, vol. 1, page 9. [2] Idem, page 12.

to have the opportunity of determining their own groupings and federations according to their affinities and interests. If they think fit they are free to substitute a free federation of Danubian states for the Austro-Hungarian Empire.[3]

Concern with the internal arrangements of the monarchy, combined with the recognition on the part of the western Allies that it would survive, made a deep impression among the Czechs and the South Slavs. The radicals in Prague realized that the Epiphany declaration[4] had anticipated international events: they had believed that the Entente Powers took the dissolution of the Habsburg state for granted. Šámal, the organizer of the secret society in Prague, sent a highly agitated message to Beneš; although it never reached him, it was the opening move in a clandestine correspondence that had a profound effect on the development of the political situation inside Austria–Hungary. Šámal's message of 13 January[5] is valuable because it shows the current concerns of the radicals, their ignorance of the achievements and commitments of the exiles up to date, and the value they placed on the contacts with the political exiles. Šámal wrote, in the cryptic style of the secret correspondence:

Prague [the secret society] informs you that it is desperate and that it has no news from the National Council in Paris. Its trustworthiness suffers, and nobody believes that it has any connexions at all. . . . Prague begs for detailed and exact answers to the following questions:

1. Does the National Council in Paris know, officially or unofficially, the attitude of the Entente (of each particular Power) to the solution of the Czech question?

2. If it is known officially, how?—a treaty, gentlemen's agreement, etc.?

3. Has the Entente a minimal and maximal programme in the Czech question?

4. What is the minimal programme, which the Entente will carry out at any price? (This is important for our policy in Vienna.)

5. The frontiers of the Czechoslovak state?

[3] *USFR*, 1918, Supplement 1, vol. 1, page 162.

[4] See above, page 173.

[5] *Dokumenty*, pages 141–147.

6. Is the National Council agreed on the form of the state—monarchy or republic?

7. Who for the king?

8. Has the National Council agreed with the Entente (*a*) the amount of national debt the Czechoslovak state will have to carry (*b*) help by aid, currency reform, supply of raw materials, etc?

9. What will be the position of the Germans in Bohemia? Should the Czech parliamentary delegation in Vienna start making far-reaching promises to the Germans?

10 Has the National Council reckoned with the possibility of armed resistance of Bohemian Germans and Magyars against the Czechoslovak state?

11. How does the National Council evaluate Czech policy from 30 May 1917? Is there anything that should be changed? Directives!

12. Will the Czechoslovak army in France really consist of 120,000 men and where from? (America?) Does this army imply an official guarantee by the Entente (or only by France) of a Czechoslovak state?

13. What about a separate peace with Russia?

14. The Pope's attitude towards the Czechoslovak state?

15. Does the Entente (who?) still tolerate the Habsburg dynasty?

16. The attitude of Entente press and Entente working classes towards the Czechoslovak state.

17. How many and which newspapers have been won over for it?

18. What will happen to the Czechoslovaks in Russia in the case of a separate peace?

19. Does an agreement exist between the National Council and the Entente about Czech representatives at a peace conference? (*a*) only the National Council's representatives? (*b*) also from Austria–Hungary? (*c*) both? We beg you to answer the same questions concerning the Jugoslavs.

Although this message never reached the National Council in Paris, Beneš was not, in January 1918, in a position to supply answers that would have satisfied and encouraged the radicals in Prague. The members of the Mafie had, on the other hand, compelling reasons for closely questioning the council's secretary: they had not heard from him since the middle of July 1917 and they were unprepared for the new revolutionary wave spreading from Bolshevik Russia. Now, more than ever before, it was essential for them to be well informed about the activities of the exiles in the West. Nevertheless, until they had more concrete results to show, the emigrés were not very communicative; the first message from Beneš, after a gap of seven months, was dispatched from Paris on 8 February 1918; it merely informed the members of the Mafie that

> ... politically, we rely on France in particular, although we enjoy real sympathies from other allies as well ... it would be a great error to draw pessimistic conclusions from the speeches of Lloyd George and Wilson; in Italy, a vigorous movement has come to the surface for an agreement with the Slavs against Austria.[6]

In his request of 13 January for detailed information on the work of the exiles in the Entente countries, Šámal also asked Beneš to answer the same questions concerning the South Slavs: they had no such means of communication at their disposal as the Czechs; their exiles were still working in isolation, without any contact with the politicians at home. This, as we have already seen,[7] had facilitated their activities early in the war. After a good start, however, the South Slav exiles ran into serious difficulties. Wickham Steed, the British journalist, who took a keen interest in the Habsburg Slavs, remarked in his autobiography[8] that the South Slav committee was 'far less efficient than the Czechoslovak National Council under Masaryk and Štefánik'; its work was seriously hampered, early in 1917, by differences with Pašić, the Serbian Premier, on the organization of the future united state. Pašić was reluctant to accept the idea of a federation: he wanted Belgrade to play the leading role in a centralized state. Supilo, one of the founder members of the committee, left it several months before his death in September 1917; Trumbić, its chairman, complained that there was no future for him in politics and that he was thinking of emigrating to Buenos Aires and earning his living there as a taxi-driver.[9] The differences between the Serbian government and the exiles' committee were patched up in July of 1917; in the 'Corfu agreement', signed by Pašić and Trumbić, the Serbian Premier made certain concessions to the exiles. It attended to the

[6] *Dokumenty*, page 148. [7] See above, page 72.
[8] *Through Thirty Years*, vol. 2, page 165, London 1924.
[9] Idem, page 166.

desire of the Serbs, Croats, and Slovenes to form an 'independent national state' but it made no specific mention of federalism. Apart from a common flag there would be special Croat and Slovene flags and emblems. This concession may well have been interpreted by Trumbić as implying federal organization of the future kingdom, which it was agreed at Corfu, would 'include all territory compactly inhabited by our people'.

Pašić had had powerful supporters in Tsarist Russia; the disappearance of autocracy in Petrograd contributed to making the Serbian Premier more understanding towards the ambitions of the Habsburg South Slavs, and propelled him in the direction of an agreement with Trumbić. But the two men were agreed in their attitude to the Habsburg monarchy; they thought in terms of detaching large tracts of territory from Austria–Hungary. They were therefore bitterly disappointed when they found that the western Allies did not share their ideas. At Corfu, the temporary seat of the Serbian government, the American diplomatic representative interviewed the Serbian Acting Foreign Minister soon after the speech of Lloyd George of 5 January had become known to him; the American summed up his reactions in this manner:

> The speech of the British Premier as far as is known to me by apparently conclusive extracts has surprised, disillusioned, and given anxiety for the future and liberty of Servian people, having apparently renounced the principle that every people should have the right of self-disposition and of determining its destinies. Nothing is said of the desire and struggle of Servian people to unite, nor of Jugo-Slavia, which alone could be a strong bulwark against Austrian–German eastern pressure. . . . There is mention only of restoration of Servia and not of reparation as for Belgium although Servia has suffered more. The Serbs, Croatians and Slovenes have shown far greater determination for union and have made far greater efforts and sacrifices than peoples of the Trentino and Transylvania.[10]

When Pašić returned to Corfu a few days later, he spoke to the American representative in the same vein as his Foreign Minister had done: he added that if the Austro-Hungarian Empire was pre-

[10] *USFR*, 1918, Supplement 1, vol. 1, pages 790–791. Telegram of 22 January 1918, from the Special Agent at Corfu (Dodge) to the Secretary of State.

served, while its Polish, Rumanian, and Italian parts were separated—as both the British Premier and President Wilson had suggested—the Germans and the Magyars would become a majority capable of achieving complete Germanization of the Empire.[11]

In Corfu, the situation was regarded as extremely grave; several ministers in the Serbian government threatened to resign. Nevertheless, after the bitter disappointments, which the Czech radicals at home and abroad shared with the Serbs, Allied policy towards Austria–Hungary began to take a new shape: under the pressure of the events in Brest-Litovsk, and with the knowledge that Germany would soon be in a position to throw a considerable amount of troops from the East on to the western front, the Allies turned to the problems that had been created by the withdrawal of Russia from the war.

In Britain, the press lords were in control of the Ministry of Information: the Minister, Lord Beaverbrook, was assisted by Lord Rothermere, in charge of propaganda in neutral countries, and Lord Northcliffe, the Director of Propaganda in enemy territories. Although Northcliffe's acquaintance with the territories covered by his department was slight, he was assisted by a number of dedicated men, among them Wickham Steed and R. W. Seton-Watson.

Apart from their official activities as experts and propagandists, both men were engaged in journalism as well: Steed was the foreign editor of *The Times*, and Seton-Watson, since October 1916, had spent much of his time and money editing and writing the monthly *New Europe*. They were friends and protectors of Masaryk, Trumbić, and other emigré politicians and they were in complete agreement with the plans of the Czech and South Slav exiles. The Habsburg monarchy was Steed's principal enemy; although it is difficult to establish what exactly he had thought about the chances of Austria–Hungary's survival before the war,[12]

[11] *USFR*, 1918, Supplement 1, vol. 1, pages 790–791. Dodge's telegram to the Secretary of State of 28 January 1918.

[12] In the preface to the first edition of *The Hapsburg Monarchy*, published in London in 1913, Steed wrote on page ix: 'Errors, weakness, or prejudice on the part of the Monarch, of statesmen, or of races may, it is true, bring the monarchy to the verge of ruin; disaster may seem to portend the fulfilment of prophecies of disintegration; but I

in his memoirs,[13] he summed up his and Seton-Watson's position:

> From the outset, nay, even before the declaration of war, I was persuaded that Austria–Hungary would be the pivot of the struggle, and that, unless she was discomfited and transformed, if not dismembered, Germany could not be truly defeated. This persuasion I shared especially with my friend Dr. R. W. Seton-Watson, a young Scottish historian who had studied Austro-Hungarian problems assiduously for a decade and who, like me, enjoyed the confidence of the principal leaders of the non-German and non-Magyar races.

Steed and Seton-Watson became, in 1918, the first official practitioners of psychological warfare in Britain; although General Ludendorff congratulated the Allies, after the war, on their propaganda effort,[14] there is evidence that the Allied experts were, early in 1918, impressed by the German achievements in this field. At the inter-Allied propaganda conference in London at the end of February M. Henri Moysett, a student of central European affairs and the private secretary of the French Minister of Marine, who had been invited to London by Steed, argued that the Allies must launch a 'war of ideas' on Germany. He pointed at the success, since August 1917, of the German propaganda effort in Russia, which produced disastrous effects; he is reported to have said that this propaganda

> . . . had been conceived and carried out by a metaphysician who had clearly foreseen the shattering effect of Bolshevik doctrine on Russian minds.

M. Moysett added that:

> . . . in view of the military position, Allied propaganda must aim on the one hand at quick results, and, on the other, at the transformation

have been unable to perceive during ten years of constant observation and experience—years, moreover, filled with struggle and crisis—any sufficient reason why, with moderate foresight on the part of the dynasty, the Hapsburg dynasty should not retain its rightful place in the European community. Its internal crises are often crises of growth rather than of decay.' In a letter to *The Times Literary Supplement* of 13 August 1954, Steed wrote 'When I left Vienna in July, 1913, it was with a feeling that I was escaping from a doomed edifice.'

[13] Op. cit., vol. 2, page 38. [14] *My War Memoirs*, London 1919, vol. 1, page 367.

of the state of mind prevailing in enemy countries. Therefore it should be directed in the first place against Austria–Hungary and be based upon the aspirations of the subject Habsburg races without forgetting that even among the Magyars there were potentially anti-Habsburg elements.[15]

Indeed, as the Allied propaganda campaign against the Habsburg monarchy developed, it came to resemble the activities of the 'metaphysicians' in the *Wilhelmstrasse*. The western Allies came to use the exiles from the Habsburg monarchy in the same manner as the Germans had used Lenin and the nationalist movements in Russia.

Wickham Steed had, however, been working on the lines suggested by M. Moysett before the meeting of the Allied propaganda experts in London. In the middle of February, he drafted a memorandum for Northcliffe; the policies it advocated came to be accepted gradually as the basis of the British and Allied policy towards Austria–Hungary. The foreign editor of *The Times* wrote:

> There are two conceivable policies for the Department of Propaganda in Enemy Countries. They are (*a*) to work for a separate peace with the [Austrian] Emperor, the Court and the aristocracy, on the principle of not interfering with the domestic affairs of the Hapsburg monarchy and of leaving its territory almost or quite intact; or (*b*) to try to break the power of Austria–Hungary, as the weakest link in the chain of enemy states, by supporting and encouraging all anti-German and pro-Ally peoples and tendencies.
>
> The (*a*) policy has been tried without success. The Hapsburgs are not free agents. They have not the power, even though they may wish to break away from Germany because, (1) they are controlled by the internal structure of their dominions [the Dual System] which gives Germany decisive leverage over them through the Germans of Austria and the Magyars of Hungary; and, (2) because the Allies cannot offer them acceptable terms without breaking with Italy. It remains to try the (*b*) policy. This policy is not primarily, or even, in the last resort, anti-Hapsburgian; it is not opposed to the interests of the Roman Catholic religion; and it is in harmony with the declared aims of the Allies.

[15] W. Steed, op. cit., vol. 2, page 192.

After giving a brief description of the ethnic composition of the Habsburg monarchy, Steed concluded:

There are thus in Austria–Hungary as a whole some 31,000,000 anti-Germans and some 21,000,000 pro-Germans. The pro-German minority rules the anti-German majority. Apart from questions of democratic principle, the policy of the Allies should evidently be to help and encourage the anti-Germans.[11]

Before incorporating Steed's memorandum in a letter to Balfour, the Secretary of State for Foreign Affairs, Northcliffe asked his adviser to recommend the means by which the anti-German group in the Habsburg monarchy could be encouraged: Steed willingly complied with the request. He advocated that the Allied governments should insist on 'democratic freedoms' for the Habsburg peoples, while dropping expressions like 'self-government' and 'autonomous development' from their pronouncements. Although Steed was of the opinion that the Allies should stop making statements that they did not wish to dismember Austria–Hungary, he said that the Habsburgs, under Allied pressure, might be driven to assist in a radical transformation of their dominions. He also recommended the utilization, for propaganda purposes, of the various exile organizations such as the Czechoslovak National Council, the South Slav Committee and the various Polish organizations, and the encouragement of the

. . . present tendency of the Italian government to shelve the policy embodied in the London treaty of 26 April 1915 and to adopt a policy of agreement with the anti-German races of Austria–Hungary.

Finally, Steed announced that the aim of the Allied policy should not be the creation of a 'number of small disjointed states', but that a non-German federation of central European and Danubian states should be formed, and that, on the other hand, the 'Germans of Austria should be free to join the Confederated States of Germany'.[17]

In his memorandum and in the subsequent recommendations to Northcliffe, Steed was guided by several and in some respects

[16] Steed, op. cit., vol. 2, pages 187–188.
[17] Idem, pages 188–189.

contradictory considerations: while he was genuinely trying to assist the military effort of the Entente, he was also moved by a desire to help his emigré friends; he was also expounding his private views on the post-war organization of eastern Europe; finally, he did not want to offend the sensitivities of the Foreign Office. Steed must have been aware of the fact that Balfour had no particular liking for either the Minister or the Ministry of Information, and that he was going to be suspicious of the suggestions emanating from Crew House.[18] This was why Steed tried to hold his views on the inevitability of the break-up of the Habsburg monarchy in check by suggesting that his policy was not necessarily anti-Habsburg and that the dynasty might, under pressure, adopt a policy of reform. At this time, Steed was convinced that the monarchy could not survive, that the policy of a separate peace was pointless, and that there was every reason for doing everything to speed up Austria–Hungary's final agony. Although Steed tried hard not to let this conviction jeopardize the acceptability and smooth passage of his memorandum through the Foreign Office, it nevertheless came to the surface when he advised against the employment of terms such as 'self-government' and 'autonomous development'. He argued that they 'should be avoided because they have a sinister meaning in Austria–Hungary, and tend to discourage the friends of the Allies'. Steed simply meant that, when such terms were used, the continued existence of the Habsburg monarchy was taken for granted. There were, however, more serious flaws in his reasoning: in contemplating the possibility of a non-German Danubian federation on the one hand, and of the Austrian Germans joining the 'Confederated States of Germany' on the other, Steed not only ignored the ethnic realities of central and eastern Europe, but he also underestimated the refractory force of unbridled nationalism. He clearly had not consulted his Czech friends about the future of the Austrian Germans: the exiles, as much as the politicians in Prague, would have abhorred his suggestion.

Indeed, Balfour's reply of 26 February to Northcliffe's letter[19]

[18] Lord Beaverbrook, *Men and Power*, page 289, London 1959.
[19] Steed, op. cit., vol. 2, page 189.

either misunderstood or deliberately rode roughshod over Steed's painstaking subtleties. It also demonstrated that the Foreign Secretary neither believed that the fate of the Habsburg monarchy could be settled in London, nor that he had any intention of having his policy dictated by the Ministry of Information. He wrote:

> Your very lucid memorandum raises in one shape or another the fundamental problem of the Hapsburg Empire. A final and authoritative answer to the question you put to me can be given (if given at all) by the Cabinet, speaking in the name of the Government. . . . If the two alternative policies of dealing with the Dual Monarchy set forth in your paper were mutually exclusive, and if they involved distinct and even opposite methods of propaganda, our position would be more difficult than it is. . . . Fortunately, our position is not quite so embarrassing. As you point out with unanswerable force, everything which encourages the anti-German elements in the Hapsburg dominions really helps to compel the Emperor and the Court to a separate peace, and also diminishes the efficiency of Austria–Hungary as a member of the Middle Europe combination.

Steed tried to counter the line Balfour had taken in another letter he drafted for Northcliffe; he pointed out that

> . . . the two policies may not be mutually exclusive in the last resort, but it is very important that one or the other be given an absolute precedence. It would place me in an awkward predicament if, after basing vigorous propaganda on the (*b*) policy I would be confronted with some manifestations of the (*a*) policy on the part of the British or other allied government.[20]

Balfour did not reply in writing; while the inter-Allied conference of propagandists was meeting in London, Northcliffe and Steed were told simply to base their effort on policy (*b*)—that is, to support and encourage all anti-German and pro-Ally peoples in Austria–Hungary—but without promising them independence.

Steed was not satisfied with his qualified success in convincing the Foreign Office of the merits of his policy: soon, however, an opportunity presented itself for another attack on Balfour's stonewalling attitude. The importance of a *rapprochement* between the

[20] Steed, op. cit., vol. 2, page 190.

Italians and the South Slavs was one of Steed's preoccupations: he had begun to work for it at the end of 1917; soon, this approach paid dividends. The secret treaty of London had alienated the Serbian government and the South Slav Committee on the one hand, and the Italians on the other: they were allies only in name. The Jugoslavs came to look upon the Italians as the potential usurpers of the Dalmatian coast, who might become more difficult to dislodge than Austria–Hungary itself. The first attempt at improvement in their relations was made in December 1917 when General Mola, the Italian military attaché in London, Major Filippo de Filippi, the head of the Italian information bureau in London, and Guglielmo Emanuel, the correspondent of *Corriere della Sera* met Trumbić, the chairman, and three other members of the South Slav Committee at Wickham Steed's house.[21] (Steed also acted as the Chairman of the Serbian Society of Great Britain.) At the meeting Steed argued that the moment was inopportune for the cultivation of national susceptibilities, that if the Allies were defeated the promises to both parties would go by the board anyway, and that it should be possible to find a compromise between the Italian policy based on the treaty of London and the South Slav declaration of Corfu. Furthermore, if the Italians came to an understanding with the South Slavs, Steed said, it would be possible to 'stimulate a movement among the Southern Slav troops of Austria–Hungary in favour of unity, and, consequently, of defection from the Habsburgs'. After the disastrous defeat at Caporetto in September, such arguments carried weight with the Italians; General Mola said that the treaty of London was not inspired by hostility to the South Slavs and that, at any rate since the Russian revolution, the whole Slav problem had to be looked at in a different light. Trumbić, however, pertinently pointed out that the London treaty still existed and that he saw no possibility of an agreement. Sir Arthur Evans, a member of the Serbian Society present at the meeting, in order to pacify Trumbić and thus cut the South Slav–Italian knot, took a rather extreme stand: he argued that the London treaty had lost its *raison d'être* because it had been concluded

[21] Steed, op. cit., vol. 2, page 168 et seq.

at a time when it was generally supposed that the monarchy would survive the war, whereas now the Danubian Empire was certain to be dissolved. (It was, incidentally, from private pronouncements such as this one by Sir Arthur that the exiles derived their hope and optimism in the days before the official recognition of their aims.) At the meeting at Steed's house, the outlines of an eventual compromise began to emerge; in Italy itself, a group of politicians—deputies in both the Upper and the Lower Houses and a number of newspapers and newspapermen, among them *Corriere della Sera* and a young journalist called Benito Mussolini—began to work for an understanding with Serbia and the South Slavs.

This was the situation when Steed left London for Italy. Shortly after the conclusion, at the beginning of March, of the inter-Allied conference on psychological warfare in London, the foreign editor of *The Times* arrived at the Italian headquarters. Once there, he was soon able to establish the fact that Italian intelligence officers were in complete agreement with him on the best means of breaking down the cohesion of the Austrian-held lines. The Italians maintained that the various exiles' committees should proclaim the political independence of their respective peoples, and that the British, the French, and the Italian governments should 'authorize' these proclamations. At this point, however, Steed was obliged to hint at Balfour's strictures, but, he added, given two days he would try to win the British government over to promising independence to the Habsburg nationalities; in the meantime, leaflets for distribution in enemy lines should be prepared on the assumption that the British government would comply with his request.[22] Steed dispatched a telegram to Northcliffe, urgently requesting the authorization, by the War Cabinet, of the proclamation of Czechoslovak, Polish, South Slav, and Rumanian independence. Thirty-six hours later, Steed was informed of the government's agreement.

There are, however, striking inaccuracies in the story as told by Steed. He gives the impression that it was the British government that needed converting, and that the Italians did not. He

[22] Steed, op. cit., vol. 2, page 205.

glosses over the fact that the position of the Italian cabinet was, at the time, more intractable than that of the British or the French: Sonnino, the Foreign Minister, was a dedicated defender of the Pact of London; he would do nothing to jeopardize Italian prospects of territorial acquisitions on the eastern coast of the Adriatic. Thus the intelligence officers who had outlined to Steed their attitude to the problem of propaganda had either acted without the agreement of their government and in contradiction to its policies, or were prepared, in order to achieve results at the front as quickly as possible, to make empty promises. There is a third possibility: Steed, in his zeal to proceed on the lines suggested in his memorandum,[23] put his own words into the mouths of the Italians, and impressed them, once again, on the British government. But there were other reasons, apart from Steed's powers of persuasion, for the speedy assent by London. The German offensive in the West was about to be or had already been launched. (The exact date of the exchange of the telegrams is impossible to establish; Steed had left London for Italy *circa* 16 March.) The hopes for a separate peace with Austria–Hungary were also waning. At the beginning of April, the French government had an opportunity to appreciate to the full the futility of the Revertera–Armand and other secret negotiations; the exchanges between President Wilson and Emperor Karl began, by the end of March, to look unpromising and the negotiations that had taken place in December of the previous year, between Smuts and Mensdorff, clearly demonstrated to the British government the difficulties of achieving an understanding with Austria–Hungary.

The Allied propaganda offensive was conceived on a grand scale. It went into action in the first days of April under the supervision of a central inter-Allied commission set up at the Italian Headquarters, which included representatives of the South Slav, Czechoslovak, and Polish exiles' committees. It was the second onslaught on the morale of the Austro-Hungarian army in 1918; the first one had come from Russia, when Trotsky exploited the Brest-Litovsk negotiations for broadcasting subversive Bolshevik ideas westwards.[24]

[23] See above, page 185. [24] See above, page 133.

Soon after the launching of the leaflet campaign on the Italian front, the *rapprochement*, still unofficial, between the South Slavs and the Italians culminated in a meeting of the 'oppressed nationalities' in Rome. From 8–11 April representatives of Habsburg Slavs, of Serbia and Rumania, together with Italian and French politicians and journalists—the chairman of the 'Rome Congress' was Senator Ruffini—assembled in the Italian capital. In spite of Steed's insistence, Sonnino refused to take part in it: the Foreign Minister, when turning down the invitation, said that 'I should compromise the government and expose it to attacks from various quarters, were I publicly to tear up the Treaty of London, the only "scrap of paper" that exists today between Italy and the Allies.' The exiles knew that the best way of appealing to the Entente governments was by stressing the military potentialities of their movements: the most active of the four committees that carried on the work of the Congress were those dealing with the army and with propaganda. They demanded that the 'Allied states admit as combatants all those expressing their desire to be liberated from the German–Magyar yoke and made independent states'.[25] In return for their services, the exiles in Rome expected official recognition of their aims: they were disappointed when they saw that this was not forthcoming. But their cause had made some advances since January. The value of their subversive propaganda against the Habsburg monarchy had been recognized by the Allied military authorities; they had been given an opportunity, for the first time during the war, to try their hand at undermining the morale of the Austro-Hungarian troops: they could claim the full support of the Entente while doing so.

At the meeting of the 'oppressed nationalities' in Rome the South Slavs and the Czechs were more nervous than either the Poles or the Rumanians about the recognition of their aims by the Allies. Although Serbia had been promised—in the event of the Entente being able to dictate peace conditions to the Central Powers—Bosnia and Hercegovina, with an outlet to the Adriatic,

[25] *USFR*, 1918, Supplement 1, vol. 1, page 796. Telegram from the Ambassador in Italy to the Secretary of State, 12 April 1918.

the promise did not embrace the unification of all South Slavs, which, in turn, conflicted with the Italian government's adherence to the London treaty. The Czechs, on the other hand, knew that their plans implied not merely territorial losses, but the complete break-up of the Habsburg monarchy. This is why Beneš in Rome insisted that

> . . . the Empire no longer exists, it is slowly but surely falling apart; this was proved by the declaration of our deputies and by the speeches in the parliament and in Prague.[26]

The Poles were in a more favourable situation at the time; Zamorski, one of their representatives in Rome, defined the differences that set aside his nation from the rest of the 'oppressed nationalities'. Although he conceded that the Poles were united with other peoples in their resistance to the Habsburg Empire, Zamorski pointed out that without the defeat of Germany Poland could not be united, and therefore it was Berlin, and not Vienna, that was the principal enemy of the Poles.[27] Nevertheless, the presence of a Polish delegation at the congress in Rome was made possible by a radical change in the views of the Poles in the Allied countries which had begun under the impression of the momentous events in Russia. Beneš complained—quite unfairly—that no co-operation with the Poles had been possible before the revolution: they pinned their hopes either on Austria or on Russia. But Beneš had to concede[28] that as early as the spring of 1916, Roman Dmowski, the leader of the National Democrats, predicted the fall of the Tsarist régime, and criticized the western Allies and also the Czech radicals in exile for making too many concessions to Russia. Dmowski's National Committee for Co-operation with the Russian government had retreated from Congress Poland with the Russian armies; it was transferred from Petrograd to Paris soon after the Bolshevik revolution. Dmowski himself, however, went to work for the cause of a united Poland in the western Entente countries while the provisional govern-

[26] Beneš, *Světová revoluce*, vol. 2, page 109.
[27] Idem, page 109. [28] Idem, page 98.

ment was still in power in Russia. He saw Balfour in May 1917; he told the Foreign Secretary that

. . . now, when the Tsar has gone, the Entente Nations ought to announce publicly that they are going to establish an independent Poland; and if you do not do that, there is a great danger that the Germans may succeed in the future in doing what they have failed to do in the past, which is to raise a Polish army.

And Balfour went on to sum up Dmowski's arguments:

His view was, that the recruiting of this Polish army had largely failed because the magnates whether ecclesiastical or lay in Poland had taken an oath of allegiance to the Tsar and were not prepared to break it. The Tsar has gone, the oath has gone, and he declared that his view was that the constant pressure of Germany, after this particular doubt had been removed, might succeed in producing this great addition to her manpower. If it did, the effect on the Allied cause would undoubtedly be most serious. He put the number down at 700,000–1,000,000. Supposing that Poland came in in that way, on the side of the Central Powers, and supposing that Russia fell into disorganization and military chaos, the whole of the position in the East would have changed disastrously for the worse.[29]

But Balfour was not convinced by Dmowski: he commented that he would rather see an autonomous Poland under Russia, because an independent Polish state would cut off Russia from the West, and

. . . if Germany has designs in the future upon France or the West, I think she will be protected by this new State from any action on the part of Russia, and I am not at all sure that is to the interest of Western civilization.

Two months later, however, the British Embassy in Washington sent a note to the Department of State, reversing Balfour's earlier standpoint.[30] The British government pointed out that,

[29] Balfour's statement on foreign policy to the Imperial War Council. The British Foreign Secretary sent an undated copy of his speech to Lansing, the Secretary of State, on 18 May 1917. *USFR*, Lansing Papers, vol. 2, page 27.

[30] *USFR*, 1917, Supplement 2, vol. 1, page 759. The note was dated 23 July 1917.

according to intelligence reports—clearly from Polish sources—the Germans were having difficulties in Poland and that

> . . . the efforts of the Polish people to obtain their freedom and their independence should be supported in every possible way, and that they should be similarly discouraged from listening to the specious assurances of the enemy of a spurious independence.

In July 1917, the Americans hardly needed converting to this point of view. Before the United States' entry into the war, Paderewski, a famous pianist and an ardent patriot had already been active there; soon after his arrival in New York in the autumn of 1915, he embarked on a one-man crusade, during which he used his fame as an artist first to gain access to, and subsequently to influence, the highest political circles in the United States. Indeed, Paderewski was the most striking example in exile politics of the mixture of the artist and the propagandist; the sculptor Meštrović performed a similar function for the South Slavs and Masaryk was inspired, by Paderewski, to deliver an impromptu lecture on the connexions between art and politics. In November 1915, the pianist met Colonel House, the influential adviser of President Wilson; the following month Paderewski achieved his first political success when he persuaded the Colonel that the American voluntary aid should be distributed by the Polish National Committee, and not by an international organization. In the summer of the following year, Paderewski visited the White House for the first time.[31] These were the beginnings of an extremely important association for the future of Poland, which started bearing fruit early in 1917. In a speech on 22 January Wilson maintained that 'statesmen everywhere are agreed that there should be a united, independent, and autonomous Poland': statesmen were not altogether agreed on this, nor did many of them—especially in Petrograd—approve of the President's remarks. Nevertheless, he emerged as the most powerful advocate, among the politicians of the neutral countries, of the Polish cause. A year later, when the United States were taking part in the war

[31] T. Komarnicki, *Rebirth of the Polish Republic*, page 144 et seq., London 1957.

and Soviet Russia was in the process of withdrawing from it, the thirteenth of Wilson's 'fourteen points' stated:

> An independent Polish state should be erected, which should include the territories inhabited by indisputably Polish populations, which should be assured a free and secure access to the sea, and where political and economic independence and territorial integrity should be guaranteed by international covenant.[32]

The Rumanians also enjoyed a special position. Like Italy, Rumania had been tempted to try its luck in the war by a secret treaty with the Entente governments that promised it territorial acquisitions at the expense of Austria–Hungary; the Rumanians, perhaps more than any other nation represented at the Rome congress, knew that the fulfilment of their ambitions depended on the military success of the Allies. After the disastrous failure of Rumania's war effort, its government was, in March 1918, about to conclude a peace with the Central Powers; in Rome, apart from a small number of exiles from Transylvania, there were deputies from the Bucharest parliament who wanted to keep alive their country's alliance with the Entente. Although there was no Rumanian organization comparable to the Polish or Czech national committees in exile, the Rumanians maintained good relations with other political emigrations, and with the Czech in particular. Indeed, they appear to have been the only group in exile that contained men concerned with the post-war organization of the Danubian area. This was rather a neglected feature of emigré politics. In his memorandum for Northcliffe, Steed had recommended the creation of a non-German federation of central European and Danubian states;[33] the idea fell into abeyance during the fast-moving final months of the war. The majority of the exiles, on the other hand, had no constructive plans: they were absorbed in an essentially destructive task, and they gave little thought to political arrangements after the war. Beneš, remembering his talks in Paris with Take Ionescu—they first met in October 1917—wrote:

[32] See above, page 178; *USFR*, 1918, Supplement 1, vol. 1, pages 12–17.
[33] See above, page 186.

. . . he was one of the politicians who could discuss all the post-war problems of central Europe; I agreed with everything he said when he talked about our future co-operation; from that time I was bound to these eminent Rumanian politicians [Ionescu and Titulescu] not only by common interests, but also by common views on friendly relations, which, after the end of the war, often helped us to protect the interests of our states in our common struggles and difficulties.[34]

Such references to co-operation among the nationalities after the war are rare: in the initial stages of their work, the exiles had been too uncertain of their position in the Entente countries and of their aims; later, in 1918, they were too busy to discuss the future, not to speak of making commitments on the lines that Steed had suggested. At the same time, the first areas of friction between the exiles began to emerge: the Rumanians and the South Slavs were disputing the Banat (the Banat, apart from Transylvania and Bukovina, had been promised to Rumania by the secret treaty with the Entente of August 1916, that secured Rumania's entry into the war), the Poles and the Czechs were not agreed about the future of Teschen, and the question of who should inherit the north-eastern tip of Hungary—Carpathian Russia—threatened relations between the Rumanians and the Czechs.

Although the Allies disappointed the representatives of the 'oppressed nationalities' assembled in Rome by not officially acknowledging their aims, they had begun, in the spring of 1918, to appreciate the propaganda value of the exiles' movements. The radicals in emigration did, however, command another argument that made for the recognition of their aims: this was their direct contribution of manpower to the Entente war effort. Early in the war, the South Slavs had launched a vigorous recruitment campaign among their compatriots in the United States and South America;[35] the Poles and the Czechs followed their example. As early as May 1917—soon after the fall of the Tsarist régime in Russia—the French government allowed the Poles to form their own units; a month later, President Poincaré issued a decree that made possible the formation of a Polish army on French soil, an

[34] *Světová válka a naše revoluce*, vol. 2, page 104. [35] See above, page 71.

army that was to fight 'under the Polish flag and under the supreme command of the French'. While the Poles on the Allied side were making good progress, their compatriots fighting alongside the armies of the Central Powers began to run into serious difficulties. Many troops in Pilsudski's Legion had refused to take an oath that would have meant the incorporation of their unit into the German army; in July 1917, Pilsudski himself was interned by the Germans in the Magdeburg fortress prison, where he was to spend the rest of the war. Five days after the conclusion of peace between the Central Powers and the Ukraine, in February 1918, the second Brigade of the Legion, commanded by General Haller, an Austrian officer of Polish descent, deserted the Austro-Hungarian front line in Bukovina. A few months later, Haller became the commander of the Polish Army in France. In December 1917, Beneš succeeded in convincing the French government that the Czechs were also capable of organizing their own units; on 7 February a detailed convention, signed by Clemenceau and by the secretary of the Czechoslovak National Council, and similar to the French–Polish agreement, was published.[36] In Italy, the Czech prisoners of war formed their own unit, which was, in the spring of 1918, approved by the government and successfully employed on the front; those Poles in Italy who wanted to volunteer for service were sent to join their army in France. Of all these units, the Czecho-Slovaks in Russia came to play the most prominent role in the war effort of the Entente.

The Czech Legion had rapidly expanded in the period between Masaryk's arrival in Russia in May 1917 and the Bolshevik revolution in November; together with his aides, the chairman of the National Council had succeeded in persuading some 30,000 prisoners of war to take part in the struggle against Austria–Hungary.[37] The Russian provisional governments had recognized the usefulness of the Czech troops but the situation changed when the Bolsheviks came to power. The men in the Legion were intensely imbued with national ideals; their leaders had little sympathy with the Bolshevik aims; they were determined to fight the same Powers with which Lenin—if his régime were to survive

[36] *Dokumenty*, page 329 et seq. [37] See above, page 131 et seq.

—had to conclude peace. At the time of the Bolshevik revolution there were some 37,000 volunteers concentrated on the front in southern Ukraine, west of the river Dnieper. They were formally a part of the French army; their political leaders were hoping to have them transferred to the western front. Masaryk was determined that his troops should remain neutral towards Russian internal developments; two days after the Bolshevik seizure of power, on 9 November, he sent a circular to the commanding officers of the Legion, reminding them that 'the Czechoslovak army cannot be employed in Russian internal conflicts, but only against Russia's external enemies'.[38] The first opportunity to put this policy into practice presented itself shortly after the November revolution, when a Czech unit, commanded by a Russian officer, was withdrawn from the front and took part in the defence of Kiev against the Bolsheviks; after a few days' fighting, the unit was recalled and the officer deprived of his command.[39]

Indeed, both the Bolsheviks and the Czechs tried, in the first months after the revolution, to maintain scrupulously correct relations. Lenin's government did not oppose the transfer of the Czech troops to France: in the middle of February, the representatives of the Russian branch of the National Council concluded an agreement with Muraviev, the Soviet commander in the Ukraine, that guaranteed the Czechs a free withdrawal from the territory under his command; further negotiations were carried on in Moscow. On 26 March Stalin, at that time People's Commissar for Nationalities, telegraphed the National Council:

> The Council of People's Commissars regards the suggestion of the Czechoslovak army corps as justified and completely acceptable, if the Czechoslovak units immediately set out on their journey to Vladivostok and if all counter-revolutionary commanding officers are removed. The Czechoslovaks will not travel as fighting units but merely as a group of free citizens, carrying a certain amount of weapons for self-protection against the counter-revolutionaries.[40]

Although no armed conflict flared up before May, the temporary peace between the Czechs and the Bolsheviks was far from

[38] *Dokumenty*, page 629.

[39] Margarete Klante, *Von der Wolga zum Amur*, Berlin 1931, page 118.

[40] *Dokumenty*, page 635.

stable. The collapse of the eastern front was a matter of profound concern to Russia's Allies; the Czech radical leaders, on the other hand, were entirely dependent on the goodwill of the Allied statesmen and therefore unlikely to resist their decisions—if these conflicted with their own plans—as to the employment of the Legion in Russia; finally, a number of the Czechoslovak officers were inimical to the Soviet régime, and disapproved of the policy of non-intervention.

After the November revolution, the attitude of the western Entente Powers to Russia was divided: the desire to re-establish the front in the East was the only unifying factor in their policy and it was bound to come into conflict with Lenin's peace plans. Nor were the Allied missions agreed on their attitude to the Bolsheviks; whereas the British and the Americans were at first inclined to explore the chances of co-operation, the French, and their military mission in particular, gave active support to the adversaries of the Bolsheviks. With their policies based on conflicting, and frequently misleading, reports from Russia, the Allied governments found it impossible, until July 1918, to achieve agreement.[41] However, the arguments against a conciliatory policy towards the Bolsheviks were powerful; nor were they derived from the Russian situation only. At the beginning of February, the Allied representatives to the Rumanian government reported that Mr. Bratianu, the Premier, was reminding them of the sacrifices that his country had made for the Allied cause and particularly of its difficult situation arising from the rupture with the Bolsheviks. Bratianu recalled that '. . . it was in agreement with us that he undertook police action against the Maximalist elements on the Russian front'.[42] The police action by the Rumanians preceded the landing of the first Allied forces on Russian soil. On 11 March the British Navy sailed into Murmansk; the Royal Marines later

[41] It is outside the scope of this study to attempt to trace, in detail, the hardening of the Allied policy towards the Bolshevik régime; this has been done with consummate skill in George Kennan's *The Decision to Intervene* (London 1958) the second volume of Soviet-American relations, 1917–1920. Cf. page 345 et seq.

[42] *USFR*, Supplement 1, vol. 1, page 75. The Ambassador to France [Sharp] to the Secretary of State. Telegram of 6 February 1918 based on a joint telegram from the Ministers of the United States, France, England, and Italy, dated Jassy, 5 February.

landed with the consent of the local Soviet to protect the valuable military stores; the landings in Vladivostok at the beginning of April completed the Allied blockade of Russia.

These operations had taken place before the governments in London, Paris, and Washington agreed to embark on the course of intervention in Russia; reaching the agreement to intervene was as half-hearted a process as its subsequent execution. The attention of the French and the British governments was riveted on the military developments on the western front, which absorbed all their military potential; although Japan was the only Power able and willing to dispatch considerable forces to Siberia, Washington resolutely opposed such action. The Czech Legion therefore became—apart from the indigenous Russian counter-revolutionary forces—the only potentially effective instrument of intervention. But the conflict between the Czechs and the Bolsheviks also anticipated the Allied decision to intervene: indeed, the easy initial victories of the Czechs over the weak forces of the revolution were to become a powerful argument in the hands of the advocates of intervention.

The vacillations of Allied policy in Russia were reflected in the attitudes of the Czech revolutionary leaders. Masaryk was not in a position to pursue a policy contrary to the wishes of his protectors; his genuine desire to keep the Legion out of Russian entanglements could be put into practice only with the approval and help of the Allies. When he left Moscow on 7 March to continue his work in the United States, he believed that the future of the Czech army was settled: that it would be withdrawn as speedily as possible and transferred to the western front. But at the time of Masaryk's departure there were already signs that the Allies had different plans for the Legion. The chairman of the National Council missed, by a few days, a communication from the French Foreign Ministry, signed by Paul de Margerie and dated 11 March:

The Minister of War informed me on 4 March that, according to the reports of the Czech delegates imparted to General Niessel in Russia, M. Masaryk arrived at a compromise with the Bolsheviks which would make it possible for the Czech units to remain. In these conditions the chief of the French military mission in Russia gave the Czechs the freedom to negotiate, and closed the negotiations that he himself had opened at the order of the Minister of War, on the transfer of these units to France.[43]

Masaryk would have been puzzled by the communication had he received it when still in the Russian capital; it completely misunderstood the nature of the Czech agreements with the Bolsheviks. Soon, the American State Department became interested in Masaryk: while he was still undertaking the long and perilous journey across Siberia, Lansing, the Secretary of State, advised the Ambassador in Tokyo to intercept him; the conversation between the two men took place in the middle of April.[44] Masaryk gave the Ambassador his views on the situation in Russia; they were, in fact, arguments against the policy of intervention. He gave it as his opinion that the Bolshevik government would survive for some time, and that it would then be replaced by a coalition of Bolsheviks, Socialists, and Liberals; he saw no future for the Cadets and other 'moderate elements'. The Czech leader, in the words of the Ambassador's telegram, thought it 'possible that the Bolsheviks, with aid and sympathy of Allies, could organize within a year a substantial army to oppose German aggression'.

In the meantime in Paris, Beneš, the secretary of the National Council, came to understand that the French and the British views on the employment of the Legion were different from those of Masaryk; he was clearly aware of the possibilities the situation offered for the strengthening of the position of the National Council. Whereas Masaryk had had a better opportunity of observing the Legion against the background of the events in Russia, Beneš, who himself remarked that he 'had no connexions with the army in Russia',[45] had a keener understanding of the Allied plans. From the beginning of March, he had negotiated with the French government and the Allied military authorities at Ver-

[43] *Dokumenty*, page 633.
[44] *USFR*, 1918, Russia, vol. 2, page 122. Telegram of 13 April 1918.
[45] *Světová revoluce*, vol. 2, page 184.

sailles about the employment and the transport of the Legion; on 1 April he received a message from the French military attaché in London, expressing doubts as to whether the army could reach Europe. The British War Office had indicated that there was a serious shortage of shipping facilities and that, at any rate, if the Czech army was really of any military value, it could be used in Russia itself.[46] Beneš commented on the communication from the military attaché: 'The document is also of historical interest. It inaugurates our politically important negotiations about the army, which I used for our political recognition in France and in England.'

Masaryk's task in Russia was far from finished at the time of his departure for the United States. The speedy withdrawal of the Czech forces from the Ukraine became a still more pressing necessity after the German armies began their advance at the end of February. At this time, the command of the Legion was by no means unified; separately, the units did their best to emerge unscathed from the Ukrainian chaos. Most of them hastily withdrew from the danger area; some of them fought, alongside the Bolsheviks, against the Germans; at least one unit had to enter into an agreement, in order to be able to retreat, with the local German commanding officer.[47] Nevertheless, by the middle of March, the Czechs had largely succeeded in extricating themselves from the Ukraine and in concentrating their forces, before setting out on their journey to Vladivostok, in south Russia.

At this point—in order to understand better the political situation inside the Legion—it is necessary to discuss two other movements that attracted some of the Czech prisoners of war in Russia. These were the monarchist counter-revolutionary movement, the other the internationalist communism. They are both little-known features of the Czech action in Russia; their impact on the Legion,

[46] *Světová revoluce*, vol. 2, page 182; cf. *Dokumenty*, page 636.

[47] The last incident was usually neglected by the Czech nationalist historians of the Legion. Jaroslav Kratochvíl, a Social Democrat writer, described this agreement, concluded in Kiev on 3 March as the 'sore point of Czechoslovak revolution' in his *Cesta revoluce*, page 38, Prague 1928. Later, the communist historians used it to show that the leadership of the Legion was not interested in fighting the Germans, but the Bolsheviks. Cf. Jiří Muška and Jaromír Hořec, *K úloze československých legií v Rusku*, page 44 et seq. Prague 1954.

the unity of which was threatened by these politically extreme attractions, was strong.

When, shortly after the November revolution, the Cadets began organizing their anti-Bolshevik front in the Don area, two Czech monarchists, Král and Captain Němeček, formed a small unit in Rostov-on-Don. They were apparently given an agreement in principle by Masaryk to recruit volunteers on the condition that they, like the Legion, would not interfere in the internal affairs of Russia. But at a meeting of Král's unit in January it was decided that they 'will go to the front as soon as it is established that there are Germans and Hungarians among the Bolsheviks'.[48] It was, of course, common knowledge that the Bolsheviks were conducting a vigorous propaganda campaign among the prisoners of war, and that the Germans and the Magyars were joining the Red Army. At the meeting, a Russian general implored the Czechs to 'help Russia against the Bolshevik terror'; Professor Milyukov, the former Foreign Minister in the provisional government and Masaryk's friend, wrote to the Czech leader asking him to join the anti-Bolshevik movement. After one of the messengers from the South had been intercepted by the Bolsheviks, Masaryk denounced Král's activities; he replied to Milyukov that although he criticized Marx, he was himself a socialist and that he would continue to maintain a strict neutrality in the civil war. Seeing that there was no possibility of persuading Masaryk to approve his action, Král began to look for another figurehead: Dürich, the Agrarian deputy, willingly obliged. When the unit fought the Bolsheviks, alongside the Russian counter-revolutionary army during the defence of Rostov in March, it was given to understand that the Legion would soon come to join it; its troops were led to regard themselves as a part of the Legion. This was the reason why they did not recognize Dürich as their leader: Kramář's erstwhile protégé was as unsuccessful in his martial activities as he had been in his bid for the leadership of the Czech movement in Russia under the protection of the Tsarist government in 1916.[49] The Czech monarchists in south Russia were subsidized by the French mission in Rostov; Král remained,

[48] J. Kratochvíl, op. cit., page 29. [49] See above, page 131.

until his assassination at the end of 1918, the moving spirit behind the organization.[49a]

In contrast to their leadership, not many troops in Král's unit were likely to have been monarchists themselves: most of them joined simply because they were unable to find their way to the Legion. The Bolsheviks, at the other extreme of the political spectrum, had more success among the Czechs than the monarchists. Not only the left-wing Social Democrats, but also some National Socialists and anarchists among the prisoners of war were receptive to Bolshevik propaganda, that impressed on them the necessity to concentrate on class—rather than national—struggle. Soon after the November revolution, groups of Czech communists began to form in Kiev, Moscow, and Petrograd. In January, prisoners of war started to join the Red Army; the town of Penza later became one of their most important centres. According to communist sources, 150 Czech and Slovak prisoners formed a Red Guard unit in Tsaritsyn (Stalingrad) as early as November 1917; in the Ukraine, 4,000 troops, mainly prisoners but apparently also some members of the Legion, 'joined the Red Army and continued to fight for the liberty of their country'.[50] But Bolshevik internationalism, even when it found a receptive audience among the Czechs, soon became diluted by their deeply ingrained nationalist ideas. They tended to form their own 'internationalist' groups; among the Czech communists in Penza, apart from the orthodox 'love of the proletariat', there was much affection for the 'fraternal Russia, which we, the Czechs and the Slovaks, must not desert'.[51] Indeed, their most important difference with the leaders of the Legion was that they were not prepared to desert Russia for France. They regarded Russia, where

[49a] The later history of the unit is largely a story of insubordination and mutiny. During the fights around Rostov a part of it led by Král was forced to retreat to the Caucasus mountains; in October 1918, when they received news about the events at home, most of the Czech troops refused to go on fighting and insisted on repatriation. They were, however, retained in south Russia, taking part in sporadic fights against the Bolsheviks, until in February 1919 they came under direct French command. Král's death was very likely due to French munificence; the large amounts of ready cash he carried on him proved a strong temptation to some members of his unit, who robbed him and then shot him dead.

[50] J. Muška, op. cit., page 47.

[51] J. Kratochvíl, op. cit., page 51.

the Red Army was in the process of being formed, and where volunteers were in short supply, as the obvious place to spring to the defence of the revolution. Their views were, in fact, in contradiction to Lenin's policy of peace with the Central Powers; a leaflet, printed in Samara at the beginning of March, was characteristic of the tone of their propaganda:

> To all Czechoslovaks! Comrades! They were telling you that there was nothing more to do in Russia and that you would carry on your revolutionary fight on the French front. Issues of vital importance are concerned with this departure for France. With the greatest enthusiasm they describe to you France, America, England. We are certain that you notice the events that are taking place around you and that you will interrupt the journey to the French front. Comrades! Austrian and German armies are advancing further and further into the Russian Federal Republic. Many Czechs, who could not retreat and remained in their way, were shot. The Austrians and the Germans have occupied Kharkov and the armies of Emperors Wilhelm and Karl are advancing towards Kursk. Must it be recorded in the history of the world that the Czech armies have, at this time, so dangerous for the liberty of all nations, retreated before the Austro-German bands and left the Russian revolutionaries without help?[52]

The Czech communists concentrated on persuading their compatriots to remain in Russia; there are indications that Trotsky, early in the spring of 1918, regarded the Legion as a possible nucleus of his revolutionary army.[53] Nevertheless, until the outbreak of hostilities between the Legion and the Bolsheviks, there was little enmity between the Czech 'internationalists' and Masaryk's army; both sides were convinced that their respective actions were the best means of furthering their similar revolutionary aims.

After Masaryk's departure, the leaders of the Russian branch of the National Council had to steer a middle course between the rival attractions of counter-revolution and Bolshevism: their task was made more difficult by the loose discipline that was imposed on the volunteer members of the Legion. Before the withdrawal from the Ukraine, there were already signs that the Czech poli-

[52] J. Kratochvíl, op. cit., page 51. [53] *Dokumenty*, page 636.

tical leaders were uneasy about the effect the Russian situation might have on their troops; the general congress that was to have taken place between 2 and 4 February was postponed indefinitely.

For a short time, the National Council succeeded in maintaining the precarious balance and adhering to the policy of neutrality laid down by Masaryk and to the agreements with the Soviets on the conditions of their transit. On 16 March the first voluntary surrender of arms by the Czechs to the Bolsheviks took place at Kursk; on the same day Antonov-Ovseienko, the Red commander in south Russia said:

> . . . the revolutionary armies will never forget the fraternal help rendered by the Czechoslovak army corps in the fight of the working people against the hordes of miserable imperialism. The arms, given up by the Czechoslovaks, are accepted by the revolutionary armies as a fraternal gift.[54]

Antonov-Ovseienko's speech was the first and the last of its kind. A week later, on 23 March Klecanda, the secretary of the Russian branch of the Czech National Council, then negotiating with the government in Moscow, intimated to his council, based on Penza, his suspicions as to the sincerity of the Bolshevik government; he added that the Legion should retain as many weapons as possible. Klecanda's early suspicions were further reinforced before the armed conflict between the Czechs and the Bolsheviks finally flared up in May. The transports of the Czech troops encountered too many difficulties on their way to the East, and it was obvious that not all of them were due to the inefficiency of the technical personnel. There was also the intrusive Bolshevik propaganda intended to undermine the unity of the Legion, and the restrictive measures taken by the Soviet authorities against the Russian branch of the Czechoslovak National Council and finally the arrest of one of its most prominent members. The Bolsheviks, on the other hand, also had their doubts as to the good faith of the Czechs: at the end of March, the local Soviet government in central Siberia discussed the possibility of the Legion's being used against it; it suggested to the

[54] Kratochvíl, op. cit., pages 41 and 607.

Council of Commissars in Moscow that the Czechs should be diverted to Arkhangelsk. On 2 April Trotsky told a member of the Moscow government that the Czechs should cross Siberia in small, completely disarmed, units.[55] The distrust between the Czechs and the Bolsheviks deepened further when, soon after Trotsky's decision, the landings of the Japanese troops in the Russian Far East were announced.

Although the Czechs began hoarding and hiding the weapons and ammunition they should have surrendered at Penza, the uneasy armistice was maintained for another six weeks. Yet already during this time two officers of the Legion were planning to break the impasse, and win the army over for an action against the Bolsheviks. They were Radula Gajda, commanding officer of the seventh regiment of the first division, and Captain Kadlec of the same unit. Gajda was an adventurer with a taste for conspiracy; Kadlec was a professional soldier, without political interests. The skills of the two men were complementary; they were united by their distaste for the Bolshevik régime. During the second half of April Gajda began paying attention to the advances of the ostracized Russian political parties and the underground organizations of former officers; he started setting up his own intelligence service in which both the Russians and the Czechs took part. Soon, he became convinced that an anti-Bolshevik action had a good chance of success.

On 2 May Gajda's 'plan of action', the military details of which had been worked out by Kadlec, was ready; a day later it was dispatched to the subordinate officers in his regiment and those in the second engineer's platoon. In the plan Gajda insisted that

. . . either we shall take a united action against the Soviet committees in agreement with the National Council, or we shall act without such an agreement.

Further on, Gajda ordered the first unit that came into conflict with the Bolsheviks to

'substitute the Soviet by a local government consisting of parties that wish us well, such as the Mensheviks, Cadets, Social Revolutionaries, etc.'[56]

[55] Kratochvíl, op. cit., page 56. [56] Idem, pages 65–67.

Soon, an incident occurred that sparked off the conflict and gave Gajda and his accomplices the opportunity of putting their designs into practice. At this time, when the most advanced units of the Legion were approaching Irkutsk, the half-way post on their journey to Vladivostok, the delegates of the first division were about to open their congress, which was originally to have taken place in Kiev in February, at Chelyabinsk.[57] It was here, on 14 May, that two trains were standing side by side at the local railway station; a Czech train and one full of prisoners of war. A piece of iron, flung by a prisoner, hit and seriously injured a Czech soldier, whose friends took it upon themselves to lynch and kill the man whom they believed to have been the culprit. Chelyabinsk did not provide a conciliatory background to this incident; the local Soviet, dominated by Hungarian 'internationalists' had, on several occasions before 14 May, hindered the eastward transports of the Czech troops.[58] On 14 May it detained the train and ordered an enquiry. Three days later the Czech sentries who had witnessed the lynching were invited to give a statement to the Soviet; they were arrested on their arrival, and the members of a deputation from the Czech train who went to negotiate the release of the sentries were also imprisoned. In the evening of the same day the Czechs disarmed the Red Army guards at the station, and marched into the town where they forced the Soviet to release the prisoners.

The congress of the first division's delegates thus took place in a tense atmosphere. Four members of the Russian branch of the National Council were present; Gajda took part in the meetings as the representative of his own regiment. Between 18 and 20 May the delegates agreed that the Legion should proceed to Vladivostok 'in their own order'; this meant that, if necessary, they would fight anyone who might try to disarm or detain them. Although the decision did eventually sharpen the conflict between the Czechs and the Bolsheviks, and although men like Gajda must have been aware that it would have precisely this effect, Zmrhal, the chairman of the congress, wrote about it:

[57] See above, page 207.
[58] J. Kratochvíl, op. cit., page 73.

At the moment when the decision was made no one of course had any notion that it would basically alter the attitude of the Czechoslovak army towards Soviet Russia. On the contrary, the delegates were convinced that the decisiveness of the congress would affect the Soviet government and the local Soviets in particular, and that these would release the Czechoslovak army trains for their journey to the East.[59]

The stormy situation itself in Chelyabinsk set off Zmrhal's interpretation of the decision of the Congress as rather naïve. However, apart from agreeing to proceed to Vladivostok in their own way, the delegates refused to split the Legion's forces and direct the First Division to Arkhangelsk. In view of the acute shortage of manpower on the western front, the French military insisted that one of the two Czechoslovak divisions in Russia should come to France, as speedily as possible, via Arkhangelsk. The Supreme War Council approved the plan on 2 May; a week later, Bohdan Pavlů, the vice-chairman of the Russian branch of the Czech National Council, began preparations for the transport of the first division from Chelyabinsk to the North. Although Professor Maxa, Masaryk's deputy in Russia, who was still negotiating and trying to smooth out difficulties in Moscow, sent a telegraphic order on 21 May to the commanders of the Legion asking them to surrender their weapons to the local Soviets,[60] the officers on the Trans-Siberian railway saw the situation in a different light. On 22 May, the congress at Chelyabinsk sent identical telegrams to Maxa, to the council of commissars, to the Soviets on the Siberian railway and to the French mission at Vologda. It informed them that the congress of the Czechoslovak revolutionary army declared:

. . . its sympathies with the Russian revolutionary nation in its hard struggle for the strengthening of the revolution. Nevertheless, the congress is convinced that the Soviet government is not strong enough to guarantee a free and safe transit to our armies to Vladivostok, and therefore it unanimously agreed to give up no weapons until such

[59] Karel Zmrhal, *O samosprávu a demokracii v sibiřske armádě*, pages 134 and 135, Prague 1923.
[60] K. Zmrhal, *Armáda ducha druhé míle*, page 46, Prague 1927.

time when it can be guaranteed free departure and personal safety against counter-revolutionary trains.[61]

The following morning, Colonel Voiciekhovski, the commanding officer of the sixth regiment, dispatched a part of his unit from Chelyabinsk to Omsk 'in their own order'; the hidden machine-guns were brought out and mounted on the tender behind the engine.

On 25 May Gajda rejoined his unit at Novonikolaevsk; soon after his arrival he began issuing orders for the capture of the town, and he also sent Kadlec a coded telegram ordering him to occupy Mariinsk, a small town further east on the line. At 6 p.m. Kadlec reported that the order had been carried out; encouraged by his fellow-conspirator's success, Gajda issued an order to 'all echelons between Omsk and Irkutsk' to fortify their positions, detain all armed Bolshevik transports, take over control of communications, and release only those telegrams addressed to himself.[62] On the night of 25–26 May, Gajda ordered the dissolution of the Novonikolaevsk Soviet and set up a 'provisional Siberian government' in its place.

While some of the Czech echelons at Irkutsk continued their journey to Vladivostok—they finally reached the shores of the Sea of Japan on 29 June—the bulk of the Legion proceeded to strengthen their hold on the Siberian railway and the neighbouring countryside. In spite of conciliatory efforts by the members of the Russian branch of the National Council and American diplomatic and technical staff along the line, and in spite of Trotsky's sharp order to disarm the insurgents, the Czechs went on fighting the Bolsheviks, usually with striking success. On 26 May Thomson, the United States consul at Omsk, telegraphed his Ambassador at Vologda that 'attempts to disarm nine echelons Czecho-Slovaks approaching Omsk caused severe fighting here'.[63] In the evening of the same day, Voiciekhovski's troops occupied Chelyabinsk; later that night, Nizhneudinsk was taken. On the morning of 28 May the Czechs captured a train carrying a load of armoured

[61] J. Kratochvíl, op. cit., page 80. [62] Idem, page 84.
[63] *USFR*, 1918, Russia, vol. 2, page 177.

cars for the Red Army at Penza; a day later they occupied the town itself. On 31 May Petropavlovsk and Tomsk fell.

The die was cast: the ease with which the Legion fought the Bolsheviks and overthrew their institutions involved them, against the better judgement of their political leadership, in a protracted and bloody struggle. They became irrevocably tied down in Russia; their chances of taking part in the fight against Germany and Austria–Hungary on the western front—however small they may have been—disappeared. The conflict strengthened the conviction of the majority of Allied diplomats as to the necessity of intervention in Russia. On 29 May Francis, the American Ambassador, telegraphed the State Secretary:

I have not changed from expressions in my 140, May 2, except to grow in the conviction that Allied intervention advisable from every viewpoint. Red Army organization is a failure and Trotsky influence rapidly waning. . . . German Ambassador endeavouring in every way to establish closer relations with Soviet government and effectually succeeding. Am convinced that if we wait for Bolshevik invitation Allies will never intervene.[64]

By the end of June, the highest Allied military authorities were convinced that intervention was not only necessary but also possible; on 2 July the American liaison officer at the Supreme War Council informed Washington:

The Supreme War Council considers that since its last meeting a complete change has come over the situation in Russia and Siberia, which makes Allied intervention in these countries an urgent and imperative necessity. In the first place the recent action of Czecho-Slovak troops has transformed the Siberian eclipse. There is now a force of 50,000 troops, of Slav nationality, totally disinterested in the internal politics in Russia, yet determined to fight Germany for the liberation of their own country, in control of the railway in western Siberia. . . . To fail in bringing support to these faithful troops, now desperately fighting for the Allied cause, would not only forever discredit the Allies, but might have a disastrous effect on the Slav population both of Russia itself and of Austria–Hungary and the Balkans as

[64] The Ambassador's telegram to the State Secretary, in *USFR*, 1918, Russia, vol. 1, page 519, in which Francis opined: 'in my judgement the time for Allied intervention has arrived'.

> proving that the Allies are unable or unwilling to exert themselves effectively to save the Slav world from falling wholly under German domination.[65]

The Allies in spite of their intentions were unable to dispatch troops to the Legion's relief; from a plan to re-establish the front against the Central Powers, the intervention of necessity degenerated into a rearguard action against the Bolsheviks. The Czechs, on the other hand, partly by accident and partly by design, became involved in a protracted and frustrating action. They regarded themselves as revolutionaries; revolution had for them not only national, but also social connotations. Their fight against the Bolsheviks could be regarded as an armed clash—the only one in the process of the dissolution of the Habsburg monarchy—between the forces of national and social revolution: a fact that, as far as the rank-and-file members of the Legion were concerned, first puzzled and later embittered them; finally, the army became an object of sharp political controversy in the new Czechoslovak state.

Although the leaders of the National Council in the West (and to a certain degree the leaders of its Russian branch as well) lost control, during the May events, over the Legion, they readily exploited its political value in the changed circumstances. Beneš, as we have already seen, was more alert than Masaryk to the ways in which the Allies were interested in the army. On 18 May, when the first conflict between the Czechs and the Bolsheviks flared up in Chelyabinsk and the members of the army's congress began deliberating on their policy, Lord Robert Cecil wrote to Clemenceau:

> The War Cabinet has asked me in the absence of Mr. Balfour . . . with regard to the question of intervention in Siberia. At present things are rather at a deadlock. . . . I have seen M. Beneš, a member of the Czechoslovak National Council and asked him his views. He says that he is quite sure that the Bohemian troops who are well-disciplined will carry out any orders sent to them by the National Committee and he is prepared to get the necessary orders sent on condition that we

[65] *USFR*, 1918, Russia, vol. 2, pages 241–242.

make a declaration recognizing the Czechoslovaks as our Allies and the justice of their claim to independence.[66]

When Beneš talked to Cecil—around 14 May—he may still have believed that the Allies would transport the Legion to France. But Allied policy changed and so did that of the secretary of the National Council. The change of Beneš's attitude towards the problem of employment of the Czechoslovak army in Russia was dramatically reflected in two of his messages to Prague. On 14 June he informed the members of the Mafie that 'the Allies wanted to use our people in Russia for the purpose of intervention, but we are opposing it because it is dangerous'.[67] But soon after this message, on 8 July Beneš wrote from Paris: 'Military negotiations are being conducted here about intervention in Russia, which is now bound to take place and in which we shall play a certain role.'[68]

Whereas Beneš confined his activities, in the last months of the war, to dealing with the French and the British governments and to informing his friends at home of his successes, Masaryk's tour of the United States began with a triumphant progress through the towns with large Czech and Slovak colonies of immigrants. It was, incidentally, in Pittsburg that the unity of the two peoples received their blessings: on 30 June Masaryk signed the 'Pittsburg Convention' which promised the Slovaks their own Diet and autonomous administration. The President had received Masaryk, for the first time, on 19 June; a month later, Masaryk wrote to the Acting Secretary of State:

> You will understand our wish that the great American Republic would join the French Republic in recognizing our National Council (in Paris) as the representative of the future Government of the Czecho-Slovak free State. I think that this recognition has become practically necessary: I dispose of three armies (Russia, France, and Italy) I am, as a wit said, the master of Siberia and half Russia, and yet I am in the United States formally as a private man.[69]

[66] *The Milner Papers*, at New College, Oxford.
[67] *Dokumenty*, page 165. [68] Idem, page 176.
[69] *USFR*, 1918, Supplement 1, vol. 1, page 818. The letter was dated 20 July 1918.

The summer months brought the fulfilment of the dearest wishes of the exiles. On 29 June the French government recognized the right of the Czechoslovaks to independence and the National Council in Paris as the 'first basis of the future government'. On 14 August the British acknowledged the Czechs as an Allied nation and their military units in Russia, France, and Italy as an 'allied and belligerent army waging regular warfare against Austria–Hungary and Germany'.[70] On 3 September the United States government followed suit and recognized the National Council as a 'de facto belligerent government'. Finally, on 14 October Beneš announced the formation of a provisional government with its seat in Paris and proceeded to nominate its representatives with the Allied Powers.[71] Five days later, in his reply to the Austro-Hungarian peace note, the American Secretary of State informed Vienna bluntly that the tenth point of the President's January address had been invalidated by subsequent developments. Lansing wrote:

> The President . . . is no longer at liberty to accept the mere 'autonomy' of these peoples as a basis of peace, but is obliged to say that they, and not he, shall be the judges of what action on the part of the Austro-Hungarian government will satisfy their aspirations and their conception of their rights and destiny as members of the family of nations.[72]

The ambitions of the exiles and the plans of their well-wishers found their expression in the decrees of the Allied governments only in the last months of the war. Although as late as February 1918 Balfour doubted whether the fate of the Habsburg monarchy could be settled in an Allied capital, a few months later the Entente governments signed the death warrant of Austria–Hungary. The recognition of the exiles' aims had far-reaching effects (these will be discussed in the following chapter) inside Austria–Hungary itself. The exiles not only had the backing of the victorious Powers, but their plans for the break-up of the Habsburg Empire were much more advanced and articulate than those of their compatriots at home. Of all the 'oppressed

[70] *USFR*, 1918, Supplement 1, vol. 1, page 824.
[71] Idem, page 846. [72] Idem, page 368.

races', the Czech political emigrés had faced the most formidable task: the right of the Poles to a united state in one form or another had long been recognized in both the belligerent camps; the South Slavs had had the Serbian, and the Austro-Hungarian Rumanians the Rumanian government to back them up. The Czechs, on the other hand, enjoyed no such advantages; their ambitions, if fulfilled, would have had the most disruptive effect on the *status quo* in central Europe. Nevertheless, the task of all the political emigrés was facilitated when the German spring offensive impressed upon the Allies the usefulness of nationalist propaganda directed against the Austro-Hungarian army: the Czechs were further helped when their Legion in Russia began to play an important role in the policy of intervention. The Allies had thus sanctioned the break-up of the Habsburg monarchy before the actual event took place; they did so at a time when military necessity outweighed all other considerations.

VIII

END OF THE EMPIRE

By midsummer, the German offensive on the western front had spent itself. Its last thrust had failed on the Marne; the shelling of Paris stimulated the French to an all-out effort to hold and drive back the Germans. American troops were now pouring into France at the rate of a quarter of a million a month. The opening move of the Allied counter-stroke was made by General Haig on 8 August: its objective was to free Amiens and the main line to Paris. But even after its initial success, no Allied soldier or statesman thought of the offensive as the last encounter of the war; it had been conceived as a mere preliminary to the final effort to come in 1919. Nevertheless, at the end of August, the Allied commanders realized that the decision could be forced in the same year; the weakness of the German army had been fully plumbed and the combination of infantry and tanks proved a formidable offensive weapon. Ludendorff was not allowed to withdraw his divisions to the Hindenburg line at his own pace; the attack launched on 29 September disrupted the positions and the morale of the German army still further. On the same day, Ludendorff demanded that peace and armistice offers should be made to the Entente; a week later, Prince Max von Baden, the new Chancellor, requested the American President to 'arrange the immediate conclusion of an armistice on land, by sea and in the air'. However, the armistice took another five weeks to conclude; while notes were being exchanged, the war cost the belligerents another half million casualties.

The evidence of the failures of the German army on the western front speeded up the defection of Berlin's allies. On 14 September the Austro-Hungarian Emperor published a peace manifesto without consulting the German government; the Entente statesmen simply ignored it. A day later, the Allied attack on the Bulgarian front began to unfold; the pro-Entente Sofia ministry signed the armistice on 29 September. On the Italian front, where the majority of the Austro-Hungarian combat forces were concentrated, apart from a week's hard fighting in June and then again in October, both sides were content to remain on the defensive. But it was here that the fighting spirit of the Habsburg army was broken, and its cohesion frittered away in two futile attacks spread over too long a front.

When the Allies launched their offensive on the western front, the Austro-Hungarian armies were still fighting or stationed on enemy territory; in Italy and Serbia, in Rumania and Albania, in Poland and the Ukraine. Yet its morale, only partially restored after the events in the spring,[1] was now declining week after week. Protected against economic privations longer than the civilian population of the monarchy, it began to suffer not only hunger but also acute lack of military supplies; the number of deserters was increasing rapidly. The 'human material' began to show grave signs of fatigue. And the military knew that Germany could no longer come to the rescue, as it had done before, of the Habsburg army.

Despite the numerous and far-flung fronts and outposts the army had to man, the demands that internal security made on its resources were also heavy. Whereas the Germans were able to transfer some forty divisions from the eastern to the western front after the Bolshevik revolution, seven of the Austro-Hungarian combat divisions that were supposed to have been moved from the Russian front to Italy were employed, after urgent requests from the civil administration, to break the January strikes. But even this large drain on the resources at the disposal of the front line commanders did not satisfy the civil authorities. Requests for more military assistance continued to flood the Ministry of Defence. On 6 February—shortly before unrest broke out in Galicia as a result of the peace with the Ukraine—the Governor wrote from Cracow to the Ministry of Interior that he had asked the

[1] See above, page 143.

Ministry of Defence for more troops; he needed at least sixteen companies for the Cracow and Lwow districts and nine for the Przemysl district; 8,000 troops in all to meet emergency situations in his province.[2] The seven combat divisions remained in Austria-Hungary: the Ministry of Defence had to resist frequent demands from the High Command to return them, especially at the time of the preparations for the offensive in Italy in June.[3] A sharp exchange of views on the respective merits of the home and foreign fronts continued throughout the summer; on 8 July General Arz ordered all combat divisions to go to the front; the Ministry of Defence countered the order by an appeal to the Emperor. One thing became certain during this correspondence: the struggle against the internal enemy had become at least as important as waging the war itself.

In the last months of the war, as the threats to the internal stability of the monarchy were gaining in force, the army was becoming an ever blunter instrument; it eventually failed the Habsburg dynasty in its hour of need. By suppressing the mass strike movement early in the year—set off by economic privations and inspired by the Bolshevik revolution[4]—the Austro-Hungarian army had in fact rendered its last service to the national leaders: in the following months they were able to consolidate popular support for their policy, and thus to prevent the revolutionary movement from splitting into socialist and national streams. As long as the national leaders were able to control the masses and prevent them from precipitating futile encounters with the army, they had nothing to fear from it. Apart from military force, the dynasty appeared to know of no means of persuasion.

It was also during this intervening period—between May and October—that the radicals in the Habsburg monarchy became aware of the extent of the exiles' achievement in the Entente countries. Although some of the information of the activities of the political emigrations was available in the press, and the Poles had a useful connexion abroad through the emissaries of the Warsaw Regents Council, the underground channel between Prague and

[2] *VA*, 3203 MI ex 1918. [3] J. Opočenský, op. cit., pages 495–496.
[4] See above, page 135.

the National Council in Paris was the most effective means of communication. It served not only the Czechs, but, as the meetings of the Slav politicians became more frequent after the beginning of the year, all the radicals in the monarchy. After the long silence between July 1917 and February 1918,[5] exchange of messages grew more frequent and reliable; during the four last months of the war, twenty-seven long messages passed between Prague and Paris. Apart from reporting on the progress of the exiles' activities in the Entente countries, Beneš frequently advised the politicians in the monarchy on their tactics. His hints—this had not been the case earlier in the war—were often taken.

Although in May Beneš was still unable to inform his friends in Prague that the aims of the National Council had been officially recognized by the Allies, his messages, after his return from England at the end of the month, were becoming increasingly optimistic. On 27 May he wrote from Paris:

> Beneš . . . negotiated with Balfour and Robert Cecil. Both promised him absolute support for our cause. . . . Robert Cecil promised that he would speak publicly against Austria and for our independence. He did so on 22 May. . . . After his return from London Beneš had discussions with ministers Pichon and Clemenceau. Pichon categorically declared that France will now go most decisively and ruthlessly against Austria. He said: 'We want you to be free. We want to destroy Austria. You have done what you could, and we are expecting still more help from your people at home.'

At the end of the message, Beneš intimated that the proclamation of the Czechoslovaks' right to independence was imminent, and he went on to say that

> . . . after the declaration of independence a provisional government may be set up. Be prepared for it and *do not publish a disavowal at any price* [Beneš's italics] and especially bear in mind unity with us. The provisional government will be regarded here as a delegation and as a part of the provisional government, *the second half of which will be in Bohemia.*[6]

Beneš wanted to prepare the ground in Prague for the recog-

[5] See above, page 181.
[6] *Dokumenty*, pages 162–164.

nition, by the Allies, of the National Council in Paris as the provisional government of the future Czechoslovak state: he was aware that there were politicians in the monarchy, popular leaders of powerful parties, who would themselves aspire to high honours in the new state, and he was uncertain of their reception of the news. Nevertheless, on 8 July, Beneš was able to describe the 'greatest political success, of 29 June, we have so far achieved', that is, the letter from Pichon to himself, in which he

> . . . recognizes our independence, all our historical rights, the Slovak situation, binds France to support us at the peace negotiations, and that the National Council is regarded as a delegation of the provisional government.

And again, he underlined the sentence: *Therefore unity and co-operation between us are essential.*[7]

At the same time, Beneš revived his old plan for a meeting between the Prague politicians and the representatives of the National Council. Early in 1917 he had asked the Mafie to begin planning such a meeting in a neutral country; in July 1918 he became insistent on its necessity.[8]

The Czechs both at home and abroad expected the Austrian government to make difficulties: Beneš originally planned an illegal exit for the politicians. But when Kramář, Klofáč, Staněk, Habrman, and Kalina applied for their passports, the government of Hussarek gladly obliged; the Premier would do nothing to antagonize the Czechs or appear to furnish further proofs of his government's restrictive policies towards the Slavs. The delegation, consisting of the five politicians and two financial experts, finally left Vienna for Geneva on 25 October; they were the last Czechs to carry Austro-Hungarian passports.

Indeed, by the end of the summer, it seemed as if the Austrian government had lost its conviction of its right to govern. Its enemies were numerous; there were far too few allies. The Slav politicians were able to make the most outrageous anti-Habsburg speeches in the *Reichsrat*; after a while they wearied of abusing a lethargic government. In October Hussarek made a final bid to rally at least some of the Slav politicians around his government.

[7] *Dokumenty*, page 174. [8] Ibid., page 168.

The Imperial Manifesto of 16 October had been in preparation since the beginning of the month; it was intended to satisfy the demand for self-determination. But Burian and Wekerle, at the time the two most influential Hungarian ministers, secured the guarantee from the Emperor as to the integrity of the Hungarian part of the monarchy, and turned down his suggestion that a similar manifesto should be published in Budapest. Hussarek's belated attempt at federalism would hardly have satisfied the demands the Slav deputies had made at the time of the reopening of the parliament in May 1917;[9] it would have prevented the unification of the South Slavs in the two parts of the Empire, and it would have made the union between the Czechs and the Slovaks impossible. The manifesto, instead of pacifying the peoples of Austria, in fact opened the floodgates of separatist tendencies. When asking the Austrian peoples to support the implementation of the principles of the manifesto, the government turned to the National Committees for assistance: their existence was thus recognized and given official blessings. The Emperor and the government, however, overestimated the loyalty of the National Committees to the monarchy: by now, they were largely dominated by radical politicians who regarded a clean break with Vienna as the only way of preserving the national identities of their peoples.

While Hussarek was preparing the Manifesto, the Czech politicians were getting ready to take over power in their lands. They knew that it was going to be a difficult task. The administration of the Czech lands was still conducted by the old civil service under the direction of loyal governors. In Brno and Opava, the capitals of Moravia and Moravian Silesia, the town councils were dominated by German majorities. In Prague, there were no Czech military units; German, Hungarian, and Rumanian troops were stationed there. In Brno, apart from one Czech regiment, the troops were German; the garrison in Opava was largely Polish. Faced with such obstacles, the National Committee decided on a policy of peaceful transfer of power, preferably on the day of the armistice; it also set up an economic council, under the chairmanship of Švehla, the Agrarian leader, which was to prevent the ex-

[9] See above, page 126.

port of food, coal, and other products from Czech territory. There was, however, another reason for the circumspect policy of the radicals; they were afraid that a violent upheaval might assume forms they could not control. On 11 October Šámal wrote to Beneš in Paris: 'We cannot even contemplate a revolution; it is quite likely that because of the general starvation it would soon acquire Bolshevik forms.'[10]

The National Committee tended to be rather secretive about its plans which were nearly jeopardized by an action of the Socialist Council. The council, on which the Social Democrats, National Socialists, and other left-wing elements were represented, decided to declare a general strike on 14 October. It was to be a protest, in support of meetings organized by the economic council of the National Committee, against exports of food and coal from the 'territory of the Czechoslovak republic'. Soukup, the right-wing Social Democrat deputy and secretary of the National Committee, prepared a draft speech to be read at the protest meetings of the economic council; the members of the Socialist Council, on the other hand, expanded Soukup's draft, without his or the National Committee's knowledge, to include the following paragraph:

> We declare ourselves, of our free will and with the knowledge of the democratic world, the executives of a new state sovereignty, and citizens of the Czechoslovak republic. . . . We declare that every export from our country is a robbery and a crime against the sovereignty of our state as was the attack on Belgium at the beginning of the war.[11]

On 13 October both the National Committee and the Austro-Hungarian civil and military authorities got to know about the Socialist Council's plan. Švehla and Rašín, fearing that the action of the socialists might interfere with the plan of the National Committee for a peaceful transfer of power, immediately started telephoning their committee's branches in the provinces, informing the local leaders that the Prague National Committee disapproved of the planned demonstrations. On the same day, they

[10] *Dokumenty*, page 206.
[11] F. Peroutka, *Budování státu*, vol. 1, page 40, Prague 1933.

were also banned by an order of the Governor. Nevertheless, the meetings were held and backed up by a token strike on 14 October; in several provincial towns—Plzeň, Moravská Ostrava, Písek, and Strakonice—the formation of the republic was announced, while at other meetings the paragraph proclaiming the new state was suppressed.

Although the Socialist Council had no desire to destroy the unity of the National Committee, its members clearly intended to prove the potential strength of the socialist movement to the middle-class radical leaders, and to indicate the necessity of social reforms in the new state. They may have resented the air of exclusiveness and secrecy that surrounded the committee; they also knew that monarchists were represented on it, and they wanted to forestall them by declaring a republic. On 14 October the socialists, in fact, were conducting a struggle on two fronts: they were fighting against Austria–Hungary for an independent state; at the same time, they were joining the fight for political influence in this state. But the main weakness of the socialist action lay in the fact that they had merely planned a political demonstration; they left the problem of the transfer of administrative and military control unsolved. The National Committee was successful in defending its authority against the pretensions of the socialists: it strengthened its position in Bohemia, and also in regard to the Austrian authorities. It condemned the action of the Socialist Council; Machar, the poet, chauvinist, and a co-opted member of the National Committee said that on 14 October the 'whole action gave the impression of having been ordered from Vienna'.[12] The Austrian administration, on the other hand, began to regard the National Committee as a body capable of resisting anarchy and preventing violence and bloodshed; the government in Vienna hopelessly confused the incident and interpreted the action by the Socialist Council as a Bolshevik attempt to usurp power in the state.[13]

Soon after the excitement created by the socialists had died down, the delegation left for their meeting with Beneš in Geneva.[14]

[12] Peroutka, op. cit., page 52. [13] Z. Tobolka, op. cit., vol. 4, page 383.
[14] See above, page 221.

Klofáč had left a few days before the other members of the delegation for an Imperial audience in Vienna; as a result of their conversation on 22 October, the Emperor became convinced that there was no hope of retaining the Czech lands for the monarchy.[15] The other Czech leaders—Kramář, Staněk, Habrman, and Kalina—also broke their journey in Vienna. They wanted to sound the views of Austrian politicians and of Lammasch, the Premier designate, in particular; there are also signs that Kramář and Staněk were in search of allies. These two men were convinced monarchists; Kramář made no secret of it in his talks with the Austrians and Staněk expressed his doubts to Baron de Vaux as to whether the Czech state could exist as a republic.[16] Nevertheless, the Czechs left the Habsburg capital on 25 October with the impression that the Austrian politicians expected them to break off their ties with the dynasty; nobody seems to have made the slightest attempt at persuading them to revise their decisions.

At the Geneva meeting, which took place between 28 and 31 October, Beneš was aided by three secretaries. He needed all the support he could get: he was confronted with a formidable group of men, all senior to him in age and political experience, who entertained not only high hopes as to the future of their people, but also high personal ambitions. But Beneš held the trump card in his hand: his and Masaryk's policy, which they had pursued in face of many vicissitudes since the beginning of the war, had proved successful; it had the backing of the victorious Powers. He secured an agreement that the politicians in Prague would do nothing without the consent of the National Council, which implied the subordination of the National Committee to the organization of the exiles.[17] He also removed the doubts any member of the delegation may have had as to the certainty of the establishment of an entirely independent Czechoslovak state, and as to its right to be represented at the peace conference.[18] He assured them that the National Council had no commitments towards the Allies as far as the form of the future state was concerned, but at the

[15] Z. Tobolka, op. cit., page 385. [16] Idem, page 396.

[17] Beneš, *Světová válka*, vol. 2, pages 583 et seq.; cf. *Dokumenty*, page 175.

[18] Idem, page 381.

same time he pointed out that Masaryk in his Washington declaration of independence had made it clear that the state should be a republic and that this was the feeling of the majority of the Czechs abroad. There were some differences on this point between Beneš and Kramář; but Kramář conceded that 'if our state is to be a monarchy, it must be an extremely democratic one, like England'.[19]

In Geneva, the actions of the radical exiles were approved, for the first time, by a representative delegation from their home country. The rough outlines for the development of the future state were laid down there. In a sense, the stigma of defeat clung to the politicians—especially to Kramář—who had come from the defeated monarchy. Kramář's policy of Pan-Slavism had been shattered by the disappearance of the Tsarist régime, and Masaryk's pro-western ideas were vindicated; Kramář monarchism had to be toned down in the face of the socialist opposition at home and of the exiles' views. It was in Geneva that Kramář must have come to realize that it was Masaryk who would play the leading role in the new state.

The elder statesmen had gone to Geneva; the younger politicians—Švehla, Rašín, Stříbrný, and Soukup—were left in control of the National Committee in Prague. The younger men were more energetic; their nationalism was perhaps even more pronounced than that of their colleagues, who had spent their long political careers in the *Reichsrat* and who, even on their way to Switzerland to meet Beneš, were unable to by-pass Vienna. Before the delegation's departure they agreed with the men left behind in Prague that these should, if need be, carry out the transfer of power themselves. This was precisely what they did.

In Prague the National Committee observed the actions of the army command carefully; the soldiers, for their part, were apprehensive of the Czechs. On 27 October, however, two events occurred which convinced the National Committee that the time was ripe for resolute action. On that day Lammasch became the new Premier; his Foreign Minister, Andrassy, made an offer of a separate peace to Wilson; he also asked the President for an im-

[19] Beneš, *Světová válka*, vol. 2, page 392.

mediate armistice, on the basis of the note of 18 October, which implied the discontinuation of Austria–Hungary's alliance with Germany and the recognition of the right of the Czechoslovaks and the Jugoslavs to independence. On the same day the Supreme Command requested the National Committee through Tusar, its representative in Vienna, to send a delegation to the front which would try to persuade the troops to remain at their posts, at any rate until the time of the armistice. Tusar telephoned Rašín, informing him of the Supreme Command's request, on the evening of 27 October.[20]

The administration and the military authorities were by now thoroughly confused, by both the Imperial Manifesto and Andrassy's note, as to the aims of the government; they regarded the National Committees as officially recognized instruments for the transformation of the monarchy. Early on 28 October Švehla and Soukup had no difficulty in taking over the administration of the Office for the Distribution of Corn in the name of the National Committee, an action that made it possible for them to control food supplies to both the civil population and the military. A few hours later, the representatives of the National Committee informed the Governor's deputy (Coudenhove was in Vienna at the time) that they had decided, in the interest of the maintenance of public order, to take over the administration of the country; they told him that existing laws would remain valid. From the Governor's office they proceeded to visit Count Schönborn, the chief of the Land Administrative Commission, who offered his services to the National Committee, believing that the committee intended to implement the Imperial Manifesto of 16 October.

In the meantime, the text of Andrassy's note had become publicly known in Prague. Demonstrations against the state and the dynasty took place in the main square: Imperial insignia were torn off public buildings and even off soldiers' uniforms. Rašín, when he was informed of the demonstrations, disapproved of them.[21] Like the rest of his colleagues on the committee, Rašín was afraid that the demonstrations might take the form of

[20] J. Opočenský, *Konec monarchie*, page 727.
[21] Z. Tobolka, op. cit., vol. 4, page 387.

anti-German and anti-Jewish riots, which might make an unfavourable impression abroad. At the same time he feared that the frankness of popular excitement might jeopardize the line the National Committee was taking with the official agencies—that it was acting in the interests of public order and for the implementation of the Imperial Manifesto.

In the evening of 28 October a general meeting of the committee took place which unanimously passed a 'law on the establishment of an independent Czechoslovak state'. Although the law neither specified the form the future state was to take, nor defined its relations with the monarchy, it was an act which repudiated the plan for an Austrian federation as expressed in the manifesto. With each successful transfer of power into its hands, the strength of the National Committee had grown considerably during the day; the state in the name of which Švehla had negotiated early in the morning was a different entity from that declared by the committee in the evening.

To round off an eventful day, Soukup and Scheiner, the leader of the *Sokols*, called on the military commander of Prague. General Zanantoni, who had been instructed by Vienna to enter into contact with the National Committee, and who had no insight or interest in the political situation in the capital, soon reached an agreement with the two emissaries. The two parties pledged themselves to co-operate in the restoration and maintenance of public order and agreed that the committee would take over the functions of the Governor's office; the *Sokols* were to post their own guards at military establishments and ammunition factories, and the committee was expected to send liaison officers to the military command.

The agreement was favourable to the Czechs; the military authorities no longer believed in their ability to influence the developments in Prague. At 9 a.m. on 28 October, the commander dispatched a hopeless telegram to Vienna:

> In present circumstances the declaration of martial law seems impossible, because we have no means of making it publicly known. . . . It would also further irritate the masses. . . . It is necessary to take into

account the imminent danger that insubordination and riots which occurred in several military units will spread. . . . The commander is of the opinion that if military units remain exposed to this atmosphere any longer he may lose the remainder of the reliable troops.[22]

Although on the following day the Ministry of War changed its views on the desirability of co-operation with the national committees, the Czechs had used the respite they gained by their agreement with General Zanantoni. They had equipped the *Sokol* volunteers with arms from the military stores; the Rumanian troops in Prague had received an order from Maniu, their national leader, to give every support to the Czech committee which, in its turn, promised to facilitate their return home. After the Rumanians, the Hungarian troops also refused obedience to their commander. By 30 October the Austrian government had lost the last remnants of its power in the Czech parts of Bohemia; the National Committee took over the military commands in Prague, Plzeň, and Litoměřice.

The events in Moravia developed in a similar manner to those in Bohemia, but without the thorough preparation of the Bohemian revolution. No equivalent of the National Committee existed in Brno; it had to be created, in a hurry, on 28 October. A day later the members of the committee asked Heinold, the Governor, to hand over the administration of the country. The Moravians were in telephonic contact with Švehla: they used the same tactics as those that had been employed successfully in Prague; they alleged that they were working for the implementation of the Manifesto. Heinold resignedly handed over his office to one of his Czech subordinates; owing to the presence of Czech troops in Brno, the committee had no trouble in taking over the military command. The town council, on the other hand, with its German majority, presented a more difficult problem. But the Brno tradition of amicable settlement of differences between the two nationalities finally asserted itself: after negotiations lasting several days the German city fathers agreed on 7 November to participate in a new council with a Czech majority.

On 30 October even the government in Vienna could no

[22] Quoted by F. Peroutka, op. cit., vol. 1, pages 121 and 122.

longer have any doubts that the Czechs meant to break off all their ties with the monarchy. The National Committee gave Tusar full powers to negotiate on the liquidation of the Habsburg state in Vienna. When Lammasch, now the Prime Minister, received the Czech emissary, he told him: 'Your Excellency, I have the pleasure of welcoming you as the Ambassador of the Czechoslovak state', to which Tusar replied, with a touch of irony, 'Sir, the pleasure is mine.'

The 'Czechoslovak state' was, however, far from being a political reality. The idea of such a state had originated in Prague; the Czechs fought for it, but without being given much encouragement from the Slovaks themselves. Even at the very end of the war, the thin crust of Slovak intelligentsia which thought in Czechoslovak terms had little popular support behind it; it was also faced with a tougher and more resolute government than the Czechs. In exile, the practical co-operation of the two peoples had made some progress; Štefánik was a member of the National Council and, after the Allied recognition, of the provisional government; Masaryk had concluded an agreement on the common state with the Slovak immigrants in the United States.[23] Inside the monarchy, Vavro Šrobár, the leader of the Slovak National Party, went to Prague as soon as he was released from a Hungarian prison on 20 October; he was the only Slovak to become a member of the National Committee and to sign the 'law on the establishment of an independent Czechoslovak state'. In the meantime, in Slovakia, Matúš Dula, another prominent member of the National Party began, on 24 October, to organize a meeting at Turčanský Sväty Martin. It took place on 30 October; the assembled Slovak patriots knew nothing of the events in Prague. (Derer, who returned from Vienna for the meeting and who had been in touch with Tusar there, came back with the message 'do nothing rash'; since the Slovaks did not expect anything either interesting or important to happen in their own country, Šrobár remained in Prague and Hodža, one of the most active of Slovak politicians, in Budapest.) They decided to set up a National Committee consisting of twelve members, on which

[23] See above, page 214.

the national, socialist, and clerical factions were represented. A resolution was agreed on at the meeting, which declared the Slovaks to be 'linguistically, culturally, and historically a part of the Czechoslovak nation', and it demanded self-determination for this nation.[24]

The government of Wekerle in Budapest showed neither the same degree of weakness nor of understanding towards the ambitions of the Hungarian nationalities as the cabinet of Lammasch had done. Two companies of Magyar troops, dispatched from the capital, arrived at Turčanský Sväty Martin on the day of the meeting; a delegation of Magyar ladies, who were expected to influence Slovak politicians through their women in favour of moderation, also made their appearance. (The troops had probably been dispatched by Wekerle and the women by Karolyi, whose government came into power on 31 October.) At a meeting on 2 November, the National Committee in Prague decided to occupy Slovakia, without waiting for the decision of the peace conference. But the Czechs had planned for an easier enterprise than it proved to be. Šrobár, the head of the first Slovak local government left Prague, together with three colleagues, on 4 November. Even with the help of about a hundred Czech gendarmes they did not succeed in making their way to the Slovak capital: the seat of the first Slovak government was in Uherská Skalica in Moravia.

Apart from redeeming Slovakia for the new state, the national committees in Prague and Brno had to contend with the problem of considerable German minorities in Bohemia and Moravia. Indeed, had the right to self-determination of the Germans in the Czech lands been recognized, the Czechoslovak state would have lost some 1,700 square miles of territory and nearly 3,000,000 inhabitants. The Czech politicians were sensitive on this point; when Coudenhove, the Governor of Bohemia told Rašín on 29 October that the National Committee could not hope to control *Deutschböhmen* (the German parts of Bohemia), Rašín angrily silenced the Governor and told him that this was a concern of the committee. The Germans, for their part, showed no intention of becoming citizens of the Czechoslovak state. Their deputies met

[24] Peroutka, op. cit., vol. 1, page 168.

in Vienna on 29 October, where they agreed to set up a German province in northern Bohemia, with Liberec (Reichenberg) as its capital. The deputies from southern Moravia declared themselves for the incorporation of the Znojmo district into Lower Austria, and those from southern Bohemia demanded the incorporation of Böhmerwaldgau into Upper Austria. The German deputies from northern Moravia and Silesia declared that they would set up a province—Sudetenland—with Troppau (Opava) for its capital.[25]

Faced with the Czech demands, the nationalist German politicians were the most active in Bohemia and Moravia; in Vienna, however, the Social Democrats came to dominate the political scene. They were the only party in Austria that had faced the possibility of the Empire's break-up, that had a programme which could be put into practice in such an event, and that looked towards the future with a certain amount of confidence. Indeed, the German middle class parties, after their war-time policies had come to grief, asked the Social Democrats whether they would be willing to join a united national front. On 3 October the socialists replied that:

> The representatives of the German workers in Austria recognize the right to self-determination of the Slav and Latin nations in Austria and they claim the same right for the German nation. We recognize the rights of the Slavs to form their own national states; we resist, however, resolutely and for good, the subjection, to these national states, of German territories. We demand that all German territories in Austria should be unified in one state which would regulate its relations to other nations of Austria and to the German Empire according to its needs.[26]

Since unity of the German nation—referring to Germans outside the Austrian provinces—was specifically mentioned in the Social Democrats' declaration, the German nationalist parties decided the following day to accept it as the basis for further negotiations. The Christian Socialists acknowledged the declaration on 9 October, with the reservation that the monarchy should be transformed into a federation of nations which the Austrian Ger-

[25] *Hlas*, 29 and 30 October.

[26] O. Bauer, op. cit., page 74.

mans would join of their own free will. If any of the German politicians were still vacillating, the audience with Count Wedel, the German Ambassador to Vienna, and the American note of 18 October, which declared the Czechoslovaks and the Jugoslavs the sole arbiters of their own future, clearly indicated their course of action. The Germans in Vienna were the first people in the Austrian part of the monarchy to set up their own National Assembly, in which all former *Reichsrat* deputies of German nationality, including those from Bohemia and Moravia, took part. The assembly's chairman, deputy Waldner, said in his opening address:

> History made our nation the founder of the old state of Austria, and we gave it faithfully and unselfishly all the best achievements of our people in the fields of civilization and economy throughout the centuries. We are parting company with this state without any misgivings . . . we will rely on the vital forces of our own nation.[27]

At the same meeting Victor Adler, the Social Democrat leader, declared that the Austrian Germans were faced with the choice between a federation of all the nations of the monarchy or an *Anschluss* of the Germans to Imperial Germany. For Adler this demand was the natural outcome of the doctrine of national self-determination; for other Austrian politicians, and the nationalists in particular, this was the only way of preserving the national identity, and even political power, of their people.

Germany's leaders shared the preoccupations of the Austrian Germans. The collapse of the Habsburg state threatened to deprive them of their political power, while leaving them at the mercy of the new Slav states. Berlin was therefore concerned not only with their protection, but also with the ways in which German influence in central Europe could be reinforced, and even perhaps increased. On 14 October General Ludendorff wrote to the State Secretary at the Foreign Ministry:

> The events of the last weeks direct our special attention to Austria. The Supreme Command is concerned with the question because it is of a decisive importance for our military future. It is possible that in

[27] *Die Neue Freie Presse*, 22 October.

the near future we shall be in such a position that we shall have to render the Germans in Austria our military protection.[28]

After a reference to the possibility of the formation of Slav successor states, Ludendorff pointed out that the Austrian Germans had at last recognized this danger, that their party differences among them were on the way out, and that they were against the Habsburg dynasty, because no one expected the Emperor to protect German interests.

They ask themselves [wrote the General of the Austrian Germans] whether the time has not come to begin preparing an *Anschluss* to the German Empire.

And he concluded:

There can be no doubt that, sooner or later, the *Anschluss* of German territories will take place. This development might become a valuable compensation for the disappointments that the war has brought in other fields, and we should not forget this.

Two days later Wedel sent a detailed report to the Chancellor with an enclosed memorandum by an anonymous Austrian–German politician.[29] The Ambassador, although he intimated that a direct intervention should be avoided as long as possible, insisted that his government must not desert the Austrian Germans in their hour of need. He was particularly concerned with the situation of the Germans in northern Bohemia, the territory bordering on the *Reich*. If the Czech state was set up, they would be completely economically isolated and short of food supplies, and would therefore have to rely on German help. In his memorandum, Wedel's informant pointed out the importance of the principle of national self-determination for the Austrian Germans, and he outlined the tactics of non-co-operation with the Slav peoples and their states. Whereas federal transformation of Austria would present grave obstacles to the realization of the 'central European idea', a customs union with Germany appeared the best solution to the author of the memorandum: then,

[28] *AA*, in *Oesterreich 95 sec.*
[29] *AA*, AS5628 of 16 October 1918, in *Oesterreich 95 sec.*

he added, 'we would not have to run after the Czechs and the Slovenes [*sic*] but they would have to come themselves, and come they would'.

The problem of Austria–Hungary weighed heavily on the minds of the German leaders during the final weeks of the war. The last ponderous memorandum on a matter of foreign policy by Emperor William concerned the future of the Habsburg monarchy.[30] The Emperor, the Foreign Ministry, and the military were agreed that Austria's Germans would come to regard Berlin as their rallying point; they intended to make the best possible use of this development. The belief that Germany would have to give support to its compatriots 'on the other side of the frontier' was expressed in a letter of 19 October from the State Secretary in the Foreign Ministry to the Ambassador in Vienna. Hintze realized that he was about to make an improper suggestion: 'I am approaching this problem with a heavy heart because it means, in the last analysis, a vivisection of our ally.'[31] But his reasoning was sound judged by the standards current in the *Wilhelmstrasse* during the war. He would have preferred, he wrote, to pursue Bismarck's policy of strengthening the Danubian monarchy. The Habsburgs, however, by misdirecting their patronage to lost causes like the Poles and the Czechs, and ignoring the loyal elements like the Germans, had dug their own grave. The State Secretary was convinced that the Germans in the *Reich*, their national consciousness intensified by four years of warfare, 'would not suffer their fellow-countrymen on the other side of the frontier, who have given so much blood for the honour and defence of the Habsburg monarchy, to be raped and Slavicized in return for their faithfulness'. Hintze advised the Ambassador to inform his Austrian friends that 'if Austria should, against our will and wishes, come to a catastrophic breakdown, the Germans would naturally find our protection and support'.

The possibilities of a military intervention in Austria were considered in Berlin; on 28 October the Foreign Ministry asked the Treasury for 10,000,000 marks for 'secret undertakings' in

[30] *AA*, AS5520 of 14 October 1918, in *Oesterreich 95 sec.*
[31] *AA*, A42681 in *Oesterreich 95 sec.*

Austria–Hungary.[32] For a number of reasons—the fact that a military action might jeopardize the armistice negotiations being one of them—the German army remained inactive; the Czechs, on the other hand, were able to occupy the German territories in Bohemia, Moravia, and Moravian Silesia. As long as the Germans entertained hopes of support by Berlin they proved intractable in the negotiations with the National Committee in Prague. On 31 October Lodgman, a deputy from northern Bohemia, came to the new Czech national capital; he was followed, five days later, by Seliger, a Social Democrat leader. They were both offered representation, for the Bohemian Germans, on the National Committee and on the future National Assembly; though they both were known for their moderation in matters of nationality, they refused.[33] The Czechs insisted on the administrative unity of their country: the Germans, however, pointed out that they had their own representation and that they were prepared to negotiate only as equals. The Czechs, unwisely, thought purely in terms of a national state; the Bohemian Germans also let their own nationalism override all other considerations. They might well have been attracted by the new state because it had been recognized, by the Entente, as one of its allies; it was likely to escape heavy reparations and it had better prospects of economic aid than the defeated Powers. But no such thoughts appear to have influenced the political behaviour of the Germans: even moderate politicians became, in the hour of defeat, intractable nationalists. Only in December, at a meeting of industrialists in Vienna, was it agreed that German industry in *Deutschböhmen* would be attracted by the Czech state rather than by Germany, where it could not compete on the local market.[34]

Shortly before Wedel became absorbed in trying to alleviate the position of the Germans in Austria, he had reported on the Austrian government's attitude to the Polish question: a subject that could still arouse passions in Vienna and Berlin. It had been in abeyance since the beginning of the peace negotiations in the East: unhampered by the views of their allies, Hussarek and his

[32] *AA*, AS5854 in *Oesterreich 95 sec.* [33] Peroutka, op. cit., pages 185 et seq.
[34] Idem, page 189.

cabinet were able to exercise their imagination. At the end of September the Ambassador in Vienna wrote in a private letter to the State Secretary: 'Government circles now have a fixed idea that the monarchy can be put straight and rejuvenated only through a union with Poland.'[35] The government circles were moving in the realm of fantasy. In the *Reichsrat* the Polish Circle was split; some twenty-three deputies—nearly a half of its members—were voting, together with the Czechs and the South Slavs, against the government. The meeting of the National Democrats in Cracow on 30 September approved the resignation of the deputies because their club was 'not suitable at this historic moment to lead the policy of the nation'. The resolution of the 'National Democrat party of the three parts of Poland', published after the meeting in Cracow, demanded the 'restoration of full freedom, independence, and the unity of all Poland', adding that the National Democrats approved only of those Polish institutions that adhered to the same principles: the resolution explicitly recognized the National Committee in Paris, while implying a condemnation of the Regents Council in Warsaw.[36]

But the Regents Council, the last stronghold of sympathizers with the Central Powers, was soon compelled to mend its ways. On 7 October Ugron, the Austro-Hungarian representative in Warsaw, telegraphed Vienna that the peace note and the offer of armistice to the Allies had made a profound impression in the capital, the political effect of which he was as yet unable to estimate.[37] He also reported that he had talked to Prince Radziwill and to Kucharzewski, the ex-Premier who resumed his office on 7 October for two days only; both men regarded the situation as extremely grave but they told Ugron that the Austro-Polish solution should not be dropped because of the promises of the Entente. A few hours later, the Regents Council published a declaration that dashed the last hopes of the Austrians to the ground. It had been drafted without Kucharzewski's knowledge;[38] the Council presented the Premier with a *fait accompli*. The

[35] *AA*, AS4855 in *Oesterreich 95 sec.* [36] *VA*, 22694 MI ex 1918.
[37] *HHuSA*, PA I 1016, *Krieg* 56a/7.
[38] *HHuSA*, PA I 1024, *Krieg* 56/11; Ugron's telegram of 7 October.

proclamation recognized the principles of Wilson and declared itself for the creation of an independent Poland, embracing all territories inhabited by the Poles and with free access to the sea. It dissolved the state council which had been formed in June, and announced the intention of the Regents Council to nominate a new government, based on a broad representation, which would work out the election statute for a new parliament.[39]

Three days later, a National Committee was formed in Cracow which united the Peasant's party, the Democratic party, the National Democrats, the Social Democrats, and representatives from Silesia; the conservatives, who still retained their pro-Austrian sympathies, were not invited to join.[40] Finally, at a meeting on 24 October of the deputies of the parties represented on the National Committee, it was agreed that the grounds for a common parliament in Vienna had disappeared, and that a Commission of Liquidation should be set up which would take over the administration of the country.[41] They also discussed the recognition of the National Committee in Paris as Poland's representation abroad: they decided that such recognition should be granted only after an agreement with the left-wing parties in the Congress Kingdom, and after the Paris committee's reinforcement by members of those parties in Galicia and the kingdom which were not represented on it. The take-over of the administration did not present the Commission of Liquidation with formidable difficulties: the Governor in Cracow had been complaining of the unreliability of his civil servants—most of them were Poles—since the beginning of the spring. By the end of the month, the commission was in effective control of western Galicia, eastern Silesia, and the territory under Austro-Hungarian occupation, centred on Lublin.[42]

But in other respects the Poles were, at this time, even less advanced than the Czechs on the road to the goal claimed in their public proclamations. There were difficulties of an internal political nature. The Commission of Liquidation regarded the

[39] *Wolffs Telegraphisches Büro*, Warsaw, 7 October.
[40] *VA*, 23223 MI ex 1918. [41] *VA*, 24195 MI ex 1918.
[42] J. Opočenský, *Konec monarchie*, page 751 et seq.

Regents Council as a political anachronism, a relic of the occupation régime which it was reluctant to recognize as the leading organ of Poland. Dmowski's National Committee in Paris, on the other hand, had failed in the bid for its recognition by the Entente as the Polish government. The French cabinet gave it this recognition only on 15 November, the British and American governments refused theirs.[43] In Galicia and in Congress Poland only the National Democrats were inclined to recognize Dmowski's committee as the government of the new state. At a meeting of the Warsaw City Council, they in fact announced their recognition of their party leader's organization.[44] This action deepened the differences between the right- and the left-wing parties in the capital; whereas the socialists defended the principle of Poland's neutrality the National Democrats, both abroad and at home, favoured the policy of the closest possible co-operation with the Entente.

The left-wing parties in Warsaw, now supporting the Regents Council, demanded the release of Pilsudski, who was still incarcerated in the Magdeburg fortress. On the day the Council issued its proclamation, Prince Radziwill telegraphed the German Chancellor on its behalf, requesting Pilsudski's release. In spite of Ludendorff's and Beseler's objections, the Foreign Ministry decided, after a talk between Kessler and Pilsudski in Magdeburg at the end of October, that the Polish leader should be released. The decision was taken on the basis of Kessler's report, which was concluded by the following paragraph:

> On the whole the conversation gave me the impression that Pilsudski, should he command a Polish army organized by himself, would obey the orders of any Polish government, even in the case of a declaration of war on Germany. But he wants neither a war nor the occupation of Posen or western Prussia, and therefore he may become a moderating influence in Warsaw; he knows what war and Bolshevism means and he desires wholeheartedly peace for the building of Poland into a state and an economic entity. It does not, however, seem plausible that Pilsudski could work or even live together with General

[43] T. Komarnicki, *Rebirth of the Polish Republic*, page 230 et seq., London 1957.

[44] *HHuSA*, PA I 1024 Krieg 56b/11; Ugron's report of 13 October.

Beseler; the animosity between Beseler and Pilsudki, who, as an army chief and because of his popularity, would become the most powerful figure in Poland, would be fatal for Polish–German relations. Pilsudski's release would, in my opinion, have to be followed by Beseler's recall.[45]

Assured that Pilsudski was planning no military action in the German part of Poland, Prince Max von Baden's government ordered his release on the eve of the armistice: the following day, Pilsudski triumphantly returned to Warsaw. But the government nominated by him on the one hand, and the National Committee in Paris on the other—representing the two main streams of the Polish national revolution—were to be reconciled only at the beginning of the following year. The fact of the impending peace conference and the mediation of Paderewski aided the agreement.

There were, however, weightier problems that had to be solved before Poland could make claims to existence as an independent and unified state. The problem of departure of the German armies of occupation had to be settled: the territorial integrity of both the Congress Kingdom and of Galicia had to be defended against the ambitions of the Ukrainians. There were a number of ominous differences between the new state and Germany: finally, on 19 December, the Polish government broke off all diplomatic relations with Berlin; Wasilewski, the Minister of Foreign Affairs, informed the Germans that 'because of the short time that is dividing us from the peace conference, the Polish government regards all negotiations outside the framework of the conference as unnecessary'.[46] Like the Czechs, the Poles had to fight for the territory they claimed as their own: only their fight was longer and more arduous. Although there were to be differences between the partisans of a federal integration of national minorities into the new state—Pilsudski was one of them—and the protagonists of a national state—led by Dmowski—they were finally settled, as in Czechoslovakia, in favour of the views of the latter group.

[45] *AA*, Report from Kessler, the Foreign Ministry's representative, to the Chancellor, of 1 November. A46496 in *WK 20c sec.*

[46] The text of the note was printed in the *Norddeutsche Allgemeine Zeitung*, of 20 December 1918.

In the meantime, the revolution began to undermine the positions of the Magyar oligarchy which did not, however, renounce its claims to power and privilege without a hard struggle. Until the last of the war, it fought a rearguard action on two fronts against the demands of the 'minority' nationalities on the one hand, and against the Hungarian reformist elements on the other. Stefan Tisza, the former Premier and still one of the most powerful men among the Magyar ruling class, had the courage of his convictions when he condemned in an uninhibited public speech in Sarajevo early in October, the aspirations of the South Slavs to form their own state. He described the principle of self-determination as an 'empty phrase', and added that Serbia would be so exhausted after the war that the Bulgars would have no difficulty in 'eating it up after breakfast'. Two weeks later, on 17 October, this time in the Budapest parliament, Tisza turned his attention to the Czechs; he remarked that the 'Czechoslovak problem is nothing but the thieving desires of the Czechs'. The following day Wekerle, the Premier, declared that the relations with the nationalities in Hungary was his government's own business—a criticism aimed at both the Imperial Manifesto on federation and at the plans of the National Committee in Prague for Slovakia.[47]

The concentration of political power in the hands of the landed nobility was maintained in Hungary until the last weeks of the war. But there were three parties which could be described as reformist, which were opposed to the Magyar oligarchy, and which were able to attempt to exploit popular unrest: the Social Democrats, Michael Karolyi's Independent party, and the Radical party. The Independents sent a small number of deputies, about twenty-four, to the parliament, where neither the Social Democrats nor the Radicals were represented. But only the Social Democrats ran a party based on solid mass support, with an efficient organization. Karolyi's group, on the other hand, was an almost exclusively parliamentary party; it never attempted to become a vital political force outside the chamber of deputies. Karolyi, this 'noble political sportsman', was temperamentally unsuited for the role of the leader of a mass movement: by birth a candidate for an influential

[47] W. Böhm, *Im Kreuz feuerzweier Revolutionen*, page 36, Munich 1924.

position among the ruling class, he would have been a dissenter with or without popular support. Yet it was he who was alone capable of assuming the responsibilities of forming the first Hungarian revolutionary government when the time came.

On 8 October, after the successful conclusion of the Allied offensive against Bulgaria and a week after the conclusion of the armistice on the south-eastern front, the Social Democrat executive published an address to the Hungarian people, which denounced 'national oppression' and anticipated the formation of the successor states, and which demanded the government's resignation, the dissolution of the parliament, and the formation of a national assembly elected on the basis of universal, equal, and secret suffrage, and which suggested a thoroughgoing land reform and the nationalization of certain industries.[48] On 24 October, when the news of a revolt among the Croat troops in Rjeka (Fiume) reached Budapest, Hungarian officers demonstrated in favour of peace and of a government led by Karolyi; on the same day the Independents, the Social Democrats, and the Radicals formed a National Committee. Its political programme was similar to that of the Social Democrats: but the demand for an independent state was accompanied by the announcement of the committee's intention of recognizing the principle of self-determination while maintaining the 'territorial integrity' of the Hungarian state.[49] Wekerle's government and, later, the short-lived cabinet of Hadik existed for a few days side by side with Karolyi's committee. But the authority of the official government gave way to the quickly increasing prestige and power of the National Committee: on 29 October the Budapest garrison pledged its loyalty to the committee; the following day the police, the postal services, and the railwaymen followed suit. On 31 October Archduke Josef appointed Karolyi, in the name of the Emperor, the Prime Minister of Hungary; on the same day Stefan Tisza, whose name was the symbol of the old régime, was assassinated. Karolyi's government stood and fell with the support of the Social Democrats who, after some hesitation, joined it. Nevertheless, the cause of demo-

[48] W. Böhm, *Im Kreuzfeuer zweier Revolutionen*, page 47, Munich 1924.
[49] J. Opočenský, *Konec monarchie*, page 722.

cracy in Hungary—and Karolyi's cabinet was well-intentioned on this count—became identified with national disaster and the inevitable consequences of war. The government based on the policy of the National Committee soon gave way to rule by the Soviet, which, in its turn, was substituted by a régime that reversed the policies of Michael Karolyi and which ruthlessly stamped out the founders of the Bolshevik state and their doctrines.

Contrary to the expectations in Budapest, Karolyi's reputation as a resolute opponent, throughout the war, of the policies of Tisza, did not save Hungary from the most painful consequences of defeat. The revolutionary government wanted to preserve the country's territorial integrity: Oscar Jaszi, one of the leaders of the Radical party, and now in charge of the nationality affairs—although he doubted the ultimate success of such a policy—made a determined effort to uphold it, at any rate until the time of the peace conference.[50] But vague offers of autonomy and self-determination satisfied no one. Only Milan Hodža, the Slovak politician present in Budapest at the time of the revolution until his sudden recall by the National Committee in Prague, showed himself willing to negotiate with the new government. The Rumanian politicians in Austria–Hungary had discussed, at the beginning of the year, the future of a unified Rumania attached to the Habsburg monarchy by a personal union, over the head of the Hungarian government.[51] This move had been directed, in the first place, against Budapest; a few months later, the Rumanians, while retaining their plans for a unified state, abandoned hope for its support by the Habsburg dynasty. Otherwise, the developments in Transylvania and Bukovina followed the usual pattern of national revolutions in Austria–Hungary. A radical committee was established at Chernovtsy in Bukovina on 17 October; the Rumanian deputies stated their demands in the Budapest parliament the following day, after which they quietly withdrew from the chamber, never to return. In Bucharest Marghiloman's government—which was responsible for the conclusion of peace

[50] O. Jaszi, *Magyarens Schuld Ungarns Sühne*, page 59 et seq., Munich 1923.
[51] *HHuSA*, PA I 1044 Krieg 59i, a report of the Foreign Ministry's liaison officer at the Supreme Command of 17 February 1918.

with the Central Powers in March—was forced to resign early in November; soon, the Rumanian troops, aided by the Allied units under Berthelot, began to follow in the wake of Mackensen's retreat, thus extending the power of the Bucharest pro-Entente government westward, into Austro-Hungarian territory.

But the gravest threat to the frontier of Hungary came from the south. The government in Budapest, both before and after the revolution, was confident as to its ability to continue controlling Slovakia and Transylvania; it never entertained the same hopes with regard to Croatia. Here the Jugoslav revolution was to be given an added edge by the presence, South of Hungary's frontier, of the Allied army under General d'Esperay, and of the Serb troops now returning to their home country. The National Committee in Zagreb had been set up in August, during a visit to the Croat capital by a delegation of Czech politicians; on 5 and 6 October all political parties in the South Slav provinces of both parts of the monarchy agreed to set up a wider National Committee, which demanded the unity of the Serbs, the Croats, and the Slovenes in a free, democratic, and independent state.[52] In Croatia, the serious political differences between the Croat–Serb Coalition and Frank's party[53] had disappeared: the formation of a national front in Croatia made possible an effective resistance to the Budapest government. When, on 5 October, Wekerle's government decided to replace Ban Mihalović—the leader of the Croat–Serb Coalition—by Baron Unkelhäuser, the National Committee simply sent Unkelhäuser back to Budapest.

The Hungarians had already been unable to enforce their decisions in Zagreb at the beginning of October; the influence of the Budapest government, together with the power of the local military authorities, continued to decline throughout the month. On 27 October the National Committee requested the military command, which incidentally was headed by two Croat generals, to provide arms and ammunition for a civic guard; as the army was unable to maintain order without assistance from the civil population, the request was granted. Two days later the Zagreb Diet passed a law drafted by Svetozar Pribičević, one of the Serb

[52] J. Opočenský, *Konec monarchie*, page 745. [53] See above, pages 57 and 166.

leaders of the Coalition, which discontinued the constitutional ties of Croatia, Slavonia, Dalmatia, and Rjeka with Austria–Hungary, and which declared these lands a part of the 'state of the Serbs, the Croats, and the Slovenes'. On the same day, the Slovenes in Ljubljana also celebrated their independence. On 1 November General Sarkotić handed over the administration of Bosnia and Hercegovina to the National Committee. But the progress of the unification of all South Slavs was interrupted three days later when the Italians occupied, in accordance with the Pact of London, parts of the Dalmatian littoral.

The events in the South Slav territories followed the pattern of other national revolutions in Austria–Hungary: it was partly executed under the guidance of the Czech radicals. The National Committee in Zagreb had been set up in August, during a visit by the Czech politicians; in and out of the *Reichsrat*, the South Slavs and the Czechs had been co-operating closely for nearly a year.

Like in other lands of the Habsburg monarchy, a broadly based political movement led to the formation of an anti-Habsburg united front and the establishment of a national committee, which began piecemeal, taking over power from the Austro-Hungarian authorities. Nevertheless, like the rest of these rudimentary governments of the successor states, the Committee faced the manifold difficulties of the exact delimitation of the new state's frontiers, of the form it should take, and of its political and economic consolidation.

CONCLUSION

At noon on 11 November Emperor Karl signed, in pencil, his abdication. The epitaph on the demise of the House of Habsburg was a gentle, apologetic document: there was no bitterness in it, but nor was there a trace of inclination to carry on the burden of the government.

> Since my accession to the throne, [it read] I have unceasingly tried to spare my nations the horrors of the war, for the outbreak of which I bear no responsibility. I have never hesitated to restore constitutional life, and I have opened the way for my nations to their independent political development. Since I am filled now, as before, by unchangeable love for all my nations, I will not place my person as an obstacle to their free evolution. . . .

Having signed this informal document, Karl found the majestic surroundings of Schönbrunn, the Imperial residence in Vienna, unbearably oppressive. Early in the evening a fleet of seven cars took him and his family, together with their now depleted court, to the Eckartsau hunting lodge. Here the former Emperor of Austria–Hungary spent the last months before going into exile. The windows of the baroque house overlooked Marchfeld, the battlefield where the victory of his thirteenth-century ancestor, Rudolf Habsburg, had laid the foundations to the fortunes of his family.

During his stay at Eckartsau, Karl was the detached observer of a hopeless scene: the insignia of his House torn down everywhere in his former dominions; the Imperial anthem half-forgotten and no longer sung; the oath of loyalty disregarded, and superseded by new ones. He saw the Hungarians, the Poles, the Czechs, and the Austrian Germans renounce the dynastic form of government in favour of republican institutions, and the South Slavs adopt the Serbian Karadjordjević dynasty as their own.

Nevertheless, the legislation enacted in the successor states at the end of the year 1918, concerning their form of government and depriving the House of Habsburg of every vestige of power, merely formalized a situation that had existed for some time. On 29 October *The Times* commented on the Austro-Hungarian Foreign Minister's reply to President Wilson's note of 18 October:

> It is clear that, whatever they may do about an armistice, the Allies and the United States cannot deal solely with the Austro-Hungarian government in regard to the future of the peoples composing the Monarchy. The Czecho-Slovak people is already recognized as a belligerent and Allied nation. President Wilson has recognized in the fullest manner the justice of the nationalistic aspirations of the Jugo-slavs for freedom: 'and it is, for every reason desirable that they should no longer be left by the Allies in the position of a people technically enemy.' The French government has recognized the National Committee of Rumanians and Transylvanian Rumanes in Paris. The Poles are also recognized. The Ruthenes may need recognition, and the Italians in Austria naturally find their champion in Italy. The right of the Austro-Hungarian 'Government' to speak even for the German Austrians is not clear, and Count Andrássy himself can hardly have a valid mandate to represent anything save the Magyar Junker oligarchy.

The leading article in *The Times* bore every mark of Wickham Steed's authorship: he was the foreign editor of the newspaper and, as a member of the staff of Lord Beaverbrook's Ministry of Information he had exerted himself, earlier in the year, to convince the British government of the necessity of recognizing the radical exiles' aims. Apart from indicating that an Austro-Hungarian government no longer existed, and that the Allies should deal direct with the representatives of the Austro-Hungarian peoples, the leader intimated subtle distinctions in the achievements, in the eyes of the Allies, of these peoples. The 'Czecho-Slovak people' had done extremely well, and they were recognized as belonging to the Allied camp; so had the Poles; the Austro-Hungarian Rumanians had got themselves 'recognized' in Paris; President Wilson had said that it was a pity that the South Slavs should be treated as 'technically enemy'; the government in Rome was expected to look after the claims of the Italians in Austria. The

Ruthenes, on the other hand, had done rather badly; the Austrian Germans got an honourable, and the Magyars a dishonourable mention.

The political reality behind the fluent and plausible description of the situation in *The Times* was one of extreme complexity; in addition, the leader-writer made no distinction between the peoples in central Europe and the politicians regarded as their representatives in the Allied countries. Indeed, by the end of October, there were few differences between, say, the South Slav politicians at home and those abroad. But this situation had taken some time to develop. Most of the political exiles had had, throughout the war, very few connexions with their home countries; the Czechs were a notable exception. Until the spring of 1917, and in many cases until the beginning of 1918, the politicians in Austria–Hungary were not easy to convince that the break-up of the monarchy was one of the Allied war aims. On several occasions, in fact, the exiles had to anticipate events in order to convince their compatriots still loyal to the Habsburg dynasty of the error of their ways. When, shortly after the launching of the German offensive in the West in March 1918, the western Allies recognized—on military rather than on political grounds—the necessity of encouraging refractory national movements on the territory of Austria–Hungary, there was a marked decline in the stability of the Austro-Hungarian government. The radicals inside the monarchy found it now plain sailing to convince their vacillating friends that the monarchy had no chance of surviving the war; largely due to the smoothly functioning underground communications apparatus, developed by the Czech Mafie early in the war, they were well informed on the achievements of the politicians in exile. In this sense, the western Powers can be said to have made a considerable contribution to the demise of the Habsburg Empire. The argument—still expounded in some quarters nowadays—that the Allies wilfully broke up the monarchy in October 1918, or still worse, at the peace conference, completely lacks substance. By October there was a powerful anti-Habsburg movement among most of the Austro-Hungarian nationalities which would not accept concessions, however far-reaching, from the government in Vienna and Budapest; by the time the peace conference met the monarchy no longer existed.

The Allied policy of 'national incitement' would, on the other hand, have very likely proved a failure had there not been a receptive audience inside Austria–Hungary already. The ultimate responsibility for the disappearance of the Habsburg monarchy rests squarely on the shoulders of its rulers. They alone had the power to reconcile or repel their peoples: they used it badly, or not at all. Where peace had tried them, war ruined them; they had lost conviction in their right to govern some time before its end.

There had been radical, anti-Habsburg movements among the Austro-Hungarian peoples before the war; they did, however, either disappear during the hostilities, or change beyond recognition. The pro-Russian movement among the Ruthenes in eastern Galicia, Bukovina, and Carpathian Russia, that had caused the government the gravest concern, did not long survive the outbreak of the war. Its leaders were either arrested or fled to Russia. Finally, when the military weakness of the Tsarist Empire became an established fact, the Ukrainian independence movement, encouraged and protected by Berlin and Vienna, proved attractive to the Ruthenes. The Serbian terrorist activities in Bosnia, which had pushed the monarchy into its last war, was swallowed up in the greater violence of the battlefield; the ambiguously anti-Habsburg Neo-Slavism of the Czechs, as formulated by Karel Kramář, could not survive the demise of the Tsarist Empire.

The national movements that eventually rent the state apart had little in common with the radicalism of the pre-war days. They developed in the hot-house conditions generated by the war; they were political mass movements headed by determined, if not always courageous, leaders. Their strength was different, in kind and not only in degree, from the high treason, motivated by a puzzling mixture of religious and national feelings, that was to be found among the Ruthenes before the war, or the heroic hooliganism of the Serbian terrorists. Their growth was often stimulated by the blunders of the government.

The dualist arrangement of the Habsburg dominions—the

sharing of power between Vienna and Budapest—had, since 1867, complicated the treatment of national problems. It had ossified into a rigid system; it made a uniform approach to the questions of nationality impossible. But the original intention behind the *Ausgleich*, that is the establishment of the Magyar and German supremacy respectively in the Hungarian and the Austrian parts of the monarchy, fell, in the subsequent decades, by the wayside. Although the original plan did not work out, it misled many historians into dividing the Austro-Hungarian nationalities into two categories, the 'ruling' and the 'oppressed'. In fact, by the outbreak of the war, the nationalities had found their place in an intricate hieratic system.

Although the Magyar oligarchy was more successful in retaining power in its hands than the Germans in Austria, it too had had to compromise—in a similar manner to their own compromise with the dynasty in 1867—with the South Slavs in Croatia, who came to enjoy a considerable degree of autonomy. The Slovaks, the Rumanians, and the Ruthenes of Carpathian Russia, on the other hand, were too weak to make any successful political demands. They were on the lowest rung of the hierarchy, and they remained there until they found allies either inside the monarchy, like the Slovaks, or outside it, like the Rumanians, and until the machinery of the state began running down in the last months of the war.

In Austria the Poles and the Czechs had made successful bids for political power. They sent strong representations to the *Reichsrat*; the Poles provided many Austrian governments with some of their most influential members; the Czechs were also frequently represented in the cabinet. Indeed, without Polish support, constitutional government in Austria would have been impracticable; on several occasions it ground to a standstill in the face of Czech opposition.

The balance of nationalities inside Austria–Hungary was seriously disturbed by the war. Attempts were made, from a number of quarters, to restore German hegemony in Austria. The alliance with Berlin, the absence of constitutional remedies, the prospects of rule by Imperial decrees, and the increased powers of the military all helped to make the Slavs, and the Czechs in particular, suspicious of the intentions of the central authorities. Although the successive governments in Vienna did their best to resist the concerted pressure from the German side, this feature of their policy was not very clear to a number of Slav politicians. They were denied the opportunity of meeting in the *Reichsrat*, which was not summoned until May 1917; most of them spent the four years of the war in the rumour-ridden atmosphere of the provincial towns.

At the same time a serious conflict flared up between the civil and the military authorities. In the first months of the war it looked as if the very power in the state was at stake: the military attempted to take over political control in Bohemia and Croatia. Although this aspect of the conflict was eventually settled in favour of the civil authorities, its underlying causes—two sharply opposed approaches to the treatment of the Slav peoples—were not easy to reconcile.

On the whole, the civil administration could be said to have acquired, through their long experience of work in the Slav territories, a certain amount of tolerance. The men who ran it knew that forbearance was necessary when dealing with the delicate problems caused by excessive national zeal. They realized that not every Serb in Croatia favoured the Great Serbian ambitions of Belgrade, or that not every Czech was impatiently waiting for the moment when he could welcome, a flag in his hand, the Tsarist armies on their arrival in Bohemia. The military authorities disapproved of so tolerant an attitude of mind; they tended to generalize isolated instances of treason and make a whole people responsible for the misdemeanour of a few of its members. The constitutional situation brought about by the war gave them the powers to deal with treason among the civilian population; they used them to the full, and often with stupidity and unnecessary brutality. The treatment by the military of the Slav peoples of the monarchy, and of the Czechs and the Serbs in particular, was one of the most convincing arguments against the good intentions of the rulers of Austria–Hungary.

It was employed by the political exiles from the very beginning of their activities in the Allied countries. They made no distinction between the attitudes of the civil authorities and of the military, but the line they took was on the whole justified. The other, and more powerful, argument they frequently employed concerned the relations between Vienna and Berlin; it has since found its way into modern European historiography. The exiles maintained that the rulers of the Habsburg monarchy were nothing but a tool in the hands of Germany, and that they were hopelessly committed to the expansionist plans of Berlin. This was not the case. The relations between the two allies during the war were far from smooth; the German Ambassador to Vienna often complained about the 'spirit of Sadowa' among the ruling circles of the monarchy. There were, however, more serious differences between the allies. Most of them occurred in the sphere of the eastern policy of the two states.

The Austrians perhaps expected too much from Berlin: they were, for instance, confident that the war would make the 'Austro-Polish' solution of the Polish question possible. Although, at first, the German leaders indicated that they would not object to most of the Polish territories (apart from their own) being united and placed under a rather loose control of the House of Habsburg, they were to change their minds. There was initially a strong support for this solution among the Poles themselves; in time, however, they learned to hope for little from Vienna and for less from Berlin. In this sense, Austria–Hungary's alliance with Germany was extremely costly—it lost them the support and good will of the Poles. At the beginning of the war there were a number of Polish troops who fought the Russians on the Austrian side; some of them ended the war by fighting the Germans on the western front.

Finally, there was another aspect of Germany's eastern policy that contributed to alienating the Poles from the monarchy. The policy of support of the Ukrainian national movement, which was expected to weaken the military potential of Russia, was adopted both in Berlin and in Vienna early in the war. It was consummated by the peace treaty with the Ukraine, concluded, on Germany's initiative, in February 1918. It conceded territories the

Poles regarded as their own to the Ukrainians: after this event only the staunchest conservatives among the Poles remained pro-Austrian.

Whereas the Polish problem was international in its wider implications, the Czech radicals had to work hard to break out of the confines of the Habsburg monarchy. In the months immediately before the war, there was only one party in the Czech lands with a radical policy; it was extremely small, but its activities intimated the shape of things to come. Its leaders believed that the Czech question would be solved by a war, and then only by the creation of a completely independent state. They issued appeals to the Great Powers in order to draw their attention to their aspirations. But they were not excessively pro-Russian, and Russophilism usually spelled opposition to the very foundations of the Austro-Hungarian state.

This movement was, of course, represented in the Czech lands; its significance has, however, often been misread. It was limited to sections of urban middle and lower middle classes, receptive to extreme forms of chauvinism; it affected neither the Agrarians nor the Social Democrats, the two largest political organizations. Kramář, the chairman of the Young Czechs, was its main exponent. He wanted an Austria–Hungary ruled by its Slav majority, and allied with Russia; failing that, he evolved a plan for a federation of Slav states with the Tsar at its head. The war made up Kramář's mind; he did, however, refuse to go into exile, confidently expecting the arrival of the Russian armies in Prague.

The majority of the men who eventually went to work against the monarchy abroad—Masaryk and Beneš among them—relied on the strength of the western Powers; they spent most of their time in exile in England and France, and later in the United States. Even in exile they had to contend with Russophil tendencies among the colonies of Czech immigrants in the Allied countries; but in the long run the course of the war proved their views right, and disappointed Kramář and his friends. Masaryk and Beneš set themselves an exacting task; they worked without sparing themselves, and they never lost sight of their aim. Although their propaganda sometimes sacrificed veracity for effect, their contribution to the break-up of the Habsburg Empire was of a momentous importance. Without the efforts of the exiles the Czechs would have never secured such an advantageous peace for themselves. But they were perhaps too absorbed in their immediate aim—the destruction of the Habsburg monarchy and the creation of a Czechoslovak state—to raise their sight to the wider issues. They gave little thought to the post-war organization of central Europe; their reliance on the western Powers implied, in terms of the foreign policy of the future state, lifting the problems of their nation out of their central European context.

There were certain similarities between the development of the Czech and the South Slav attitudes to the monarchy during the war. Pre-war radicalism among the South Slavs was a minority movement; they suffered, perhaps more than the Czechs, from maltreatment by the military, and in Croatia they witnessed the struggle for political power between the military and the civil authorities. Soon after the outbreak of the war, some of their politicians and journalists went into exile; after the reopening of the *Reichsrat*, the Czechs and the South Slavs formed a united parliamentary front. But there was a Serbian state on the other side of the frontier, and the central problem of South Slav nationalism was whether Serbia should be regarded as the nucleus of the future Jugoslav state, and if so, what kind of a state it should become. The radicals gave an answer in the affirmative to the first question, without troubling themselves unduly with the second.

The South Slav exiles achieved more sooner than the Czechs; they worked abroad in a complete isolation from their home country. They were not inhibited by the same considerations as Masaryk, who insisted on keeping in touch with Prague, and who feared a denunciation by the politicians at home. Nevertheless, the South Slavs did not keep up the pace they set themselves at the outset of their activities. The attacks on them, mainly from Croatia, had a demoralizing effect; they expended a lot of energy agitating against the Pact of London; their relations with Pašić's government gradually deteriorated.

On the whole, the exiles can be said to have anticipated events in Austria–Hungary. It was not until the spring of 1917—the

March revolution in Russia and the entry of the United States into the war—that a swing towards radicalism began inside the monarchy. The demise of the Tsarist régime intimated the possibility of far-reaching changes in the Habsburg Empire; the gradual decline in the power and the prestige of the revolutionary government created a certain vacuum in the affairs of central and eastern Europe. Russia's effective interest in Polish affairs was, at any rate for the time being, eliminated; the Czech Neo-Slavs could no longer hope that the Russian armies might put their plans into practice. The increase, on the other hand, of the military potential of the western Allies at the time of America's entry into the war, together with the ideas of President Wilson, provided the radicals in Austria–Hungary with a fresh stimulus. In the following months an ever-growing number of Slav politicians were turning away from the monarchy.

At the same time, the steadily deteriorating economic situation and the impact of Bolshevik propaganda, mostly generated by Trotsky at Brest-Litovsk, contributed to revolutionizing the masses of the Habsburg Empire. But the principles of President Wilson and the Bolshevik slogans were, to a great extent, complementary. From the beginning of 1918, national and social revolutions went hand in hand; national independence first and social justice second were the demands that eventually appeared on the banners of the political parties that wanted to retain, or increase, their power in the new order. The Czech, Polish, and South Slav national leaders, now contemptuous of Vienna's promises and threats, learned to control the revolutionary temper of the masses while creating the political institutions that, when the time was ripe, were to take over the power in their respective countries. Only in German Austria and Hungary proper, where radicalism lacked both the leadership and the appeal, the revolution appeared for a short time to assume social, rather than national, characteristics.

In the face of these dangers, the Austro-Hungarian government showed no political acumen. It lost valuable time before it realized that the very existence of the Empire was at stake, and it became helpless as the revolution gathered momentum. Its last chance came in the spring of 1917, when only an energetic and resolute action might still have saved the monarchy. Instead, its rulers remained irresolute and relied on half-hearted measures. The *Reichsrat* reopened in May 1917, only to become a platform for the preaching of sedition and discontent; an amnesty was granted to political prisoners who, upon their release, swelled the ranks of the radicals. Separate peace negotiations were mismanaged by the Emperor himself; although his good intentions were beyond doubt, the execution of his plans lacked the necessary decisiveness. Instead of getting rid of the burden of the German alliance, the monarchy finally became tied to Berlin more closely than ever before.

In January 1918—the time of the mass strikes—the Austro-Hungarian rulers came to rely exclusively on the army for the maintenance of internal order. From then on the Austro-Hungarian armed forces were engaged on two fronts, and the demands upon them by the home front were growing every day. By suppressing the mass strikes and popular discontent early in the year, the army rendered its last service to the radicals: it gave them a breathing space in which to consolidate their control of the revolutionary situation. But the army did not remain unaffected for long: it was fast becoming an ever blunter instrument. In October 1918 the machinery created by the radicals during the previous months went into action; by the beginning of November, the dynasty and its peoples had neither any interests nor any problems in common.

BIBLIOGRAPHY

Government Papers and Publications

Unpublished:

The documents in the *Haus*, *Hof und Staatsarchiv*, the *Verwaltungsarchiv* and the *Kriegsarchiv* in Vienna.

The documents in the archives of the German *Auswärtiges Amt*. These papers are now held by the German Federal Government in Bonn; microfilm copies of most of them can be found in the Public Records Office in London.

Lord Milner's papers in the library of New College, Oxford.

Published:

Mezhdunarodnye otnoshenie v epokhu imperialisma. Dokumenty iz arkivov carskovo i vremennovo pravitelstva, 1878–1917 *goda*. Leningrad, 1931 et seq.

Reichsgesetzblatt. Vienna, Hof und Stattsdruckerei.

Stenographische Protokolle über die Sitzungen des Hauses des Abgeordneten. Vienna, Hof und Staatsdruckerei.

Politische und parlamentarische Chronik der österreichisch-ungarischen Monarchie. Vienna, 1910–1918.

Papers Relating to the Foreign Relations of the United States, 1914–1918, published by the U.S. Department of State, Washington.

Papers Relating to the Foreign Relations of the United States, The Lansing Papers, 1914–1920, U.S. Department of State, Washington 1939–40.

Privately Published Papers

Proces dra Kramáře a jeho přátel. Prague, 1918.

Protokoll der Verhandlungen des Parteitages der deutschen Sozialdemokratischen Arbeiterpartei in Österreich. Vienna, 1917.

M. Bogitschewitsch. *Die answärtige Politik Serbiens*. Berlin, 1928–31.

S. Filasiewicz. *La question Polonaise pendant la Guerre Mondial. Recueil des Actes Diplomatiques, Traités et Documents concernant la Pologne*. Paris, 1920.

F. Nečásek, J. Pachta, E. Raisová (editors). *Dokumenty* of *protilidové a protinárodni politice*. T. G. Masaryka, Prague, 1953.

B. Nesković. *Istina o solunskom procesu*. Belgrade, 1953.
J. Papoušek (editor). *Carské Rusko a naše osvobozeni*. Prague, 1927.
J. Redlich. *Tagebücher* (edited by F. Fellner). Vienna, 1953.
F. Šišić (editor). *Dokumenti of postanku Kralijevine Srba, Hrvata i Slovenaca, 1914–1919*. Zagreb, 1920.
S. Tisza. *Briefe* (1914–1918). Berlin, 1928.

Memoirs

F. Adler. *Vor dem Ausnahmegericht*. Berlin, 1920.
J. Andrássy. *Diplomatie und Weltkrieg*. Berlin, 1920.
P. Baráček. *Vzomínky na počátek našeho odboje*. Prague, 1934.
S. Burian. *Austria in Dissolution*. London, 1925.
E. Beneš. *Světová válka a naše revoluce* (two volumes and one volume of documents). Prague, 1935.
V. Beneš. *Československá Amerika v odboji*. Prague, 1931.
——. *Masarykovo dílo v Americe*. Prague, 1925.
——. *Revoluční hnutí v severní Americe*. Prague, 1923.
——. *Z času velké víry*. Prague, 1926.
L. Biliński. *Wspomnienia i Dokumenty*. Warsaw, 1924.
L. Borský. *Před válkou o válce*. Prague, 1920.
——. *Znovudobytí samostatnosti*. Prague, 1928.
W. Böhm. *Im Kreuzfeuer zweier Revolutionen*. Munich, 1924.
O. Czernin. *Im Weltkriege*. Berlin, 1919.
J. Deutsch. *Aus Österreichs Revolution*. Vienna, 1921.
R. Dmowski. *Polityka Polska i Odbudowanie Panstwa*. Warsaw, 1926.
J. Dürich. *V českých službach*. Klášter nad Jizerou, 1921.
R. Gajda. *Moje vzpomínky*. Prague, 1920.
A. Hajn. *Česká politika za války*. Prague, 1924.
J. Hajšman. *Česká Maffie*. Prague, 1934.
L. Hatvany. *Das Verwundete Land*. Leipzig, 1921.
K. Herben. *Denník*. Prague, 1929.
——. *Kniha vzpomínek*. Prague, 1935.
H. Hinković. *Iz velikog doba. Moj rad i moji doživjavi za vrijeme svjetskog rata*. Zagreb, 1927.
——. *Jugoslavija u Americi*. Zagreb, 1922.
Conrad Hötzendor. *Aus meiner Dienstzeit*. Vienna, 1922–25.
M. Janin. *Moje účast na československém odboji*. Prague, 1930.
J. M. Jovanović. *Borba za narodno ujedinjenje*. Belgrade, 1934.
M. Károlyi. *Fighting the World*. New York, 1925.
——. *Memoirs. Faith Without Illusion*. London, 1956.

V. Klecanda. *Operace československého vojska na Rusi 1917–20*. Prague, 1921.

J. Kvapil. *Projev českých spisovatelů*, Prague, 1924.

J. Kudela. *S naším vojskem na Rusi*. Prague, 1923.

H. Lammasch. *Europas elfte Stunde*. Munich, 1919.

Lloyd George. *War Memoirs*. London, 1935–36.

E. Ludendorff. *Meine Kriegserinnerungen*. Berlin, 1922.

T. G. Masaryk. *Světová revoluce*. Prague, 1926.

A. Musulin. *Das Haus am Ballplatz, Erinnerungen eines österreichisch-ungarischen Diplomaten*. Munich, 1924.

I. J. Paderewski. *The Paderewski Memoirs*. London, 1939.

J. Pilsudski. *Pisma Zbiorove*. Warsaw, 1937–38.

K. Rašín. *Říjnová revoluce*. Prague, 1919.

M. Seyda. *Polska na Przelomic Dziejow*. Poznan, 1927–31.

C. Sforza. *Fifty Years of War and Diplomacy in the Balkans*. New York, 1940.

F. Soukup. *28. říjen 1918*. Prague, 1928.

F. Soukup and K. Rašín. *Národní výbor 28. října*. Prague, 1919.

V. Šrobár. *Oslobodené Slovensko. Pamäti z rokov 1918–1920*. Prague, 1928.

H. W. Steed. *Through Thirty Years, 1892–1922*. London, 1924.

L. Sychrava and J. Werstadt. *Československý Odboj*. Prague, 1923.

J. Szilássy. *Der Untergang der Donaumonarchie*. Bern, 1921.

V. Vaněk. *Moje válečná odyssea*. Prague, 1925.

E. V. Voska and I. Will. *Spy and Counterspy*. New York, 1940.

F. Wieser. *Österreichs Ende*. Berlin, 1919.

K. Zmrhal. *Vláda sovětů a čechoslováci*. Prague, 1919.

——. *Armáda ducha druhé míle*. Prague, about 1923.

Books, Pamphlets, and Articles

L. Albertini. *The Origins of the War of 1914*. Oxford, 1958.

Anonymous (M. Bobrzynski). *Wskrzeszenie Państwa Polskiego*. Cracow, 1920–25.

B. Auerbach. *L'Autriche et la Högrie pendant la Guerre*. Paris, 1925.

J. Auffenberg-Komarow. *Aus Österreich-Ungarns Teilnahme am Weltkriege*. Vienna, 1920.

H. Baerlein. *The Birth of Jugoslavia*. London, 1922.

E. Bagger. *Franz Joseph, Emperor of Austria, King of Hungary*. New York, 1927.

N. Basilescu. *La Roumanie dans la guerre et dans la paix*. Paris, 1919.

O. Bauer. *Die Österreichische Revolution.* Vienna, 1923.
E. Beneš. *Bohemia's Case for Independence.* London, 1917.
——. *Five Years of Czechoslovak Foreign Policy.* Prague, 1924.
——. *Smysl československé revoluce.* Prague, 1923.
C. Berezowski. *Powstanie Panstwa Polskiego w swietle Prawa Narodów.* Warsaw, 1934.
L. Bernhard. *Die Polenfrage. Der Nationalitätenkampf der Polen.* Munich and Leipzig, 1920.
V. Bibl. *Der Zerfall Österreichs.* Vienna, 1922.
H. J. Bidermann. *Geschichte der österreichischen Gesamtstaatsidee.* Innsbruck, 1889.
F. Bokes. *Dejiny Slovenska a Slovákov od najstarších čias až po oslobodenie.* Bratislava, 1946.
J. M. Cabot. *The Racial Conflict in Transylvania,* Boston, 1926.
K. Čapek. *Hovory s Masarykem.* London, 1941.
K. Červinka. *Na cestách naší revoluce.* Prague, 1920.
V. Chaloupecký. *Zápas o Slovensko, 1918.* Prague, 1930.
R. Charmatz. *Österreichs äussere und innere Politik 1895–1917.* Leipzig, 1918.
F. Charles-Roux. *La Paix des Empires Centraux.* Paris, 1947.
V. Clementis. *Panslavism Past and Present.* London, 1943.
I. Clopoţel. *Revoluţia din 1918 si Unirea Ardealului cu România.* Cluj, 1926.
K. Čulen. *Pittsburghská dohoda.* Bratislava, 1937.
J. Dabrowski. *Wielka Wojna 1914–1918.* Warsaw, 1937.
A. Demblin. *Czernin und die Sixtus affaire.* Vienna, 1920.
M. P. Djordjević. *Srbija i Jugosloveni za vreme rata, 1914–1918.* Belgrade,1922.
V. Dyk. *Vzpomínky a komentáře.* Prague, 1927.
M. K. Dziewanowski. *Pilsudski's Federal Policy 1919–1921.* Journal of Central European Affairs, July–October 1950.
M. Dzwonik. *Ohlas Velkej oktobrovej revolúcie na Slovensku (1918–1919).* Bratislava, 1957.
L. Eisenmann. *Un grand européain, Edouard Beneš.* Paris, 1934.
J. Eötvös. *Die Garantien des Macht und Einheit Österreichs.* Leipzig, 1859.
R. Fester. *Die Politik Kaiser Karls.* Munich, 1925.
J. Fiala. *Rumburská vzpoura.* Prague, 1953.
C. P. L. Finzi. *'I.T.O.' Note di un capo del servizio informazioni d'armata, 1915–1918.* Milan, 1931.

A. Fischel. *Das österreichische Sprachenrecht.* Brno, 1902.
——. *Der Panslawismus bis zum Weltkrieg.* Stuttgart, 1919.
H. Frankel. *Poland: The Struggle for Power 1772–1939.* London, 1936.
A. Frankenfeld. *Österreichs Spiel mit dem Kriege.* Dresden, 1928.
B. Frei. *Die roten Matrosen von Cattaro.* Vienna, 1927.
L. Germanov. *K istorii chekhoslovatskovo nastuplenia v Sibirii.* Moscow, 1922.
L. L. Gerson. *Woodrow Wilson and the Rebirth of Poland, 1914–1920.* New Haven, 1953.
E. Gleise-Horstenau. *Die Katastrophe.* Vienna, 1929.
R. Goldscheid. *Das Verhältniss der äusseren Politik zur Inneren.* Vienna, 1914.
F. Götz. *Jaroslav Kvapil.* Prague, 1948.
W. Graham. *New Governments of Central Europe.* New York, 1928.
G. Gratz and R. Schüller. *Der wirtschaftliche Zusammenbruch Österreich-Ungarns.* Vienna, 1930.
J. S. Hájek. *Wilsonovská legenda ve dějinách československé Republiky.* Prague, 1953.
E. Halévy. *The World Crisis of 1914–1918.* Oxford, 1930.
J. Hanč. *Eastern Europe.* London, 1943.
M. Handelsman. *Polska w Czasie Wielkiej Wojny.* Warsaw, 1932.
V. Hanzal. *Výzvědčíci v Haliči.* Prague, 1928.
E. Haumant. *La Formation de la Jugoslavie.* Paris, 1930.
R. H. Hernritt. *Nationalität und Recht.* Vienna, 1899.
F. M. Hník. *Edvard Beneš, filosof demokracie.* Prague, 1946.
M. Hodža. *Federation in Central Europe.* London, 1942.
L. Holotík. *Štefanikovská legenda a vznik ČSR.* Bratislava, 1958.
E. Holzer. *Die Entstehung des Jugoslawischen Staates.* Berlin, 1929.
F. Houdek. *Oslobodenie Slovenska.* Bratislava, 1929.
O. Jászi. *Revolution and Counter-revolution in Hungary.* London, 1924.
——. *The Dissolution of the Habsburg Monarchy.* Chicago, 1929.
E. Kahler. *Das Geschlecht Habsburg.* Munich, 1919.
R. A. Kann. *The Multinational Empire. Nationalism and National Reform in the Habsburg Monarchy.* New York, 1950.
H. Kanner. *Kaiserliche Katastrophenpoliiik.* Vienna, 1922.
G. F. Kennan. *The Decision to Intervene.* Second volume of Soviet–American Relations, 1917–1920. London, 1958.
R. Kjellen. *Die politische Probleme des Weltkrieges.* Berlin, 1916.
——. *Die Grossmächte und die Weltkrise.* Leipzig, 1921.
M. Klante. *Von der Wolga zum Amur.* Berlin, 1931.

F. Kleinwaechter. *Der Untergang der österreichisch-ungarischen Monarchie*. Leipzig, 1920.
W. Kolarz. *Myths and Realities in Eastern Europe*. London, 1936.
T. Komarnicki. *Rebirth of the Polish Republic*. London, 1957.
V. K. Korostovetz. *The Re-Birth of Poland*. London, 1928.
V. Král. *O Masarykově a Benešově kontrarevoluční protisovětské politice*. Prague, 1953.
J. Kratochvíl. *Cesta revoluce*. Prague, 1928.
K. Kramář. *Anmerkungen zur böhmischen Politik*. Vienna, 1906.
——. *Das böhmische Staatsrecht*. Vienna, 1896.
——. *Pět přednášek of zahraniční politice*. Prague, 1922.
——. *Na obranu slovanské politiky*. Prague, 1926.
A. Krausz. *Die Ursachen unsere Niederlage*. Munich, 1922.
F. Krejčí. *O Masarykovi*. Prague, 1927.
J. Kunz. *Náš odboj v zrcadle rakouské justice*. Prague, 1930.
R. Kunzl-Jizerský. *Vznik světové války*. Prague, 1923.
S. Kutrzeba. *Polska Odrodzona*. Warsaw, 1935.
R. Landau. *Ignace Paderewski, Musician and Statesman*. New York, 1939.
C. A. Macartney. *Hungary and Her Successors*. Oxford, 1937.
R. Machray. *Poland 1914–1931*. London, 1932.
——. *The Poland of Pilsudski*. London, 1936.
——. *The Little Entente*. London, 1929.
V. S. Mamatey. *The United States and East Central Europe*. Princeton, 1957.
F. Maslan. *O mírových snahách Presidenta Masaryka*. Prague, 1923.
T. G. Masaryk. *Der Agramer Hochverratsprozess*. Vienna, 1909.
——. *Naše politická situace*. Prague, 1901.
——. *Otázka sociální*. Prague, 1946.
——. *O Bolševictví*. Prague, 1921.
——. *Palackého idea národa českého*. Prague, 1926.
—. *Problém malých národů v evropské krisi*. Prague, 1926.
A. May. *The Habsburg Monarchy 1867–1914*. Cambridge, Mass., 1951.
P. Maxa. *V boji za samostatnost*. Prague, 1927.
R. Medek (editor). *Za svobodu*. Prague, 1926–29.
K. A. Medvecký. *Slovenský prevrät*. Trnava, 1930–31.
M. Menger. *Der böhmische Ausggleich*. Stuttgart, 1891.
H. C. Meyer. *Mitteleuropa in German Thought and Action, 1815–1945*. The Hague, 1955.

H. Münch. *Böhmische Tragödie*. Braunschweig, 1949.

J. Muška and J. Hořec. *Kúloze československých bqn v Rusku*. Prague, 1954.

J. O. Novotný. *Vzkříšeni samostatnosti československé*. Prague, 1932.

K. F. Nowak. *Collapse of Central Europe*. London, 1924.

J. Opočenský. *Konec monarchie rakousko-uherské*. Prague, 1928.

L. Otáhalová. *Sauhruná hlašení prazské ho mistodrzi lebustvi o protistatni, proti rakouské a proti válione cinnosti v Čechách 1915–1918*. Prague, 1957.

F. Palacký. *Österreichische Staatsidee*. Prague, 1866.

J. Papoušek. *The Czechoslovak Nation's Struggle for Independence*. Prague, 1928.

——. *Masaryk, a revolučuí armáda*. Prague, 1921.

L. Pasvolsky. *Economic Nationalism of the Danubian States*. New York, 1928.

M. Paulová. *Jihoslovanský odboj a česká Maffie*. Prague, 1928.

——. *Jugoslavenski odbor*. Zagreb, 1925.

——. *Ohlas balkánské války v české veřejnosti*. Prague, 1922.

——. *Dějiny Maffie*. Prague, 1937.

——. *Tajná diplomatická hra o Jihoslovany za světové války*. Prague, 1923.

J. Pekař. *Světová válka*. Prague, 1921.

C. Pergler. *America in the Struggle for Czechoslovak Independence*. Philadelphia, 1926.

A. Polzer-Hoditz. *Kaiser Karl*. Vienna, 1928.

K. Prchlík. *Bojovali proti válce*. Prague, 1953.

A. F. Pribram. *Austrian Foreign Policy 1908–1918*. London, 1923.

E. Rádl. *Der Kampf zwischen Tschechen und Deutschen*. Liberec, 1928.

R. Rajchl. *Štefánik, voják a diplomat*. Prague, 1948.

J. Redlich. *H. Lammasch als Ministerpresident*. Vienna, 1922.

——. *Kaiser Franz Josef von Österreich*. Berlin, 1928.

——. *Austrian War Government*. New Haven, 1929.

J. Remak. *Sarajevo*. London, 1959.

K. Renner. *Österreichs Erneuerung*. Vienna, 1916.

——. *Selbstbestimmungsrecht der Nationen*. Vienna, 1918.

J. S. Reshetar. *The Ukrainan Revolution, 1917–1920*. Princeton, 1952.

P. Roth. *Die politische Entwiklung in Kongresspolen während der deutschen Okkupation*. Leipzig, 1919.

——. *Die Entstehung des polnischen Staates*. Berlin, 1926.

R. V. Sakharov. *Das weisse Siberien*. Munich, 1923.

B. Šantrůček. *Vaclav Klofáč*. Prague, 1918.
J. Scheiner, *The Sokols*, Prague, 1920.
W. Schücking. *Das Nationalitätenproblem*. Dresden, 1908.
W. Schussler. *Das Verfassungsproblem im Habsburgerreich*. Stuttgart, 1918.
R. W. Seton-Watson. *The Future of Austria–Hungary and the Attitude of the Great Powers*. London, 1907.
——. *Racial Problems in Hungary*, London, 1908.
——. *Sarajevo*. London, 1925.
——. *The Southern Slav Question and the Habsburg Monarchy*. London, 1911.
——. *Absolutism in Croatia*. London, 1912.
——. *Corruption and Reform in Hungary*. London, 1911.
——. *German, Slav and Magyar*. London, 1916.
——. *Rumania and the Great War*. London, 1915.
——. *Masaryk in England*. Cambridge, 1943.
——. *The History of the Czechs and Slovaks*. London, 1943.
——. *The History of the Rumanians*. Cambridge, 1943.
A. Skene. *Der nationale Ausgleich in Mähren, 1905*. Vienna, 1910.
R. Sieghart. *Zolltrennung und Zolleinheit*. Vienna, 1915.
T. Sosnosky. *Die Balkanpolitik Österreich-Ungarns seit 1866*. Vienna, 1913.
R. Springer (K. Renner). *Der Kampf der österreichischen Nationalitäten um den Staat*. Vienna, 1902.
W. Steed. *The Habsburg Monarchy*. London, 1913.
F. Steidler. *České hnutí v Rusku*. Prague, 1921.
——. *Naše vystoupení v Rusku*. Prague, 1923.
N. Stojanović. *Jugoslovenski Odbor, Članci i dokumenti*. Zagreb, 1927.
E. Strauss. *Die Entstehung der Tschechoslowakischen Republik*. Prague, 1934.
D. F. Strong. *Austria, Transition from Empire to Republic*. New York, 1939.
P. Südland. *Die Südslawische Frage und der Weltkrieg*. Vienna, 1918.
A. J. P. Taylor. *The Habsburg Monarchy, 1815–1918*. London, 1948.
Z. Tobolka. *Politické dějiny československého národa*. Prague, 1936.
——. *Česká politika za světové války*. Prague, 1922.
J. S. Tomić. *La Formation de l'Etat Yougoslave*. Paris, 1927.
K. Tschuppik. *Die tschechische Revolution*. Vienna, 1920.
H. Uebersberger. *Der Salonikiprozess*. Vienna, 1942.
——. *Österreich-Ungarn zwischen Russland und Serbien*. Munich, 1958.

J. Veselý. *Češi a Slováci v revolučním Rusku, 1917–1920*. Prague, 1954.
A. Wandruszka. *Das Haus Habsburg*. Vienna, 1956.
H. Wendel. *Aus den südslawischen Risorgimento*. Gotha, 1921.
——. *Der Kampf der Südslawen um Freiheit und Einheit!* Frankfurt am Main, 1925.
F. Wichtl. *K. Kramar, der Ausbringer des Weltkrieges*. Munich, 1919.
V. Wilder. *Dva smerja u hrvatskoi politici*. Zagreb, 1919.
A. Žípek. *Světová válka*. Prague, 1923.

INDEX